WAR AND NATION IN THE THEATRE OF SHAKESPEARE AND HIS CONTEMPORARIES

Ay, now will Death, in his most haughty pride,
Fetch his imperial car from deepest hell,
And ride in triumph through the wicked world;
Sparing none but sacred Cynthia's friend,
Whom Death did fear, before her life began:
For holy fates have graven it in their tables,
That Death shall die, if he attempts her end,
Whose life is heaven's delight, and Cynthia's friend.

Thomas Kyd, *Soliman and Perseda*, 1591

You say it is the good cause that hallows even war? I tell you: it is the good war that hallows every cause.

Friedrich Nietzsche, *Thus Spake Zarathusa*, 1891

As long as war is regarded as wicked, it will always have its fascination. When it is looked upon as vulgar, it will cease to be popular.

Oscar Wilde, *The Critic as Artist*, 1891

We begin here because no life has ever been untouched by war.
Everyone loves to discuss war.
And yet its outcome, death, is shrouded in silence.

Timberlake Wertenbaker, *The Love of a Nightingale*, 1989

War and Nation in the Theatre of Shakespeare and his Contemporaries

Simon Barker

Edinburgh University Press

© Simon Barker, 2007

Edinburgh University Press Ltd
22 George Square, Edinburgh

Typeset in Adobe Sabon
by Servis Filmsetting Ltd, Manchester, and
printed and bound in Great Britain by
Biddles Ltd, King's Lynn, Norfolk

A CIP record for this book is available from the British Library

ISBN 978 0 7486 2765 3 (hardback)

CONTENTS

PREFACE

I came across the remarkable body of writing produced by Renaissance military theorists while undertaking my doctoral studies at the University of Wales during the 1980s. Maurice J. D. Cockle, a retired captain with the Border Regiment, had painstakingly gathered together the titles of various kinds of prose text for his *Bibliography of English Military Books up to 1642 and of Contemporary Foreign Works*, carefully supplying details of locations and provenance. This compendium, published in 1900, and limited to 250 copies, remains an invaluable resource for anyone interested in reading about the technical details and ideological trajectory of militarism in late Renaissance Europe. Cockle's book has an introductory note by the historian Charles Oman, and it is surprising that the treatises, pamphlets and manuals listed by Cockle remained of more interest to historians than to literary scholars for much of the twentieth century. John Hale, an inspired historian with a keen interest in the relationship between literature and history, clearly saw the potential this body of work had for an understanding of fictional representations of warfare in the early modern period. His research provides a lucid and compelling guide to the rich variety of Renaissance military writing. As far as I can tell, the first book-length study of the connections that can be made between this prose and the stage was Paul A. Jorgensen's *Shakespeare's Military World* (1956). Those who have become interested in Shakespeare's representation of militarism rightly acknowledge the immense importance of Jorgensen's work and I was very grateful to receive his advice and support during my own early research. A number of publications arose from my investigation into early modern militarism and some elements of the present book are based on these, as well as on my edition of *The Gentle Craft*, Thomas Deloney's late Elizabethan book on the history of shoemaking. Most of my earlier publications on the subject concern Shakespeare's classical plays, which is why I have not dealt with them here. I have listed these publications in the Bibliography and Further Reading.

Over the last decade or so it has been pleasing to see that this field of inquiry has expanded so that there now exists a considerable body of criticism on the relationship between warfare and the early modern stage. The work of Curtis Breight, Richard Courtney, Nick de Somogyi, Alan Shepard and Nina Taunton has been especially influential in the writing of this study. It is salutary to observe that one explanation for the increasing interest in the representation of warfare in historical writing is undoubtedly the experience critics have had of new and continuing military conflicts in their own times. Those at work in the field often express their awareness of the responsibility they have in writing about this area of human activity. Their research, like mine, is predicated on the actual (or imagined) death or injury of millions of men and women in a practice that continues to be thought of in some quarters as noble. Whilst the aesthetics of warfare clearly require critical attention, its victims deserve to be remembered as real people rather than mere subjects of academic enquiry. I should like to acknowledge the thoughtful contributions made to this study by those involved directly in a number of recent wars, either as civilian victims or as combatants. Some of those I spoke to had witnessed terrible acts of military violence and were sharing painful and inescapable memories. I have represented some of their recollections in an oblique way in parts of this book. The one person from this group whom I should like to name is Mr Stan Francis, who kindly shared his memories of people mentioned in the text.

It is important to acknowledge the support of a number of other people, organisations and institutions. Having given many papers at universities, colleges and conferences in Europe and the United States, I should like to thank those who organised the events and those who listened and responded to my work. A grant from the Arts and Humanities Research Council enabled me to finish a number of projects and allowed me to make a start on this one. I am indebted to the helpful librarians at the University of Gloucestershire, the University of Winchester, the British Library and the Bodleian Library. Paola Pugliatti generously sent me a copy of the paper she gave on Renaissance militarism at the *History and Memory* conference of the Shakespeare in Europe organisation held at the Jagiellonian University in Kraków in November 2005.

I am grateful to Jackie Jones and her colleagues at Edinburgh University Press for their assistance and to their anonymous readers who helped shape the project. My friendly colleagues at the University of Gloucestershire have been a great support – and looking further back, I am aware of how much I owe those who taught me at my universities in Scotland and Wales. The late David Goldwater, a much missed friend and comrade, encouraged me to write this book, but would have made a better job of it himself. My sister Pax, and Tim, Hannah and Tom have been very confident all the way through. I should like to acknowledge the following for their particular help and advice: Peter Barker, Hazel Bell, Nicola Gilmore, Monika Smialkowska, Ruth Willats and, as always, the *Coille Bheag* focus group.

Simon Barker
Cheltenham

Part I

Introductory Worlds

1

'KEEP IT DARK'

ॐ

Harvest time in a village in England, 1942. Raymond Peace and his friend Ronald Williams were on leave from their wartime duties with the Royal Air Force, staying for a while with the Williams family at the vicarage along the lane from the church where Ronald's father had been the incumbent Anglican priest for some twenty years. It was a beautiful day, hazy with warmth, and the two friends decided to drive the few miles to the local market town. Unusually, and in breach of wartime regulations, they also decided to make the trip wearing civilian clothes. They had sufficient petrol, an eye-catching motorcar and were many miles from their airfields in the eastern counties. Leaving behind their uniforms probably meant they thought they could further distance themselves from the increasing strains of the war. It was a difficult time for them: they were pilots attached to different bomber squadrons and had been almost constantly occupied with that summer's flying missions to continental Europe.

In the summer of 1992 I met an elderly lady at her home in the village in question. We sat for a while in the kitchen of her perfect country cottage. She complained mildly about how the area had become 'full of strangers', commuting to nearby cities, but her eyes sparkled as she recalled earlier times; and she described vividly the impact the two airmen had made during their occasional wartime visits. Ray and Ronnie, she remembered, were 'very good-looking chaps' who had entertained the locals with their RAF slang and banter. They were also kind and considerate to everyone, most conspicuously to my own mother, Ray's fifteen-year-old sister. Young Rosalind Peace also stayed for periods with the Williams family during the war. The Peace family lived in Coventry, and my mother had experienced the terrible destruction of the medieval city by German bombers in November 1940. Like many others, she lived in fear of further attacks and the Williams' home in the Warwickshire countryside had become a place of safety and somewhere to heal.[1]

Arriving in town the two men parked their car in the centre and walked around the busy streets, smoking cigarettes and chatting, perhaps about their mutual interests in rugby, flying and the cinema. But in wartime Britain two healthy men in their twenties yet not in uniform drew considerable attention, and as they strolled past the theatre to the river a woman approached them, agitated and upset. Ambushing the two men, she made a sweeping gesture back towards the town, presumably meaning also to embrace the rolling country-side beyond and all the villages and cities and peoples of the nation and the far-flung Empire. Ray and Ronnie, she called out to bystanders, were 'afraid to fight for their country' and, as a sign of her contempt, she presented the two flyers with white feathers, the universal token of cowardice.

Stratford-upon-Avon in the 1940s was not quite the tourist place it is today. Its importance as the birthplace of Shakespeare could still be balanced to an extent by its significant and visible role in the agricultural economy of the local area. Where there are now car parks and modern hotels there were still meadows and farmland. Yet in the mid-1920s, returning for the first time since before the Great War H. V. Morton had already observed what he thought of as traffic congestion, evidence in his opinion that the connection between the town and the playwright was by that time already a popular and international one:

> I drove between those well-loved Warwick hedges, through a perfect death-rattle of motor traffic, into Stratford. My old quiet Stratford was suffering from a rash of trippers. Charabancs from everywhere were piled up on the square; half the motor cars of the Midlands were either coming or going; and the hotel was full of long-legged girls from America, and sallow fathers and spectacled mothers. They gave me a bedroom called 'Love's Labour Lost' [sic] – all the rooms in this hotel are Shakespeareanized – and, as it overlooked the street, I sat a while watching more Americans arrive and thinking how amused Shakespeare would have been.[2]

So if in the sweep of the woman's hand, the town was in 1942 to stand for England, and England was to stand for Britain and the Empire, then the synecdoche was enriched by the fact that Stratford-upon-Avon was inextricably linked to the name of William Shakespeare.

Stratford was by no means isolated from the business of the war. Some government departments had been relocated there for the duration and military personnel were billeted in local hotels and in camps established in the surrounding villages. In the later stages of the war these included a considerable number of American GIs and airmen. Stray German bombs fell in Maidenhead Road on one occasion and a plaque in Evesham Place commemorates the two navy air personnel who were consumed by fire when their plane crashed there. Other bombs fell in the vicinity of the town, but local people had heard a rumour that Hitler had said he would never intentionally bomb Stratford-upon-Avon because Shakespeare was part of German culture.[3] Some of the town's men and women either joined the armed services or took part in other war work, such as travelling to local cities to fight fires or helping those injured in the raids. Stratford people also laboured in the area's munitions and armament factories.

But there was other work to be done. Replacing the earlier theatre built in 1879 but almost entirely destroyed by fire in 1926, Elisabeth Scott's Shakespeare Memorial Theatre had opened in 1932. The April to June Stratford season of 1942 saw productions in the new theatre of *A Midsummer Night's Dream*, *The Merchant of Venice*, *Hamlet*, *As You Like It*, *Macbeth*, *The Tempest*, *The Winter's Tale* and *The Taming of the Shrew*. Sheridan's *The School for Scandal* was also performed during the season. This was an ambitious sequence and evidence of the Memorial Theatre's commitment to sustaining as full a programme as possible in the face of wartime shortages and the absence of many actors and technicians called away to the war. Some of those in charge at the theatre were also 'in the know' about another possible disruption to the summer season. There were secret plans to evacuate Parliament to Stratford-upon-Avon in the event of an invasion. The House of Commons, which met almost daily throughout the war, would continue to sit for as long as possible using the public seating of the Memorial Theatre.[4] This plan invites the fanciful image of Members of Parliament making a last-ditch stand against an invading army amid the paraphernalia of Shakespearean production. Although never executed, of course, the symbolism of the location might be seen as an intense reminder of the centrality of Shakespeare to the minds of some wartime planners, and the contingency is certainly a tribute to the facilities afforded by Scott's design.

The two airmen drove back to Ronnie's family home in Temple Grafton, a village itself associated with Shakespeare because, according to one theory, it was where the playwright had been married in 1582.[5] One can imagine them retelling the white feather incident at the vicarage that afternoon, just as it was to be retold in family circles across the years. According to my mother, the accusation of cowardice, although unwarranted, contained a paradoxical truth.

She made no secret of the fact that by the summer of 1942 her brother was indeed 'afraid to go to war' in the sense that he had become fatigued and distressed by the frequent missions he was flying to bomb Germany and German-occupied territory.

Raymond Peace's many surviving letters from the 1930s and 1940s are a rich and powerful testimony to the love he had for his family and friends, and in particular his absolute devotion to his much younger sister. They also include vivid descriptions of what it felt like to fly in those still comparatively early years of aviation. For example, having been rested for a short while from his bombing duties, he wrote while on detachment to RAF Kinloss, near Forres, Scotland:

> As I mentioned earlier I flew to Ireland to take some people on Saturday & returned again on Sunday. Owing to weather we could not go over the hills & instead went all around the north of Scotland & down the coast (west) by the Isle of Skye, etc. It was a lovely trip in spite of rain showers, & I can say I have seen a lot of Scotland & the beautiful scenery. Actually it's very rocky & bare in the north, but there must be some beautiful drives round about. It's rather good for one's geography.

He writes well, in the idiom of the time. There are touching accounts of the routines of military life: long train journeys to a new base; the importance of letters and parcels from home; the indignities of daily life in wartime, first in a sergeants' mess in the early part of the war, and later in the officers' mess.[6] It is a world of dances, the pictures and early nights storing up sleep ahead of missions. It is also a world in which comrades suddenly disappear. None of the letters contains anything remotely jingoistic, anti-German or boastful, although on one occasion, having 'limped' home across the sea on one engine, he does say that he and his crew planned to take their 'revenge' the following night. They had been caught by searchlights and anti-aircraft fire and had considered bailing out, but had been as afraid of the sea as they were of crashing.

The letters contain what seems a surprising depth of detail about particular operations, including bombing destinations, accidents, lost planes and missing personnel. Writing to his parents and his sister on the 27 August 1942, Peace begins by noting that there had been renewed German raids in the Midlands:

> I have been rather worried about you recently because of news that B'ham & Coventry has [sic] been bombed. Please do take cover & if possible below ground level, & don't watch what is happening for it is a foolish

entertainment & dangerous, especially if he starts machine gunning as is his wont.

He is afraid for his family and, by this time, desperately afraid for himself. His letter concludes with an account of the dangers involved in his work, whether in the air or on the ground, during the day or at night:

> We have had a very hectic week, full of changes & unrest. It was impossible to carry on at the other place, no-one was getting any sleep & nerves were not too good. Dust and glass everywhere, the trees quite flat, etc., etc. Too near the coast you see. Fortunately I was over Germany the other night when they had 4½ hours of it, in broad moonlight. I did not enjoy the daylight do about ten days ago. I had just landed, go outside the hangar, when the first one dropped [*sic*]. Three of us dodged back inside & got in a corner which they tried to hit it [*sic*]. Both the others were hurt, one died & I had only a scratch but it shook me up. Still, we're OK here.

In the margin of this letter, realising he has said too much about events, or even too much about his own fear, he scrawls in capitals: 'KEEP IT DARK'.

Studying the sequence of letters it seems clear that Peace, like his friend Williams, was in ever-increasing danger as missions became longer, more complex and more vulnerable to accident and enemy assault. Understatement and euphemism disguise his anxiety, but not entirely successfully. Reading the letters against recorded histories of the bombing missions in which Peace participated suggests that he found himself working ('work' was what he called his duties) very much against the statistical odds of survival. And in this context, his experience of this work was defined by anticipation of his own death. This is why the woman's accusation in Stratford-upon-Avon had a ring of truth about it. By the late summer of 1942, Peace was 'afraid to go to war' but managed mostly to 'keep it dark' – just as he urged others to 'keep dark' those other kinds of detail about operational matters. My mother told me that by the late summer of 1942 her brother had developed an unsteady hand, which shook as he lit his cigarettes. He had seemed suddenly to grow older than his years and often lapsed into long silences. His letters reveal other evidence of his growing unease.

His was by no means an uncommon response to wartime duty at home or abroad – in the air, on the land or at sea. Nor does such a response diminish the bravery of those who, despite the immense psychological strain, performed unselfish acts in the war against

Nazism.[7] Indeed, it somewhat enhances it. Yet central to this book are those responses and attitudes to war that are carefully 'kept dark' in order to perpetuate its orthodox narratives.

War is such a constant in the way that humanity is constructed, defined and experienced that it seems a statement of the obvious to remind readers of its recurrent representation in a variety of cultural forms. The subject of this book is the representation of war in some of the literature of the late sixteenth and early seventeenth centuries. I shall be focusing mainly on texts produced for the public theatre of the period. However, since war is represented in a wide variety of fictional and non-fictional texts from this period, I shall also examine some examples of contemporary prose that the theatre's audiences might also have had an interest in. These will include treatises discussing the theory and methodology of war, but also a prose fiction, Thomas Deloney's *The Gentle Craft*, which contrasts with these military texts' attitudes towards war.[8] What these various forms of writing have in common is that, as far as we know, they were immensely popular at the time – the prose widely read and the drama widely seen. It is not my intention to deal specifically with the 'Court' literature of the period despite the fact that it too clearly contains representations of militarism, helping, for example, to shape the ideal aristocratic subject. There are representations of war in texts such as Baldesar Castiglione's *The Book of the Courtier*, widely read in England, and Edmund Spenser's *The Faerie Queene*, but my emphasis is on this more popular writing, designed to be read or performed, in which war was theorised and subjected to critical examination.[9]

REPRESENTING WAR

It is not surprising that war is a common topic across a range of different types of popular writing in the early modern period. Over the centuries, in each new and repeated form of cultural representation, war inspires creative acts that occupy space within that form, alongside other seeming constants, such as love and desire, matters of spirituality and faith, or the endless conceptual quest for apparent absolutes like truth and beauty. It should be remembered that in the late sixteenth century, although it had evolved from earlier forms of drama, the publicly performed secular play was really an entirely fresh genre – one that worked best when performed in the innovative outdoor amphitheatres. The new form attracted poetic plays about war. And the increasingly efficient printing presses turned out a conspicuous amount of prose fiction, non-fiction or a blend of the two for a readership seemingly keen to read of earlier battles, or of how to win battles, or even perhaps of how to avoid them.

Writing and warfare have had a long relationship with each other, but one might ideally want to resist, as an explanation for this, a concept as general as 'the inevitability of war' as a condition of 'humanity'. However, it would be hard to challenge the consistent scope that war offers as a source for narratives of what it is like to 'experience' being subject to such a generalised if artificial concept as 'humanity'. Taking a traditional (i.e. Western) approach, we can see that the early classical canon of stories from the societies that evolved in and around the Mediterranean is almost entirely bound up with accounts of military conflict. As the Greek theatre evolved as a new form of cultural expression, it found itself at once working through and retelling the blood-drenched legends of earlier times. I shall return later to Homer as a kind of origin for this phenomenon. At this stage I should like to emphasise a wider articulation that can be seen to develop between warfare and new cultural forms. Homer's stories found a place in the new theatres of the ancients. Shakespeare and his contemporaries, in the new theatres of the Renaissance, rehearsed not only the war stories of the classical period, but also dramatised the war-torn chronicles of their own recent history.

An important point can be made about this sequencing, one that links Ancient Greece to the early modern period, and the early modern period to our own. The ideological force of this dramatisation of earlier dramatic conflicts surely affected subsequent attitudes to war just as, say, a representation of the experiences of some Second World War airmen, forged in the compelling post-war cinematic narratives of the RAF campaign, has resonated down the years. If this is the case, then the influence might be said to be strongest when there is a new or relatively new kind of cultural form through which that influence can be channelled. Whilst there are many forms of written and graphic representations of the war in the air, it was in the cinema that the campaign was most widely re-fought for posterity, 'keeping dark' some elements of the experience of war and reshaping others, as tragedy or even as comedy. The cinema – a kind of electric theatre – retold the Second World War in a way that is analogous to the ancient theatre's retelling of Homeric myths. As far as the RAF was concerned, films such as *The Dambusters* (1954), *Reach for the Sky* (1956), *633 Squadron* (1964) and *The Battle of Britain* (1969) produced a narrative of the conflict that helped define and consolidate the relationship between war and nation.[10]

War is thus mediated for those who come later by a mixture of overlapping narratives that influence each other and determine, or at least sway, attitudes towards subsequent wars. In the case of the Second World War there are many general written histories. Examples from Britain range from Winston Churchill's six-volume account to more recent interpretations, such as Joanna Bourke's *The Second World War: a People's History*.[11] There are also autobiographical accounts by various participants, usually those in charge, which seek to describe the conflict through the eyes of individual witnesses.[12] Fictional prose based on the Second World War is an ever-expanding canon, and one with a complex aesthetic history that has to embrace everything from the serious novel to comics, aimed at school children, that were so pervasive in the cultural environment of the decades following the war.[13] Yet it is cinematic fiction, including those films about the RAF mentioned above, that has most powerfully reworked the war for succeeding generations. Such films have sat alongside documentary accounts, such as Jeremy Issacs' *The World at War*, although occasionally the two forms have been fused, when fictional accounts have used documentary footage. *The Longest Day* (1962) and *The Battle of Britain* included such wartime cinematography in order to imply a high level of verisimilitude.[14] Advanced cinematic technology has been used in fictional accounts of the war in order to attempt to present a more 'realistic' impression of 'what it was like to fight' than actual footage allows, most notably in the opening sequence of Stephen Spielberg's *Saving Private Ryan* (1998).

Alongside these carefully designed narratives exist less formal accounts of war: personal, often familial, usually anecdotal and fragmented, and with no greater claim to an objective truth than those of printed or celluloid fiction. It is to the credit of organisations such as the Imperial War Museum and the BBC that such accounts have been given of late (and before it is too late, of course) considerably more prominence than in the past, and are now being preserved in electronic form. There is a clear implication that what is on offer here extends, and at least occasionally counters, both the more 'official' histories and the fiction produced in the immediate aftermath of the war.[15] These stories told among friends and within families, these marginal narratives that are not necessarily supported by documentary evidence, belong to a more casual historiography. They have a special importance as they lie somewhat beyond the more official accounts; but they have to be seen in relation to the adjacent narratives of remembrance and ceremony where past campaigns feed into continuing displays of militarism in times of peace. I shall argue later that the influence of fiction on these displays is paramount to their role in maintaining images of warfare that do little to forestall notions of the inevitability of further war.[16]

My handed-down account of Peace and Williams, their afternoon in Stratford-upon-Avon and Peace's response to war, is in itself a story – difficult to prove as absolute fact – but nonetheless resonant for some who hear it. It is a response that contests the dominant image of the RAF pilot as more or less 'fearless' without in any way detracting from the commitment Peace and Williams had to their duty – their 'work' in the war against Nazi aggression. It may seem odd to have started a book about the representation of war in the literature of the sixteenth and seventeenth centuries with this intimate family story from the Second World War. Yet the time, the place and the event offer a particular set of conjunctions with some of the book's main themes. Part of the aim of the book is to discuss the influence of narratives of war upon national identity, so it is worth stating that it seems impossible to underestimate the importance of the Second World War (and its stories) in the development of the post-war British state and its narratives of identity. It is from within this war-formed state that one looks back at its political and cultural evolution for points of connection across the centuries.

NARRATIVES AND CONNECTIONS

Thinking about these narratives of war it is worth noting the obvious irony that a man named 'Peace' had to make his work the business of war. Raymond Peace was apprenticed to the RAF at Cranwell in 1932 as a specialist instrument mechanic involved in the production of the sophisticated equipment on which modern aviation increasingly depended. Like many young men and women of his time he was an enthusiast for all aspects of flying, yet his ambitions were initially linked to his trade, and his trade was determined by his background and the promising solidity of the professional opportunities offered by engineering in the English Midlands. It was the threat of war in the later 1930s that led Peace to be trained as a pilot and assume the kind of identity revealed in family memories and through his correspondence. War was not his 'natural' element any more than the air was, yet he took to the new work in a dutiful way and at the same time fell in love with the sensations and aesthetics of flying. A number of issues proceed from this unexpected opportunity that will be developed in the historical scope of this book.

The first is the fundamental question that is widely considered so absurdly innocent that it is often restricted to the queries of children. Alternatively, it is dismissed along with the other slogans of anti-war activists and their over-idealistic (perhaps over-'intellectual') theorists. The question 'Why war?' has been raised periodically over the centuries and has produced a range of responses.[17] Whether the answer lies in some kind of genetic impulse, an enjoyment of war, the excesses of masculinity, greed, colonialism, economic competition or a mixture of these, less time has been spent on the question itself than on the procedures and aftermath of war. A skilled, intelligent, trainee aviation engineer who doted on his family and whose principal political interests were, like his enemy's, mostly shaped by the governments endorsed by his parents, was intensively trained and quickly promoted to the controls of a Halifax bomber. This he flew across the sea to drop explosives onto German cities just as similarly promoted young Germans were flying in the other direction to bomb British cities. His contribution helped destroy the grip of European fascism and kept most members of succeeding European generations out of further such large-scale wars, if not entirely out of uniform and further conflict. Yet the relatively comforting if complex tenets of the just war still obscure the fundamental question of why human beings should settle their disagreements in this way. The question is put aside, or belittled, or narrowed to fit the mouths of conscientious objectors – individuals at best treated ambivalently, but often seen as morally perverse as they lie beyond the common cause. Yet this fundamental question did arise, and was not easily dismissed during the period that this volume will address. It was discussed in the writing of those involved in the practice of war – and those who negotiated the shape of political practice in relation to the Reformation and the emerging British nation. And, in a questioning and unsettling way, the issue can be traced in the work of those writing fiction in the late sixteenth and early seventeenth centuries, in both popular prose and in poetry written for the stage. In other words, the question that those free from war on the scale of 1914–18 or 1939–45 might ask of the generations that fought those wars belongs to a fundamental agenda that was much more evident and critical to those who thought about war in the early modern period.

Of primary importance in thinking about the causes and results of war is the role of religion. Ray Peace and Ronnie Williams set out that afternoon in 1942 from the vicarage attached to the Anglican Church of St Andrews, Temple Grafton.[18] Nothing may have seemed strange or disturbing to them or their families about the connections between their work and this location. Indeed, the church and its services surely offered to these individuals, and countless others in the war, a degree of comfort and security.[19] Prayers for those engaged in the fighting were offered in the Anglican Church and in the congregations of many other denominations and faiths. As in most wars, the Church sanctioned the killing in the name of necessity and as a response to evil. If there were expressions of doubt, they were mainly confined to those objectors whose opinions were often met by scorn (and white feathers). Most churches stood by the campaign, congregations prayed for the combatants and received the bodies of the dead with solemn ceremony that is almost always reserved for the 'fallen' in military conflicts around the world.[20]

In terms of the much wider history of war and its representation in a variety of cultural forms, the association between war and religion is an intimate one. In the private realm of individual faith and redemption, and in the public realm of liturgy, the just war and the remembering of the dead, there is often at stake some kind of mediation of religious doctrine. An issue to the fore in this book is the way that expressions of Christianity, the principal faith system of the people of the period under examination, evolved in order to accommodate the new kinds of war that can be found discussed in early modern literature and drama. The period saw considerable anxiety about the inconsistency between Christ's teachings and the practice of war. Yet it also saw uncertainty swept away and the matter pretty much settled for centuries to come with any doubts smothered, or 'kept dark', in the relativist values and conditional philosophies of the just war.

Another factor linking Ray Peace to the arguments of early modern commentaries on war is that of national identity. In Stratford-upon-Avon in 1942, his accuser was able to evoke a clear sense of the relationship between his supposed cowardice and his duty towards the modern concept of the nation (and Empire), symbolised by the town itself and, presumably, by its famous theatre. Peace and Williams received their white feathers not because they were non-combatants but because they were not wearing uniforms of the state. In the early modern period, such a concept of the state was still in the earliest stages of its development, and clearly the relationship between militarism and the evolution of the state was a close one, played out in the formal political discourse of the time but also dramatised on the contemporary stage. While it is true that Peace and Williams fought in a war against fascism, it is likely that their principal justification for the conflict and their part in it was the defence of an established twentieth-century concept of nation that was, in the early modern period, still being cultivated. Moreover, the relationship between the early modern 'state' and its military was still very unclear. In 1942 civilian conscription to the forces was a given, with the exception of the 'reserved occupations'.[21] In the early modern period the idea of the 'civilian soldier', which I shall return to, was an ideal to some commentators but a violation of a vision of militarism to others. Some early modern writers, as we shall see, advocated a national standing army (as opposed to the more or less private armies of the medieval period), while others preferred a militia of citizens in constant preparedness for war. What seemed a conventional relationship between the state and the citizen in the 1940s was, then, one that was carefully forged in the early modern period. Amid conflicting arguments about militarism, the state and the subject – seen developing in a dialectical relationship with one another – the early modern period fostered the conditions for the militarised nationalism of modernity.

Another issue that this volume will address is the relationship between warfare and gender. Throughout modern history the militarised individual has stood for a particular kind of idealised masculinity. This may well have been part of what was at stake in Stratford in the summer of 1942. Peace and Williams, dressed in civilian clothes, adhered to a certain standard that would, given the assumptions of the period, have been aesthetically and socially pleasing in the opening months of 1939. They were well-dressed, 'good-looking chaps' with their cigarettes, easy banter and smart motorcar. Their manner came from a combination of their education, their awareness of their social standing, an addiction to the cinema and a complex set of mores to do with their sexuality. Yet in 1942, to be out of uniform somehow reduced their masculinity, transforming their identity in a way that epitomises a relationship between militarism and gender which draws on a long history. It might also be said that the donning of uniform encourages the individual to relegate subjective values and instincts (including fear) in the name of a wider, corporate set of values and responses. This important issue, to do with the relations between the individual subject and the collective, and especially perceptions of these relations in terms of concepts of masculinity, were to the fore in arguments about militarism in the early modern period. Those who had an interest in the future of militarism hotly contested such issues in arguments about drill, dress and discipline. Once 'settled' they were played out by generations of military personnel across the centuries. What might be said to have been 'kept dark' in this long history is that which can be glimpsed in the arguments over militarism and gender in the early modern period. There is evidence in the literature of a clear refusal of the codes of masculinity and militarism that were to come to dominate, and this usually depended upon a parallel set of arguments about the relationship between women and war.

Women have always been involved in the business of war, usually as victims, or guardians of the 'home front', rather than as perpetrators.[22] More than anything, their role has been defined by their grief in the face of the loss of their menfolk. Non-fictional military narratives rarely dwell on the involvement of women in the extensive camp infrastructures that for centuries determined the success or failure of armies whose male combatants were engaged (more 'heroically') a little distance away on the field of battle itself. However, a new emphasis developed in the relationship between militarism and gender in the twentieth century. This was due in part to the increasing technical sophistication of warfare, which led, for example, to women's direct involvement in wartime industrial production. Women were also more formally organised for nursing duties than they had been in the nineteenth century and were increasingly recruited for other kinds of uniformed operational duties. Similarly, the bombing of civilians placed women at the heart of large-scale modern warfare.

There is, of course, a fundamental link between these strategic and technical initiatives and the struggle of women for equal rights and self-determination. Until recently in most of the armed forces of the West, women were restricted, in theory if not in reality, to what were considered 'suitable' duties away from front-line action. The ideal military subject remained irreducibly defined as 'masculine'. The controversy attracted by modern challenges to this concept of the fighting soldier (as a certain kind of male heterosexual) shows just how entrenched the ideal of the soldier had become in the state armies of the West over the centuries. The fact that the debate over women and active service continues in a twenty-first-century world of female firefighters, astronauts and political leaders (who themselves send men to war) shows something of the uniqueness and sensitivity of the ideological relations between gender and warfare.[23] It also reveals the power and entrenched nature of the corporeal identity of the ideal military subject which has provided the reference point for that debate.

This book seeks to examine the basis of the 'naturalised' soldier of modernity by suggesting that the history of the relationship between gender and militarism has, in fact, often been an inherently unstable one, particularly in the late sixteenth and early seventeenth centuries. Modern anxieties over women at the front, or gay men in the ranks, echo the terms of an historical discourse that has sought, often with considerable difficulty, to construct and maintain an 'obvious' (and therefore naturalised) ideal of the masculine military soldier. At the same time, given the equation between the ('private') military subject and the larger military body (of the public or state army), it is a discourse that necessarily theorises the purpose of war itself. Armies require an identity, which is dictated by clear purpose – and a questioning of that purpose, linked to questions of gender, has had severe implications for those larger social formations that the military institutions claim to represent.

The relationship between women and war is a sensitive one even in modern Britain. It was only after a long campaign, for example, that the wartime experiences of women were specifically recognised by the erection of a monument in Whitehall, that most symbolic of locations where an act of remembrance takes place each November on the nearest Sunday to Armistice Day. The Queen unveiled John Mills' bronze sculpture, *The Memorial to the Women of World War II*, in July 2005. Some had thought it would detract from the nearby Cenotaph to the 'Glorious Dead of 1914–1919', and the exact distance between the two memorials was finally settled (at a respectful 53 metres) only after considerable debate. Others thought the seventeen sets of clothing and uniforms, symbolic of the different jobs taken on by women in the war (many perceived as 'men's jobs'), made the monument too cluttered or ordinary compared to the simple lines of the Cenotaph itself. Many disliked the way that the project had been so determinedly backed by the women gunners of the 'Ack-Ack' Command of the Royal Artillery Association, women who had fired guns during the war. One suspects that an underlying objection was that the sculpture announced what is often kept dark, particularly at the end of a period of war. On the one hand, the design of the monument reminds the observer that there was nothing ever exclusively male about the occupations taken on by women in times of war.[24] On the other, the sculpture's preoccupation with clothing perhaps shows that the mantle of war is one that is assumed most outwardly in terms of uniform.[25] Both women and men 'dress for war' and are made uniform by war's uniforms – an act that is central to the arguments about warfare that this book will address. Modern, (uniformed) warfare grew from discussions about identity, common purpose (and dress) that were held over and over again in the pages of Renaissance prose and on the stages of Renaissance theatre.

This study will also examine matters of technology, which were as central to the development of warfare in the early modern period as they have become to the debate about military strategy in more recent periods. Military development in the early period was in many ways defined by advances in ballistics. The same is true of developments since the Second World War, such as (so-called) 'smart' missiles and bombs, considered somehow more humane because of their claimed potential to avoid civilian casualties. Raymond Peace enthused about aviation rather than warfare. As an apprentice in the highly skilled and specialist field of aircraft engineering he would have witnessed the rapid developments that were taking place in this and other branches of technology during the 1930s. He was well placed to consider the way that warfare accelerates developments in technology and how that technology enhances warfare's methodologies. Aviation, indeed, offers an extreme example of this equation. Many people living in Stratford-upon-Avon in the summer of 1942 would have remembered a time before aeroplanes. It was not yet forty years since the first powered flight.[26] Those living in the ruins of nearby Coventry might have thought about the way that technology brought them aerial bombardment so soon, but so surely, within the space of just a few decades of the invention of the aeroplane and the dirigible.[27] For centuries people had dreamt of flying, bound the dream into their myths and celebrated birds in their religions. Then came the hot air balloon, the airship, the First World War 'ace', the anti-aircraft gun, bombers and the domestic air-raid shelter. Ray Peace and Ronnie Williams were to the fore in the race that utilised human ingenuity in the pursuit of warfare. The uniforms they wore bore winged insignia representing a fulfilment of the dream of their ancestors, and the machines they flew embodied a marshalling of the very latest technology in terms of both the explosives they dropped and the means of transporting them to the enemy. In the late summer of 1942 and particularly in a town so near to Coventry, they might have been hailed as heroes rather than cowards on the strength of their command of this technology, but only if they had they been wearing those uniforms.

AFTERMATH AND REPUTATION

The remaining months of 1942 were something of a turning point in the war. Prime Minister Churchill celebrated the success at El Alamein in November as 'the turning of "the Hinge of Fate" ', after which 'we never had a defeat'.[28] In the East the Soviet Army and people held out against the Germans at Stalingrad and began to turn the tide against them over the Christmas and New Year period. This effort and the Americans' firm involvement in the European sphere of the conflict meant that Britain no longer 'stood alone' as it had during the early years of the war.

By this time the airmen described by Churchill as 'The Few' who had fought in the Battle of Britain two years earlier were celebrated, as they still are, for their decisive campaign on behalf of an isolated nation. Their efforts had a symbolic role in maintaining morale during the Blitz and, arguably, in defining a sense of 'Britishness' ever since.[29] Their exploits were lovingly cultivated in a variety of media, and especially in the cinema, in the years following the war.[30] In terms of the technology involved, their aircraft, and especially the Spitfire, became iconic reminders of a particular kind of patriotic heroism and resistance, and still make an appearance at times of national remembrance and celebration. The airmen, many of whom were not actually British, enjoy an equally secure reputation.[31]

Yet this apparently seamless continuity between past and present, between fighting machinery and those who operated it, is interrupted when close consideration is given to the post-war reputation enjoyed by Peace, Williams and their comrades in Bomber Command. By comparison with that cultivated for the Battle of Britain pilots, the bombers' legacy has been kept rather in the dark. It is not that they were simply out-dazzled by the fighter pilots; and certainly their machines are as well known as those of the fighter pilots, carefully preserved in museums, and still occasionally flown.[32] Rather, it is the scale and nature of the 'work' itself. Mass bombing, especially following the raid on Dresden in 1945 with its dreadful civilian death toll, has never sat easily in the historical canons of the Second World War.[33] Air Chief Marshal Harris, in overall charge of the bombing operations, has a reputation that seems somewhat awkward by comparison with the other wartime leaders – and certainly, with the conspicuous exception of *The Dambusters*, the few films about bombing were never as popular as those about the Battle of Britain.[34] There is still occasional speculation about the moral perspective of those involved in developing the bombing strategy. The subject arises in accounts of the war's overall moral compass, finding a disturbing place even in the narratives attached to the Holocaust because, like other Nazi leaders, Rudolf Hoess, the commandant at Auschwitz, attempted to rationalise his own activities by equating them with the aerial bombing. Laurence Rees has remarked that:

> despite all the attempts to differentiate the two methods of killing, the false comparison between them made by Hoess and other Nazis still remains emotionally disturbing. One reason is that it is well known that there was disquiet about the policy of bombing German cities inside the Allied leadership – not least, towards the end of the war, from Churchill himself. And the revelation in recent years that in spring 1945 one Allied criterion used in the process of deciding which German cities and towns to target was their 'burnability', something that helped lead to the targeting of medieval cities like Würzburg, only adds to the sense of unease.[35]

Thus Raymond Peace and Ronald Williams were marching towards a rather uncertain place in military history.

This ambivalence about certain aspects of militarism may seem a modern condition, yet it is in fact a prominent feature of early modern debate about warfare, the technology of warfare and those involved with warfare as participants (willing or unwilling) or as its advocates. It might be said that it was the particular conjunction of advances in technology and a rash of treatises about the ethics of war in the early modern period that produced the terms under which some could later cast doubt on the morality of bombing in the Second World War. And if some ex-bombers felt understandably rather indignant about the half-heartedness of their nation's post-war gratitude, then this too is absolutely resonant with the situation recorded on behalf of soldiers by those writing about war in the late sixteenth and early seventeenth centuries. Peace and Williams may have returned to Temple Grafton with their eyes firmly fixed on their next missions, but they unknowingly took with them a long history of scepticism about certain kinds of wartime work.

There is, then, an historical narrative that exists alongside the more mainstream ones of war as a necessary evil. It includes disgust at war's excesses and a contradictory set of values that simultaneously praises and condemns the warrior. It promotes and justifies war, and then pities its victims. It sees war as a badge of national identity and cohesion, but at the same time as a wasteful failure of diplomacy. It likes the idea of the manly soldier and military discipline, but it neglects its veterans. That this history is somewhat obscured, or 'kept dark' does not reduce its validity. When glimpsed, it seems important since it profoundly disturbs a sense of the inevitability of our warlike condition. My argument in this book is that this history is especially illuminated in literature, and in terms of the origins of modern warfare, in the theatre of Shakespeare and his contemporaries.

Notes

1. Coventry was home to such factories as Armstrong Whitworth, Darnlier, Dunlop and Humber. German bombers targeted the city in a sequence of raids from June 1940 to August 1942 and official figures state that 1,236 people were killed. The ferocity of one particular raid gave rise to the term 'Coventrated' as almost 5,000 homes, many public buildings and three-quarters of the city's factories were damaged by bombs, mines and firestorms in a single night. 'Operation Moonlight Sonata' began in the early evening of 14 November 1940 and lasted for over ten hours. Five hundred German aeroplanes set off from France to bomb the city, partly, it was said, in revenge for the RAF's bombing of Munich on 8 November.
2. H. V. Morton [1927] (2006), *In Search of England*, London: Methuen, p. 248.
3. Stratford-upon-Avon's proximity to major industrial cities meant that its citizens were very aware of the mass bombing in the region as planes flew near the town. The fires from 'Operation Moonlight Sonata' could be seen by incoming bombers from 150 miles way. There were many stray bombs from these raids. A 500 lb bomb was discovered and made safe in Henley-in-Arden as recently as 1998.
4. See www.thepressgallery.org.uk.
5. More properly, Temple Grafton is associated with 'Wm Shaxpere', who is named in the Latin Episcopal register at Worcester as being granted a licence to marry 'Annam Whateley' of Temple Grafton. The next entry records the marriage bond between a 'William Shagspere' and 'Anne Hathwey' of Stratford. These entries, probably as carelessly done as adjacent ones are, have produced reams of speculation over Shakespeare's sexual and matrimonial history. The inhabitants of present-day Temple Grafton, and especially those running the Blue Boar Inn, perpetuate the idea that Shakespeare was married in the village in 1582.

6. By comparison with the other services, there was less of a distinction between ranks. An aircraft captain could be a sergeant and his second pilot a pilot officer, depending on their experience. Raymond Peace had started with 'Boy Service', graduated to other ranks and was then commissioned, so he was not 'naturally' an officer.
7. I am aware that there are varied interpretations of causes of the Second World War involving the inadequacy of the settlement of the 1914–18 conflict, imperial ambition and 1930s economic conditions, yet these are also explanations for the rise of fascism.
8. Thomas Deloney [1597/8] (2007), *The Gentle Craft*, ed. Simon Barker, Burlington, VT and Aldershot: Ashgate.
9. See Daniel Javitch's review of the reception of *The Book of the Courtier* in his 2002 edition, New York: Norton, Introduction.
10. In many ways these films simply rehearsed the spirit of such patriotic wartime productions as *The First of the Few*, *One of Our Aircraft is Missing* and *Mrs. Miniver* (all 1942) and the Pathé and Movietone news coverage shown alongside them.
11. Winston S. Churchill (1948–54), *The Second World War*, 6 vols, London: Cassell; Joanna Bourke (2001), *The Second World War: A People's History*, Oxford: Oxford University Press. Bourke's work on warfare in the twentieth century raises issues about the representation of war and its motivations and practices that complement those I am addressing in the early modern period. See especially Bourke (1996), *Dismembering the Male*, London: Reaktion Books; and Bourke (1999), *An Intimate History of Killing*, London: Granta.
12. See, for example, Geoffrey Leonard Cheshire (1961), *The Face of Victory*, London: Hutchinson; and Guy Gibson [1948] (1986), *Enemy Coast Ahead*, Manchester: Crécy Publishing.
13. Examples include: *Hotspur*, 1959–81 (formerly a story paper first published in 1933); *Valiant*, 1962–76; *Hornet*, 1963–75; *Hurricane*, 1964–65.
14. See, for example, *The World at War* (1973–4), produced for Thames Television by Jeremy Isaacs.
15. Examples include the Imperial War Museum's initiative, *Their Past Your Future*, and the BBC's *WW2 People's War* project.
16. I shall return to this point, but an example of the phenomenon would be the way that the theme music of *The Dambusters* can be heard at twenty-first-century military parades.
17. Of Sigmund Freud's many writings on war the most compelling for me remains his *Thoughts for the Times on War and Death* (1915). See also Jacqueline Rose (1993), *Why War?*, Oxford: Blackwell. More historical texts include Sun Tzu's sixth-century BC *The Art of War*, and Carl von Clausewitz's *On War* [1832] (1908). For the influence of early military strategists on modern warfare, see Kenneth N. Waltz, *Man, the State and*

War (2001), second revised edition, New York: Columbia University Press.
18. The house along the lane from the church is now privately owned but called 'The Old Vicarage'. Ronnie's father, Sidney Bertram Williams, was the vicar of Temple Grafton from 1922 to 1947 (with Benton from 1945).
19. Peace's letters reveal that he often attended church services in the villages and towns near the bases on which he served.
20. Through its association with the Crusades, of course, Temple Grafton has a long connection with military conflict.
21. White feathers were often received by men involved in reserved occupations which included, in the Midlands, those involved in engineering and munitions production.
22. Without the most common experience for women as victims of war has been the use of rape and other forms of physical assault by men.
23. This was, of course, also the case in Elizabethan England where a female monarch directed men to war.
24. The clothing on the monument includes uniforms, but also the working garments of the trades previously thought of as exclusively the province of men.
25. I am aware that there are some kinds of 'soldiers' who do not wear uniforms (guerrillas, partisans, terrorists), but the history of the development of the military uniform fairly neatly coincides with the history of state armies.
26. The first powered flight by Orville and Wilbur Wright took place on 17 December 1903.
27. The first British military airship, the *Null Secundus I*, took to the air in October 1907.
28. Churchill, *The Second World War*, Vol. 4, p. 487.
29. Churchill's notion of 'The Few' was undoubtedly inspired by the St Crispin's day speech in Shakespeare's *Henry V*. Of the 2,927 allied pilots who took part in the Battle of Britain, 510 were killed.
30. Channel Four's film *The Few* (2005) demystified the assumption that the Battle of Britain pilots were uniformly of one class, noting that in preparing for war the RAF had trained men from a range of backgrounds.
31. The Battle of Britain was fought not only by British flyers but also pilots from Poland and Czechoslovakia, Australia, New Zealand, South Africa and Canada. There were a few volunteers from the United States, including Billy Fiske, whose story is being filmed for release in 2008. The film *The Few* stars Tom Cruise and is based on a book by Alex Kershaw (2006), *The Few: The American Knights of the Air Who Risked Everything to Fight in the Battle of Britain*, Cambridge, MA: Da Capo Press. The film's historical content has been described by Bill Bond of the Battle of Britain Historical Association as 'a load of bloody rubbish'. See

'Hollywood Updates History of Battle of Britain' in *The Independent*, 11 April 2004.

32. Miniature replicas were assembled by thousands of post-war children in the form of plastic kits. See Jarrod Cotter (2005), *Living Lancasters: Keeping the Legend Alive*, Stroud: Sutton.

33. This is partly because the bombing of Dresden has been seen as simply revenge for Coventry and the Blitz. For recent discussions about the morality of the bombing, see Paul Addison and Jeremy Crang (eds) (2006), *Firestorm: the Bombing of Dresden: 1945*, London: Pimlico; and A. C. Grayling (2006), *Among the Dead Cities: Was the Allied Bombing of Civilians in World War II a Necessity or a Crime?*, London: Bloomsbury.

34. The exception is the popular *The Dambusters* of 1954, which underplays the fact that 1,294 people were killed during the raids, and the much later film about American bombers, *Memphis Belle* (1990). A new version of *The Dambusters* is currently in production, directed by Peter Jackson.

35. Laurence Rees (2005), *Auschwitz: the Nazis and the 'Final Solution'*, London: BBC Books, p. 367.

2

IN THEATRE

⌒

Whether it was due to Hitler's desire to preserve the town because of the importance of Shakespeare to German culture or simply because of its military and economic insignificance, Stratford-upon-Avon remained comparatively peaceful and safe throughout the years of the war. The presence of military personnel and government officials, stray bombs, crashed aircraft and the employment of its citizens in nearby factories kept the war very much alive in the consciousness of the townspeople, yet there was very little direct threat. Indeed, the town was actually something of a vantage point from which to witness the destruction of the industrial cities of the English Midlands. With its increasingly cultivated Shakespearean associations, its residual rural aspect and its English charm as a town symbolically situated at the 'Heart of England', Stratford was geographically and ideologically unique as a place from which to observe the potential destruction of the values it had come to represent. This role invites speculation on the long-established metaphorical connection between the theatre (as a place of action and observation) and warfare in general. War is commonly thought of as 'theatre' (as in 'a theatre of war') and those involved in military activity speak of being 'in theatre' when they are transferred from the periphery to the centre of a conflict – where there is an actual 'engagement' with an enemy. Similarly, battles are 'staged', soldiers belong to 'companies' and go on 'tours' of duty, and hostilities are seen as 'action'. The 'act' of war steals from the theatre a complex of images, many of which operate, in the general lexicon of warfare, as euphemisms that distance participants and observers from its brutality. Similarly, the apparatus of military organisation depends upon a range of theatrical devices in its elaborate ceremony. There is clearly something essentially dramatic about the military parade, with its formal roles, rituals and routines, its speaking and non-speaking parts, its music, its colour and its elaborate props – as well, of course, as the costumes worn by its participants. If the relationship between war and the theatre sees the former adopting the devices and apparatus of the latter, then this is a phenomenon that becomes particularly apparent in military circles in the age of Shakespeare and his contemporaries. This relationship can, however, be seen as an equation, and this book sets out to examine what the theatre and its audiences can potentially 'give back' to the wider stages of warfare in a questioning, even subversive, way.

Returning briefly to the Stratford-upon-Avon of 1942, one looks at the list of plays staged at the Memorial Theatre for some welcome distraction for audiences preoccupied by a war that had been raging across Europe for some three years. Shakespeare's *A Midsummer Night's Dream* and Sheridan's *The School for Scandal* may have done the trick, the one 'otherworldly' and the other something of an abstraction in terms of its play upon social manners of a bygone age. But then you recall the anti-Semitism of *The School for Scandal* and think again. *The Taming of the Shrew*, with its discussion of gender roles, might have appealed to an audience that would almost inevitably have included women undertaking wartime duties that challenged the fixed nature of the relationship between gender and work. One hopes that these and other plays that summer were, if nothing else, a source of laughter for audiences seeking entertainment for a while away from the hardships of war. It is unlikely that those in charge at the theatre would have wanted to shape their productions towards the immediate concerns of the war as G. R. Wilson Knight had done with *This Sceptred Isle* at the Westminster Theatre in London in 1941.[1] Yet in 1942 the Stratford season included three plays that may well have resonated in an immediate way with wartime audiences. *Hamlet* is there, a play that starts in an atmosphere of wartime paranoia and ends with a vision of a military funeral and acts of remembrance. *Macbeth* begins with a gruesome image of the business of war and moves through battles and hand-to-hand combat that might have called to mind the actual experiences of some in the audience. And *The Merchant of Venice* evokes something of the kind of racial alienation that characterised the rise to power of the Nazi enemy itself. It has often been remarked upon by critics that this is a play whose reputation was altered for all time because of the wartime atrocities against the Jews, and it is interesting to speculate about its reception at Stratford in 1942. What the audience brings to the theatre in terms of its critical intelligence and cultural contexts and what the theatre then brings to war in terms of illuminating that which is 'kept dark' in those cultural contexts is central to this study.

Stratford-upon-Avon today seems to function for many as a kind of seaside resort with the river's banks a beach for landlocked Midlanders. A mixture of people come and go throughout the year. Although navigating the semiotics of the various attractions is probably made easier by a knowledge of Shakespeare's life and works it is possible to enjoy a day in Stratford even if you have been 'put off' Shakespeare at school. Even a Marlovian can have fun here. In other words, despite the views of some observers, a visit to Stratford-upon-Avon is not the all-encompassing, hermetically sealed experience of, say, Disneyland. Nor is it really a kind of secular pilgrimage, although admittedly many of the attractions have been grafted onto the central association with Shakespeare just as in medieval pilgrimages secular appetites were catered for alongside spiritual ones. Those visiting the theatre and/or the town have varying degrees of association with Shakespeare, from the visiting scholar to the weekend punter.

In the years between the wars, however, there was more at stake for some observers in the relationship between Stratford, Shakespeare and what is now called 'the Shakespeare industry'. The concern was with the qualitative nature of the visitor's participation. H. V. Morton wistfully remembered the Stratford of before the Great War 'as a quiet little heaven where it was always May, with the nightingales shaking silver in the dark trees at night and the Avon mooning under Hugh of Clopton's grand old bridge':

> There was Mr Frank Benson – as he was in those days – the local deity, seen often in swift and god-like transit on a decrepit bicycle, the high priest of the Stratford Festival. I remember him waving his arms at me in a storeroom hung with hams, which he used as an office, and telling me, as I sat worshipping him from a sugar crate, that only through Stratford, the common meeting-place of the English-speaking world, could we heal the pains of Industrialism and make England happy again. We were to make the whole world happy, apparently, by teaching it to morris-dance and to sing folk-songs and to go to the Memorial theatre. With the splendid faith of Youth we pilgrims believed that England could be made 'merrie' again by hand-looms and young women in Liberty gowns, who played the harpsichord. Then, I seem to remember, shortly after that war was declared . . . Stratford-on-Avon is the only town in England which can be compared with the ancient pilgrimage towns; it is, in its way, a kind of lay Glastonbury. I suppose the old religious shrines also received thousands of sheep-like pilgrims who had no idea why they were pilgrims beyond the fact that it was the right thing to do.

How I detest the word 'pilgrim' in its modern sense. Also the word 'shrine'. Whenever I hear them I seem to hear also someone saying, 'Bring a couple of Martinis – quick now – and some ice water!'[2]

Morton's account is as interesting in its own way as that of critics like L. C. Knights, G. R. Wilson Knight and E. M. W. Tillyard, who were to emerge as such dominant voices in Shakespeare scholarship in the years leading up to, during and immediately after the Second World War. Like Morton, or rather like Frank Benson, they had views about Shakespeare's role as a national figure and about his plays as representative of an idealised Elizabethan world of cultural and social harmony centred on the figure of the monarch.[3] Their influential work, much debated and even denounced since its publication, helped secure a particular place for Shakespeare at the heart of the English educational system and shape a particular approach to the study of his plays. This approach was based, among other things, on nostalgia for a world that seemed somehow innocent in the context of the political turmoil of the twentieth century. However one views these critics' approach there was something essentially optimistic about it, articulated in the years after the war with the perceived revival of national peacetime purpose and identity associated with the Festival of Britain and the new 'Elizabethan Age' that began with the coronation in 1953.

There is an ambivalence and pessimism in the sharp difference between Morton's earlier, possibly naïve idealism (irrevocably lost to the Great War), and his troubled appraisal of the situation as he found it in 1926. His evaluation of the terms of pilgrimage is critical to the history of Shakespeare and Stratford. Much of his tone is rather cryptic or tongue-in-cheek, but those who had a sheep-like relationship with the cultural core of the Stratford experience clearly offended him. He resents those who do not have the kind of (superior) qualitative relationship with the Bard and his work that he himself presumably has, or at least once had, before disillusion set in. The thinning of the cultural relationship between Shakespeare and those attending the shrine, and the overall vulgarisation of Stratford-upon-Avon by the trippers and the charabancs – Morton arrived by motor-car you will recall – corresponds to the very problem that was to be addressed by Tillyard and the others.

There is a great deal at stake here. Morton doesn't like pilgrimages that do not have a spiritual dimension: that is, the 'appropriate' response to Shakespeare and Stratford. In this approbation he predicts the ideal of the sensitive, culturally attuned respondent defined later in the work of I. A. Richards and F. R. Leavis.[4] Secondly, although rehearsing a common piece of prejudice from the time, his attack on Martini-drinkers (for which read Americans) could be said to reflect that deep vein of Englishness which Shakespeare was to represent in the New Criticism to come, but was clearly under threat between the wars.

Thirdly, the whole idea of pilgrimage is an interesting and suggestive concept in terms of both Shakespeare and warfare itself. The idea of Stratford-upon-Avon as a shrine where people go to worship the memory of Shakespeare and nation is a familiar one. Yet there is a curious correlation with a central theme of this book – the idea of the remembrance of war as a form of tragedy. If we are to look for modern forms of pilgrimage, we might indeed think of Shakespeare as an English saint and of Stratford-upon-Avon as a place to visit in search of the ghostly presence of a former, better England. But we might also consider a parallel with the way that, in ceremony and liturgy, we are asked to think of the 'Glorious Dead' of earlier wars. They are often represented (in inscription and monument) as our better but lost selves. They are suspended in time, as Shakespeare was to be in the work of the critics of the middle part of the twentieth century, with his timeless and national values. In the aftermath of war, remembrance offers a smoothing over of its harsher realities, presenting it as a tragedy with the soldier cast as the hero. Ceremony and ritual are marshalled to cover over cracks and 'keep dark' certain aspects of the practices of war.

A Shakespeare read provocatively for uncertainties, hesitations and contradictions – and against the smoothing narratives of war and nation espoused on behalf of his work by the mid-century critics – is a very unsettling experience indeed. It amounts to an assault on the reputation of Shakespeare as unequivocally supportive of the warlike hierarchical power structures of his time. In a way such a reading is almost akin to the disinterring of the war dead who lie beneath monuments, in a kind of sanitised sanctity, to find out how bodies are actually marked and torn by conflict. This parallel is especially true when it is seen how close the association between Shakespeare and attitudes to war has become over the centuries – a matter I shall turn to later.

One further point emerges from Morton's sojourn in the Warwickshire countryside in 1926. Like some of those who were to dominate literary criticism in the years that followed his visit, he seems uncomfortable with a 'lay' response to high culture. One contention in this book is that those furthest from Shakespeare and his contemporaries as emblems of high culture might well ask new and searching questions of his work. In the modern world, those distanced from 'Shakespeare' (in terms of an awareness of the writer and his work shaped by formal, educational interpretation) might wonder why he has been quite so institutionalised. In a visit to the theatre or in the cinema, they might ask very different questions of the practices and effects of dramatic representation from those asked by critics working in the formal establishments of literary or dramatic criticism. Moreover, those wandering today in and out of the Shakespeare of Stratford, or only occasionally experiencing his plays in theatre or cinema, bring with them the potential for textual readings that may be quite at odds with the formal canons of criticism. If it were not so, the difference between cultural specialist (pilgrim) and non-specialist (tourist) would collapse. One point is clear. Since they are frequently raised in the plays of Shakespeare and his contemporaries and, given the times, are increasingly likely to be of concern to many experiencing modern productions, the dual issues of war and nation should feature highly in the range of questions asked of Shakespeare in the contemporary world.

In Shakespeare's day there were spectators who were closer to him than any of us can ever be – attending early performances at Court or in the public theatres. But those people were even further than modern non-specialists from a conception of Shakespeare as 'great art', because Shakespeare had not yet been 'invented' in the terms in which so many think of him today. Since those early observers were, as we shall see, most thoroughly immersed in the experience, spectacle or philosophy of war, they would have responded differently to the plays of Shakespeare and his contemporaries when compared with later generations of theatre-goers (and readers) subject to an institutionalised Shakespeare.

THEATRE, CANON AND CRITICISM

Although it now seems to have fallen from use, the expression 'Keep it dark' was popular during the war and appeared on at least one of the government posters in the 'Loose Talk Costs Lives' series designed to remind citizens of the secrecy required in undertaking their duties. *Brewer's Dictionary of 20th-Century Phrase and Fable* notes it as:

A slogan from World War II reminding people to remember national security and not unwittingly give away any information that would be useful to the enemy. In 1940 there was a variety show playing in London called *Shush, Keep It Dark*, and later there was a radio show featuring a character, Commander High-Price, whose catch-phrase was 'Hush, keep it dark.'[5]

Interestingly, E. Cobham Brewer mentioned the term in relation to the theatre of the late nineteenth century in his original *Dictionary of Phrase and Fable*. He is defining the term '*Tace* is Latin for candle' and reminds his readers of an historical allusion 'worth remembering':

> It was customary at one time to express disapprobation of a play or actor by throwing a candle on the stage, and once this was done the curtain was immediately drawn down. Oulter, in his *History of the Theatres of London*, gives us an instance of this which occurred January 25th, 1772, at Covent Garden theatre, when the piece before the public was *An Hour Before Marriage*. Someone threw a candle on the stage, and the curtain was dropped at once.[6]

For W. C. Oulter the theatre was a place of light or darkness, and perhaps, in simple terms, a place where things that ought to be 'kept dark' (in the judgement of some) were wilfully illuminated in a potentially subversive manner. This view of the disruptive potential of the theatre coincides with the attitude to the early modern theatre assumed in this book – a view that has been helped along by the critical theory of the last thirty years or so. The fundamental shake-up in critical thinking heralded by structuralism arrested traditional criticism and set the scene for a long battle in the 1970s and 1980s over what constituted the canon of 'English literature' and what contribution a new body of theory could make to the understanding of literature and criticism. An important area of this concern over canon was inevitably devoted to the texts of Shakespeare's plays and those of his contemporaries and followers, and also addressed the manner in which theatrical performance explored the ideology of those texts. The theory that has recast criticism of Shakespeare's plays over this period is a striking but complex phenomenon and an examination of some of its key components may help to provide a context for the approach I wish to adopt.

CRITICAL APPROACHES

Three general points can be made about the kind of theory that has overturned many of the assumptions found in the earlier criticism of critics such as Tillyard, Knights and Wilson Knight. The first concerns the formerly established literary canon, the body of 'accepted' great works that privileged certain writers above others. This earlier canon has been viewed for the last thirty years or so as an ascendancy of certain authors that necessarily led to the exclusion or neglect of writers whose works did not fit an exacting but nonetheless partial, or even prejudiced, set of criteria. Thus, in the realm of Renaissance drama, Shakespeare ruled supreme, to the detriment of the dozens of writers classified solely as his 'contemporaries'. This recent sub-version of the older canon is important to the way that this book proceeds. It is part of its argument about war and nation that Shakespeare's contemporaries, although writing for similar audiences and in the same atmosphere of extended debate about war, can be read as offering a rather different set of narratives about war itself. This is not to say that Shakespeare was somehow pro-war and his contemporaries against it, but that the wider canon of texts reveals a striking complication in representations of war that depends in part upon the reaction of Shakespeare's contemporaries and followers to his work. And there are texts, marginal in the sense of the traditional canon, in which can be found narratives of war that are hard to incorporate in a view of the drama of the period as an expression of a commitment to the military orthodoxy of the period.

A second major theme of modern theory has been the overt sense of its own politics, and a recognition of the politics of the criticism that preceded it. Traditional criticism, modern theorists have claimed, was based on the apparent innocence of its assumptions and practices. It was seemingly harmless in claiming an educational and even moral purpose in 'close reading', or in recognising 'timeless values' in the literature of the past. There was in fact a political significance in the assumptions made about what constituted those timeless values and their role in reinforcing a particular social order. Thus, if a great work like *Hamlet* was read in order to show the timelessly tragic nature of the 'human condition' and the 'flaw' at the heart of even the noblest of men, then this tended to 'fix' human nature as both unchanging and unchangeable. Accordingly, modern readers and theatre audiences enjoy the play not for its sense of historical distance from their own experiences, but in terms of identification with an historical continuum: history means nothing because nothing has really changed in the core of human experience since the period when Shakespeare was alive. Implied in this kind of approach, if never clearly announced, was that the desire for societal change found at the heart of radical politics, such as Marxism or feminism, was pointless. In the context of the issues that are important to this study, a fixedly defined human nature would inevitably be bound up with a propensity to engage in warfare, as an aspect of the 'human condition' that, perhaps, tests or reveals the tragic heart of 'man'. Since I am attempting to show the instability of such a 'natural' desire or propensity, this aspect of the way that modern literary theory has unfixed a causal human nature could not be more critical. This is not to say that parallels between the 'then' of the Renaissance and the 'now' of the twenty-first century are not important. Indeed, what is striking about the relationship between attitudes to war in Shakespeare's time and in our own is exactly a sense of resonance. But it is a resonance that comes about because these attitudes were actually constructed when Shakespeare was alive; and it is in the plays that we find traces of the artificiality of an historical continuity that has been presented as natural, as part of the tragic human condition. An example of just how extensive and profound assumptions about warfare and the 'human condition' can be emerges from recent and much publicised assertions by scientists about the inevitability of war. The discourse is scientific, but its (sometimes casually expressed) assumptions might well have their origin in the triumph of 'war as tragedy' that came about in the Renaissance. For the celebrated physicist Stephen Hawking the long-term survival of the human race is at risk as long as it is confined to a single planet, and war is placed alongside natural phenomena as a source of that risk:

> Sooner or later disasters such as an asteroid collision or a nuclear war could wipe us all out. But once we spread out into space and establish independent colonies our future should be safe.[7]

This shows perhaps the importance of aligning criticism, where fictional representations of warfare are so clearly inscribed, with a politics that refuses such pessimism.

Equating critical practice with politics in the first place may seem to some absurd. Yet recent theory has been thoroughly committed to exploring the ideological nature of traditional visions of the relationship between humanity and culture, exposing the politics of the older criticism by contrast with its own, explicitly stated agenda for change. Much modern criticism has been linked to political movements at work beyond academic circles and this is recognisable in the terms that have been used to describe various subsections or varieties of modern critical thought, including feminism, post-colonialism and Marxism. And although Marxism is rarely to the fore in the realm of the most recent criticism, its influence was an important factor in the re-examination of the theory and practice of criticism in the 1980s. This was partly due to its insistence upon the de-centring of the individual as an agent in the creation and transformation of social formations and its emphasis upon structures (classes, groups, and economic systems) and the collective 'consciousness' of people subject to those systems.

Most challenging has been the influence on the study of the theatre of Shakespeare and his contemporaries of various schools of literary theory. Even if they repudiate the strictures and simplicity of Marxism, they share with it a strong sense that human beings are products of systems of language, culture and identity that generate the concept of the 'individual' or 'human nature', promoted as the source rather than the effect of those systems. The radicalism of the many strands of theory that have influenced critical approaches in the last quarter of a century has been in their understanding that meaning is not fixed or stable, but plural and contingent. Texts as diverse as a Shakespeare play, a political speech or even the signs that direct us from place to place in our everyday lives render not a set of transparent truths, but a range of sites where there are contests for meaning.[8] We may not be unduly troubled by what might simply be seen as ambiguities in signage in public places, such as arrows apparently directing us the wrong way. But it becomes clear that the meanings of phrases such as 'just war' are altogether more problematic and unstable, especially when seen in terms of twenty-first-century international relations and gender politics. This was the case in the plays of Shakespeare and his contemporaries, produced at a time when the theory of the just war was being harnessed in the service of the emerging modern state.

The theoretical approaches that have informed readings of these plays over the recent period are, then, diverse and complex. The terms that have emerged, such as 'structuralism', 'poststructuralism' and 'psychoanalysis', are perhaps better understood by readers when they are applied to literary texts, although Marxism and feminism are more easily apprehended because of their clear political provenance. However, there is common ground between the different areas of theory that is particularly significant in terms of Shakespeare's plays. The philosophical and linguistic approaches that draw to a large degree on the work of the French structuralist Roland Barthes and poststructuralist Jacques Derrida (who modified the earlier 'structuralism' of the Swiss linguist Ferdinand de Saussure) have been particularly influential with respect to texts written for theatrical performance. In proposing that meaning is not fixed, either by the intentions of the author or by the text itself, Barthes and Derrida unsettled the emphasis that more traditional criticism had placed on the author. An author produces a text, but cannot control the meanings that flow from it into the communal systems and cross-currents of language; and meanings are not his or her private realm, but operate in a public way – in what might collectively be termed 'culture'. In many respects this idea is especially true of the dramatic text – written perhaps by a single hand, but manifestly opened up in terms of the plurality of its meanings by the collaborative nature of production. If this is not the case, the impulse individuals have to see many different 'interpretations' of the same play would become meaningless. The theatre might be said to be a complex system for the production of meaning that inherently reinforces the idea of 'plurality' of meaning that theorists have ascribed to any kind of written text. The theatre is a system of signification in which meaning circulates through a range of agents, such as actors, directors or stage managers, and by means of its own mechanics – set, scenery, lighting and costume. Faced with this proliferation of devices for the production of meaning, audiences are invited to experience systems that reveal the way that meaning is 'produced' in a very practical manner. The objective may be to create an illusion of reality, but the mechanics of that illusion are very apparent, and the raw material of any production, the text, is necessarily just one component in the overall process.

The process through which meaning is produced seems especially 'open' in the plays of Shakespeare and his contemporaries, where there is an extremely close correspondence between the texts and the theatre environments for which they were written. Although this openness also has much to do with contemporary attitudes to language and meaning in a world before literacy was common, the dramatists of the late sixteenth and early seventeenth centuries seemed particularly aware of the instability and plurality of meaning. The plays are full of double-meanings, slips of the tongue and puns. In a period that valued rhetoric as an expression of scholarship, the plays constantly reflect on the power of speech itself and its potential for deception as well as truth: language seems less a transparent medium for 'truth' and more a complex of variations and uncertainties of meaning. When this phenomenon is considered in the context of the way that the plays were staged, the self-reflexivity of Renaissance drama is even more apparent. The stage was itself a system of signs, simple in its construction but complex in terms of its signification. If, as it is widely thought, the canopy in public theatres such as the Globe represented Heaven, and a trapdoor in the stage could signify Hell, then the meanings of those terms could be unfixed by being used in other pieces of stage business, or simply by being seen as part of the theatre. Meanwhile, the stage could be a platform or a forest, a castle or a battlefield, but certainly a space where meaning could be played with and played out.

Such a complex system of signification might be said to reinforce and, indeed, amplify ideas about language and meaning that have underpinned recent critical approaches to early modern theatre. Instead of searching for universal truths and timeless continuities such as 'human nature' or the 'human condition', the emphasis of recent critical thinking has shifted to the way that the theatre represents a contest between competing sets of ideas. Far from providing a smooth hierarchy of meaning, with the 'truth' of any dramatic situation as inevitable and easily accessed, the theatre tends towards inviting its audience to ponder a range of contrasting positions and viewpoints over which it has to make a judgement.

Recalling the theoretical work of Emile Benveniste, the influential critic Catherine Belsey once described the plays of the Renaissance as 'interrogative', distinguishing them from the 'declarative' texts of classic realism.[9] Writing in 1980, she argued that the 'interrogative' text:

> invites an answer or answers to the questions it poses. Further, if the interrogative text is illusionist it also tends to employ devices to undermine the illusion, to draw attention to its own textuality. The reader is distanced, at least from time to time, rather than wholly interpolated into a fictional world. Above all, the interrogative text differs from the classic realist text in the absence of a single privileged discourse which contains and places all the others.[10]

This still seems to me a valid and persuasive summary of the subversive potential of the Elizabethan and early Stuart play. Although criticism evolved into 'Cultural Materialism' and 'New Historicism', and there has recently been a return to formalist and biographical approaches, I shall be exploring the representation of war in the texts of Shakespeare and his contemporaries in terms of this idea of their interrogative nature.

SHAKESPEARE'S WAR

It is my contention that the plays of Shakespeare and his fellow playwrights from the period 'interrogate' central issues to do with war that were being constructed in this period beyond the theatre itself – notably in the military theory that this book addresses. In order to interrogate the subject of war, Shakespeare and his contemporaries had first to raise it – and this they did in as determined and focused a way as writers had in a variety of forms across the centuries since writing began. In terms of Shakespeare alone, war is such a common reference point in his work that its appearance is sometimes over-looked – or certainly marginalised – as an issue. Looking again at the 1942 Stratford season one notices the presence of war in Jacques's speech in *As You like It* where the soldier is identified as one of the 'natural' ages of man:

> Then, a soldier,
> Full of strange oaths, and bearded like the pard,
> Jealous in honour, sudden, and quick in quarrel,
> Seeking the bubble reputation
> Even in the cannon's mouth.
>
> (II.vii.149–53)

An understanding of the potential the early modern theatre has to invite subversive readings of the prevailing ideologies of its period has worked against a much older view of Shakespeare's work as straight-forwardly patriotic. The work of some recent critics has also drawn attention to the place Shakespeare obtained in relation to warfare in later periods. Much work has been done, for example, on Laurence Olivier's wartime production of *Henry V*, or of the connections seen between Shakespeare and the Cold War, the Falklands War and the attack on Iraq.

One suspects that the persistent but changing nature of war in the last two decades is responsible for the increased interest of late in the representation of warfare on the English stage of the late sixteenth and early seventeenth centuries. The book-length publications mentioned later are evidence of this, together with an impressive variety of journal articles and chapters in multi-authored collections. The issue has also been to the fore at a number of recent international confer-ences. It has been a topic for discussion in the Shakespeare Association of America, the British Shakespeare Association and at the World Shakespeare Congress, as well as in a range of more specialised, *ad hoc* conventions. There has also been a series of conferences with an his-torical or interdisciplinary theme, all showing the vitality and topical-ity of early modern warfare either as an issue in itself or as a subject in various genres of fiction. Those organising such events have pointed to recent world affairs as somehow prompting debate for those historians who, like myself, regard the early modern period as a political and philosophical source for the practices of modern warfare.

It is hard to think of a more universal topic than war and yet until recently there were few full-length volumes produced on the relationship between war and the dramatic literature of the late sixteenth and early seventeenth centuries. Written fifty years ago, Paul Jorgensen's *Shakespeare's Military World* still seems fresh because in many ways it has never been eclipsed, although it positions Shakespeare as something of a channel for Tudor enthusiasm for war.[11] Ten years ago Curtis C. Breight's *Surveillance: Militarism and Drama in the Elizabethan Era* opened up the field and has become something of a reference work for those looking for elements of coercion (military and otherwise) in the emerging early modern state.[12] Other recent texts on Shakespeare and war include: Richard Courtney, *Shakespeare's World of War: the Early Histories* (1994); Nick de Somogyi, *Shakespeare's Theatre of War* (1998); Bruce R. Smith, *Shakespeare and Masculinity* (2000); Nina Taunton, *1590's Drama and Militarism: Portrayals of War in Marlowe, Chapman and Shakespeare's Henry V* (2001); and Alan Shepard, *Marlowe's Soldiers* (2002).[13] The work of Scott Newstok is critical to an understanding of the way that *Henry V* has been used in twenty-first-century political discourse.[14] Alongside these academic discussions has been a telling amount of public interest in the staging of plays about war written by Shakespeare and his contemporaries. These range from Michael Bogdanov's 1986–89 productions of Shakespeare's history plays, with their overt references to the war between Britain and Argentina in the South Atlantic, to the recent productions of *Henry V*, which have alluded to the attack on Iraq.[15]

In the early modern period assertions about the moral righteousness of war, the 'naturalness' of the continuity between masculinity and warfare, and the necessity of the early modern state to have a standing army, had to be constructed by means of interpretations of classical models, foreign examples and biblical sources. And these assertions had to be carefully defended against an apparently powerful but increasingly occluded counter-discourse. The triumph of the pro-war, pro-soldier, pro-state army argument is evident in the range of military history that celebrates the 'origins' of the militarism of modernity in a romanticised 'renaissance' of evolving (and 'progressive') military discipline. What follows addresses this history in order to show how the early modern discourse of war was manufactured and to question its authority through an examination of some of the dramatic representations of the subject of war in the work of William Shakespeare, his contemporaries and his near-contemporaries. In this form of writing for the stage can be demonstrated the contradictions in the adjacent military prose. And glimpses can be had of the counter-discourse of, say, domesticity versus going to war, pleasure above martial prowess, and the virtue of a collective 'body of citizens' as opposed to the collective body of an army.

The book thus seeks to pursue the relationship between Shakespeare and war by setting against the drama of the period a range of contemporary foreign and domestic texts that are formally thought of as manuals on the art of war. Beyond their practical recommendations concerning tactics, weaponry and discipline, these works also describe the ideological practice of warfare in terms of its justification, ethics and purpose. These texts are evidence of and examples from an early modern international 'revolution' in the practicalities of war. They also mark an end to any real mainstream ideological (and therefore theological) doubt about the permanence of warfare as a constant in human affairs and therefore what constitutes the ultimate distinguishing practice of a well-formed modern state. The analysis of these texts shows that the military revolution which they reflect, whilst predicated on an ideal of absolute monarchy, is actually a precondition for the establishment of the conditional, parliamentary monarchies or republics of the modern era. In this evolution the inevitability and even desirability of warfare is inscribed at the expense of earlier visions of peace and co-operation espoused by thinkers such as Erasmus, Colet and More.

The study further maintains that the relationship between civilian life and military idealism was an intimate one long before the maturing of capitalism, but can be seen almost as a precondition of advanced capitalism. It looks to the theatre of the late sixteenth and early seventeenth centuries in order to trace the insecurities and contradictions in the establishment of the warlike state. The uses of Shakespeare as a symbol of patriotism are discussed as the military texts, form against form, are set against the dramatic texts. Shakespeare's theatre, like all theatre, relied on conflict, and in the pursuit of this can be read as inviting a resistance to the smooth imperative of the military prose texts, the themes of which are returned to time and time again in Shakespeare's plays. Thus my investigation of parts of the Shakespeare canon starts with the history plays and proceeds by way of tragedy to a variety of plays, all a rich source of debate about the ethics of war. In later chapters I look beyond Shakespeare to the fertile anti-war territory of his predecessors, contemporaries and those who followed him. Here there are parodies of warlike activity (and of Shakespeare's plays themselves) which invite their audiences to ponder the value and security of home and health against military organisation, foreign campaigns, sickness and death. These texts may be seen to promote crafts (and trade) against the exercise of arms, love and sex against war and destruction, and finally (and radically) to celebrate a non-violent masculinity despised by the authors of the military prose.

In terms of structure, Part II is primarily concerned with aspects of the pan-European military revolution that took place in the sixteenth and seventeenth centuries. It is also concerned with the way that texts from this period have been adopted and used in subsequent histories and representations of the history of war. The Reformation and the consolidation of a Protestant nationalist identity were thought to be vulnerable to Catholicism at home and Catholic states abroad. Spain in particular is seen as both a threat and an example of good practice in the realm of military ethics. The texts derive much of their authority from their references to classical ideals, some to what seems an absurd extent in their call for the establishment of legions of soldiers based on Roman models and equipped with Roman weapons. Yet there are also challenges for military writers over such matters as gender identity (caused by a perceived decline in codes of masculinity) and what is seen as a general sense of decadence associated with a state of peace that was seemingly undermining national confidence and political strategy.

I start with an incident reported by Desiderius Erasmus when Henry VIII of England challenged John Colet for preaching an anti-war sermon just as troops were about to embark on an expedition to France. It is a moment of considerable significance for the period, for an understanding of the texts of military theory addressed in this Part and for the innovative thinking about warfare that they reveal. My account of early modern military development is necessarily derived in part from the narratives of military historians working up archives in pursuit of a story that is coherent and compelling. The approach is of interest itself for its occlusion of what theologians such as Colet had to say about warfare. Their argument is that the pan-European revolution in militarism was not simply about technical innovation and tactical experiment. It was also about the necessity of revising military theory in the face of the imperatives that arose from colonial ambition, new economic structures and a consolidation of the idea of the early modern nation-state. Essential to this process was a reformulation of the medieval notion of the 'just war' that would accommodate the changing geopolitical environment that emerged during the era of Reformation and colonialism.

Chapter 4 starts with a description of the work of M. J. D. Cockle who, just over a century ago, undertook his taxonomy of the military prose of the early modern period. I give an account of the texts themselves (and others not listed by Cockle) and the way that military historians have responded to, and made use of, this body of writing over the centuries. Some measure is taken of the changing technology of warfare, which these texts describe in some detail. The main discussion, however, will be of the ideological commitment of the texts – their preoccupation with, on the one hand, matters of subjectivity, discipline and the body, and on the other, with establishing warfare as a necessary component of a model state and the soldier as an ideal citizen.

Part III is principally concerned with the way that war is represented in some of the dramatic work of Shakespeare. It opens with an examination of the history plays, with particular emphasis on how Shakespeare embodies aspects of militarism in the warlike figures of Richard III and Henry V. The 'vice figure' Richard, a symbol of such villainy and contempt that he has often he been compared to Adolf Hitler in modern productions, ironically expresses much of what was being called for by the military writers discussed earlier in the book. Richard's distaste for peace is the starting point for an analysis of the history sequence. The point will be to explore how Shakespeare's theatre dramatised and commented on the issues that are to the fore in the military prose, arguably registering a critique that can be thought of as undermining the force of the prose's polemic. Chapter 6 elaborates an argument about the relationship between war and tragedy, with *Hamlet* as its focus.

Part IV deals first with the radical opposition to notions of warfare, military masculinity and aggression found in the work of Shakespeare's forerunners, contemporaries and followers. Here I discuss some antecedents of the plays mentioned above, as well as parodies and analogues, and in these texts, it will be argued, are retained and dramatised the arguments against warfare that the military prose is so anxious to occlude. Chapter 7 starts with Christopher Marlowe but will mainly examine a popular prose work, Thomas Deloney's anti-war narrative *The Gentle Craft*. Chapter 8 examines some of the plays of Shakespeare's predecessors, contemporaries and followers for other instances of oppositional voices which continue a tradition of popular resistance to war that has been obscured by the promotion of Shakespeare in the terms detailed in earlier chapters. The final chapter reviews something of how some of the arguments about how to interpret early modern representations of warfare have a resonance in the present.

REMEMBRANCE, PITY AND CLOSURE

If remembering those who died in the wars of the twentieth century often involves a form of pilgrimage and a sense of theatre, then the public face of such commemoration has proved angular, masculine and, often literally, one of stone. I am thinking here of the sites of such pilgrimage that have been established in memory of British wars. There is the Cenotaph itself, but also numerous other memorials, often adorned with carved or cast images of soldiers. Then there are the beautifully tended cemeteries, mostly on the European mainland, which are sites of pilgrimage and reflection, or the bronze plaques on buildings recording the names of the dead who once worked there. It is to these sites that people return in private to grieve and remember, but also annually as part of public acts of remembrance, which almost without fail involve a form of military display. However casual the slaughter at the time, the old campaigns are recalled in formalised ritual, with marches, speeches, prayers and poppies. There is thus a kind of circularity to the proceedings: wars in the past are commemorated in a kind of theatre which implies that war will return, with the dead saluted by the very forms of weaponry that made them vanish, only to reappear in stone or metal.

The cyclical nature of remembrance is reminiscent of tragedy, and indeed the word 'tragic' is commonly used to describe the atmosphere and effects of war. In terms of remembrance there is another connection to the formal tenets of tragedy: the association between war and pity. In the latest revision to their widely adopted student textbook, *An Introduction to Literature, Criticism and Theory*, Andrew Bennett and Nicholas Royle have included a timely chapter on war. Here they contrast Alfred Tennyson's 'The Charge of the Light Brigade' with Wilfred Owen's 'Futility'. They also give an account of Homer's *Iliad*, noting that:

> Literature begins with war, with the rage of war. *Menis*: wrath, fury, rage. The first word of the first great poem in the Western literary tradition,

Homer's *Illiad* (*c.* 700 BC), declares its topic: the rage of Achilles. The Western tradition, in other words, starts up in rage and blood, the rage for war, the rage for rage – godlike, swift-footed, murderous Achilles' rage.[16]

Ranging from Homer to the war films of recent decades, Bennett and Royle explain how war has been culturally mediated in terms of its pleasures, the intensity of its experiences and the resulting aesthetics of the way that it is represented in fiction. They note that, for some, war is a delight and its heroes worthy of celebration:

> It is for this reason, perhaps, that literature is not simply *against* war, the poetry is not only in the 'pity'. And an understanding of this fact will perhaps better help us to understand the strange double-talk and double-dealings of literature, and to appreciate the deep, troubled and incessant conjunction of literature and war.[17]

We might conclude that the dominant cultural response to warfare is one that at best emphasises the Aristotelian duality of response: that we gaze upon and celebrate the heroes and 'the fallen' of war with both pity and an aesthetic pleasure at its terror. The problem with this is that it is a reading that serves to close down the fundamental question 'Why war?' Pity and terror are compelling distractions from this central question. Or we might say that pity itself is a response of such seductive power that it obscures the irrationality of war, drawing a veil over agency, responsibility or alternatives, and cementing war firmly into such continuums as 'human nature'. One would not want to dismiss pity, and certainly not in the manner of Nietzsche. Yet 'the pity of war' is one of the ways in which we keep dark the fact that those commissioned to conduct wars have been constructed – ideologically, aesthetically and culturally – partly by political discourse and partly by fictional accounts that themselves serve to perpetute war, glorifying terror and pitying the dead. After they have gone, we remember them: imaging death, idealising sacrifice, comforting ourselves with tragic stories and ceremony. In this vein, and in exemplification, I return to Ray and Ronnie whom I left in Chapter 1 marching towards their place in history.

Squadron Leader Raymond Newport Peace DFC was twenty-six years old when he died at the controls of a Handley Page Halifax bomber on the night of 20 December 1942 near the frontier between Germany and the Netherlands.[18] He is buried alongside the other seven members of the crew in the Reichswald Forest War Cemetery, near Kleve, Germany. His wife gave birth to their son in 1943. Reading his letters you know that he would rather have been flying for any purpose other than to drop bombs. Had he lived you feel he might have volunteered for the comprehensive aerial photographic survey which began in 1944 as part of the initiative to revise the Ordnance Survey maps of the United Kingdom. He could have returned to Scotland to capture images of those Hebridean islands and peninsulas which had so delighted him as he soared above them on his way to Ireland.

Acting Squadron Leader Ronald Sidney Williams DFC died on 14 July 1943 at the age of twenty-nine when his bomber was shot down over Germany. His remains lie in the Rheinberg War Cemetery and his name can be found on a memorial just inside the churchyard at Temple Grafton, a little distance from the grave of his parents.[19] Williams also left a young wife. A local newspaper report of his loss is headed 'Death of Temple Grafton DFC' and records that he had joined the RAF in 1935 as a sergeant-pilot under the short-term training scheme. The report also notes that Williams 'was exceedingly popular both in his home village and with all his crew. He occasionally played for the Stratford-on-Avon Rugby Club second team, and he was also interested in amateur dramatics.'

Notes

1. See G. R. Wilson Knight (1940), *This Sceptred Isle*, Oxford: Clarendon; (1956), *A Royal Propaganda, 1956. A Narrative Account of Work Devoted to the Cause of Great Britain During and After the Second World War*, MS, BL 11768.f.13; (1964), *Shakespearean Production*, London: Faber and Faber. For a discussion of the Shakespearean critics of the 1940s and their relation to the war, see Graham Holderness (2002), *Visual Shakespeare*, Hatfield: Hertfordshire University Press, especially Chapter 5.
2. H. V. Morton (1927), *In Search of England*, London: Methuen, pp. 248–9.
3. For an account of long post-war legacy of these critics, see Derek Longhurst (1982) ' "Not for all time, but for an age": An Approach to Shakespeare Studies', in Peter Widdowson (ed.), *Re-Reading English*, London: Methuen, pp. 150–63.
4. The best account of the work of Leavis is Francis Mulhern (1979), *The Moment of Scrutiny*, London: New Left Books.
5. *Brewer's Dictionary of 20th-Century Phrase and Fable* (1991), London: Cassell, p. 136.
6. See Ebenzer Cobham Brewer (1898), *Dictionary of Phrase and Fable*, London; and Walley Chamberlain Oulter (1818), *A History of the Theatres of London*, London: C. Chapple. I am indebted to Lorna Scott for noting this reference.

7. Professor Stephen Hawking talking to John Humphrys on the *Today* programme broadcast on BBC Radio 4, Thursday, 30 November 2006. Dr Heather Couper, former President of the British Astronomical Society, speaking to Jim Naughtie on *Today*, Saturday, 2 December 2006, said that the Royal Astronomical Society, the Royal Aeronautical Society and the British Interplanetary Society all agreed 'we were doomed'. She also remarked that Martin Rees, the Astronomer Royal, believed that of all the threats to the human race the nuclear one was the worst and most likely – we were going to 'nuke ourselves out'. To be fair, Hawking also believes that environmental damage to the earth and forms of plague further underpin a rationale for the settlement of space. See his *A Brief History of Time* (1988), London: Bantam.
8. For a clear and engaging account of these aspects of meaning, see Terry Eagleton (1996), *An Introduction to Literary Theory*, 2nd edition, Oxford: Blackwell.
9. See Emile Benveniste [1966] (1971), *Problems in General Linguistics*, Miami: University of Miami Press, p. 110.
10. Catherine Belsey, *Critical Practice* (1980), London and New York: Methuen, p. 92. Belsey offers a readable account of the influence of Roland Barthes, Jacques Derrida and Ferdinand de Saussure.
11. Paul A. Jorgensen (1956), *Shakespeare's Military World*, Berkeley, CA: University of California Press.
12. Curtis Breight (1996), *Surveillance, Militarism and Drama in the Elizabethan Era*, Basingstoke: Macmillan, 1996.
13. Richard Courtney (1994), *Shakespeare's World of War: The Early Histories*; Toronto: Simon & Pierre; Nick de Somogyi, *Shakespeare's Theatre of War*, Burlington, VT and Aldershot: Ashgate; Bruce R. Smith (2000), *Shakespeare and Masculinity*, Oxford: Oxford University Press; Nina Taunton (2001), *1590's Drama and Militarism: Portrayals of War in Marlowe, Chapman and Shakespeare's Henry V*, Burlington, VT and Aldershot: Ashgate; and Alan Shepard, *Marlowe's Soldiers* (2002), Burlington, VT and Aldershot: Ashgate.
14. See: http://www.poppolitics.com/articles/2003-05-01-henryv.shtml.
15. See Michael Bogdanov and Michael Pennington (1990), *The English Shakespeare Company*, London: Nick Hern Books. The ESC's production 'The Wars of the Roses' caused an outrage in some quarters due to its allusions to the conflict in the South Atlantic. Bogdanov writes, 'The English invade the Continent much like the marauding Celts of Old. Imperialism encourages jingoism. So the Falklands. So Agincourt. "Fuck the Frogs". The banner hung out by the send-off crowd at Southampton in our production of *Henry V* grew out of the desire to bridge nearly six hundred years of this same bigoted xenophobic patriotism' (p. 48). Nicholas Hytner's 2003 production of *Henry V* for the National Theatre

in London sparked similar controversy due to its references to the attack on Iraq.

16. Andrew Bennett and Nicholas Royle (2004), *An Introduction to Literature, Criticism and Theory*, 3rd revised edition, Harlow: Pearson, p. 272.
17. Ibid., p. 278.
18. Writing to his father on 21 December 1942 from No. 76 Squadron, Linton-on-Ouse, Wing Commander Leonard Cheshire noted that 'the target against which he was detailed was Duisberg in the Ruhr'. The raid involved 232 aircraft.
19. Ronnie's mother Lillian Sarah Williams died in March 1946, broken-hearted over the loss of her son. Sidney Bertram Williams, vicar of Temple Grafton with Benton and Honorary Canon of Coventry Cathedral, left the village shortly after his wife's death and died at Weyhill, Hampshire in 1961.

Part II

Commitment

3

GOOD FRIDAY, 1513

❧

It would have been a moment of high drama. It is certainly one that might be said to resonate across the historical period that this book addresses and throughout the fictional and non-fictional writing that it seeks to analyse. On Good Friday, 1513 John Colet, Dean of St Paul's, London preached a sermon to a congregation that included soldiers about to set off on one of many campaigns against the French. Sitting among the soldiers was their leader, Henry VIII, and, he must have thought, a figure of considerable inspiration to his troops as they prepared for the battles to come. The other source of inspiration, Henry might have assumed, would have been the deity they had assembled to worship. Also present at the service was Colet's friend Desiderius Erasmus, who coolly made a note for posterity of what happened that day.

Colet was by this time a substantial figure among the contemporary Church Reformers.[1] Many of his earlier sermons had been published, recording what he saw as the decadence, indolence and corruption of some sections of the clergy. Colet urged the development of new administrative structures for the Church and the implementation of clearer financial arrangements for the paying of its officials' stipends. He was also opposed to compulsory celibacy for the priesthood and favoured a simplification of some aspects of liturgical practice. A charge of heresy brought against him had been dismissed, but the accusations (concerning Colet's views on the worship of images and other doctrinal practices) reveal that he reflected the mood of an increasing constituency among the clergy and the laity of the day.[2] His emphasis was on individual conscience, and his preference was for the Scriptures as a source of guidance for religious practice rather than the accumulated legal writing of the Church. In matters of biblical interpretation, doctrine and ritual, Colet stood at a kind of theological and institutional threshold across which many were to pass as England became caught up with the reforming spirit that was gathering pace elsewhere in Europe. Colet died in 1519 but was instrumental in formulating the ideas that were to be drawn up by those who in succeeding decades were to manage the secession from Rome and facilitate the establishment of the English Protestant Church.[3] Moreover, Colet was exceedingly popular. His sermons were well attended and his voice was heard far beyond the confines of the ecclesiastical world, not least because of his interest in the establishment of schools and endowments for teachers and scholars.[4] Colet, it might be said, imagined a future for the Church, and therefore society, that was both progressive and conservative. It was to be progressive in its emphasis upon education, reform and individual responsibility – as well as matters to do with the use of the vernacular. But Colet's was a conservative voice in his determination to return to the Scriptures as the source of divine inspiration, over and above those whom he saw as having translated them into the rigid and, in his view, self-serving institutions of church law. Of those who had gone before, Colet may well have thought of Thomas Aquinas as a principal offender – and it was Aquinas who had laid out many of the principles of the just war.

Henry, on the other hand, was looking back. He may have fancied himself the imitator of those great warriors of the past, whose exploits he would have read and heard about – either classical figures or earlier English monarchs. He also saw himself as a rival to the continental monarchs with whom he was engaged in alliances or war. So one can imagine his growing unease during that Good Friday sermon as this most influential of clerics proceeded to undermine the understood aggregation constituted by the will of God, the figure of the king, the cause against the French and the body of assembled soldiers. According to Erasmus, Colet launched an unqualified attack on warfare in general, describing it as unChristian and, indeed, as the work of Satan himself. There may have been muttered comments among the members of the congregation, anxious for their souls or for their wages. One can imagine sideways glances to see how the king would react; or perhaps there was simply silence as the soldiers contemplated what must have seemed a daringly new attitude towards their ancient profession. Henry was indeed disturbed by Colet's anti-war tone and especially his pronouncements against those inspiring figures from the past who were models in a long chain of military leaders that led finally to his own person. Colet, it seems, spent some time urging that princes should follow the example of Christ rather than that of Caesar or Alexander. At best he may have disturbed Henry's daydream. Worse than this, though, it sounded like sedition. Erasmus reports that Colet concluded his sermon by stressing that:

> They who through hatred or ambition were fighting one another by turns, were warring under the banner, not of Christ, but of the devil. At the same time, he pointed out to them how hard a thing it was to die a Christian death; how few entered on a war unsullied by hatred or love of gain; how incompatible a thing it was that a man should have that brotherly love without which no one could see God, and yet bury his sword in his brother's heart.[5]

Commenting in the late nineteenth century Frederic Seebohm regarded this as a significant moment of discord between Colet and the monarch. He notes that Henry summoned Colet to a private meeting because he 'was not a little afraid that the sermon might damp the zeal of his newly enlisted troops', and the incident led to a long discussion between Henry and his bishop which ended with:

> [Henry] glad to find that Colet had not intended to declare absolutely that there could be no just war, no doubt persuading himself that his was one of the very few just ones. The conversation ended with [Henry] expressing a wish that Colet would sometime or other explain himself more clearly, lest the raw soldiers should go away with a mistaken notion, and think he had really said *no* war is lawful to Christians.[6]

The conversation took place in private in the garden of the Franciscan monastery next to the king's palace at Greenwich, while across the river in London the soldiers assembled for the long march to the coast, their morale somewhat dampened by the doubts that had been sown. In terms of the relationship between warfare and the evolving Tudor state the incident is without doubt something of a critical turn. It saw a leading theologian, with a position of considerable institutional authority in the see, state what he considered a fundamental principle of Christian faith. The gravity of the moment arises not so much from the fact that Colet might be questioning the evident desire of the king to regain parts of the realm lost to the French. Colet's views on the policy itself were not recorded. The important issue is, as Seebohm hints, one of absolutes. In the presence of a sovereign whose authority was thought of as guaranteed by God, one of the most material and inviolable expressions of that absolute was being denied – and in the presence of those armed subjects to whom the sovereign's will was delegated on the battlefield. Moreover, Colet's sermon had been a narrative of damnation or salvation, evoking the competing figures of Christ (peace) and the Devil (war). The soldiers might have mistaken this part of the service for a kind of Morality Play, with each of them playing the part of an 'Everyman', caught between competing authorities. The analogy seems appropriate enough since the prospect of death was so imminent. Henry and Colet apparently ended their conversation in accord, much to the annoyance of Colet's enemies in the Church's hierarchy: Henry's war was defensive and therefore just, although Seebohm notes that nobody knows whether or not a second sermon was ever preached.[7]

Much was at stake for Henry in the series of wars he waged against the French over the course of his long reign. Employing levied troops, but necessarily having recourse to foreign mercenaries, Henry's armies campaigned hard over the periods 1512–14, 1522–5 and 1543–6.[8] These wars were a material adjunct to the symbolic display of sovereignty that was being carefully fostered by Henry and his advisers. Henry's obsession with military technology, exemplified by the importation from Antwerp of the very latest kinds of cannon, was matched by a careful cultivation of images and practices derived from a chivalric past. This was in part an inheritance from his father, who after all had named Henry's elder brother Arthur in the expectation that he would succeed to the throne as the head of a quasi-mythological new order. But it was also an attempt to secure a unified national image derived from earlier military triumphs, which themselves were to be written up in Tudor chronicles in a near-mythological way. Henry VII had held on to Calais, the last remaining outpost in France, but had shown little enthusiasm in his occasional efforts to reassert English dominion over territory that had been lost since the period of Henry V's triumph at Agincourt. By contrast, his son recognised the importance of maintaining a high profile in the competing circles of European princes and saw the advantage at home in terms of prestige.

Absolute monarchy was defined and fuelled by militarism. If one of its goals was the abolition of civil war, then this was to be achieved by maintaining overseas conflicts which not only proved the worth of the institution but also kept the divided nobility occupied in a common cause. Henry stands in a long tradition of leaders who maintain authority and attempt to achieve a heightened status by summoning images of the past, recalling historical triumphs or settling old scores. Henry's armies' determined but remote efforts against the French were financially draining, beset by disease among the troops, and ended with next to nothing gained in terms of territorial advantage.[9] For Henry, they went hand in hand with summer afternoons spent at jousting matches in and around his palaces – and expensive diplomatic ceremonies based on courtly ritual and display. Henry's attempts to command a position in continental Europe's spheres of influence were not altogether successful and his fortunes changed dramatically following his excommunication from Rome. Fortunately, as far as national security was concerned, Henry wisely saw to it that he also invested in the navy and in an elaborate system of coastal defences, thus mixing propaganda with pragmatism and avoiding, although not entirely, any invasive retaliation by the French.[10]

Henry's attachment to a symbolic order derived from the past did not mean that his armies, and those of his children, were entirely ineffective. Whilst he favoured something like a revival of the medieval notion of the mounted nobility leading infantry to war, his lieutenants recognised that the practices of warfare were beginning to change. The Tudor armies that fought for English control over the Lowlands at Flodden, and at Solway, Pinkie and Leith in Scotland were successful against the armies they encountered because the English forces included an influential component of mercenaries from continental Europe. These professional soldiers brought with them, apart from their sheer brutality, weapons and skills that represented the kinds of technical and tactical innovation that have seen the period described as one that experienced a 'military revolution'.

Henry's French and Scottish campaigns set the scene for an extended period of military engagement under the later Tudor and early Stuart governments. The pattern was irregular and sporadic. The 150 years which separate the occasion of Colet's sermon at the start of Henry's wars from the outbreak of civil war in England and Wales in the mid-seventeenth century and the allied military activity in Ireland and Scotland were busy ones for English soldiers. But they were years of considerable uncertainty in matters of state military policy. It is for this reason that the later part of the period produced such an abundance of writing committed to the formulation of a clear policy that would underpin the growing confidence of the maturing Protestant state. Although the late medieval antagonisms simmered, Henry's wars of prestige in France gave way to Elizabeth's colonial wars in Ireland and the extended conflict with Spain. These campaigns were often characterised by the unauthorised participation of adventuring English soldiers – especially in the Low Countries – who reported in written accounts of their own experiences of war, on the nature, extent and fortunes of the various officially affiliated national or sectarian armies they encountered abroad. By the time a commitment to the revolt against Spain in the Low Countries had been formalised and the Armada threatened national security, the contrast between what such soldiers found abroad and the domestic military scene must have been complete. During this period over 100,000 men were raised for service in Ireland, in defence of the Scottish border and for the wars in continental Europe. Ian Roy suggests that this figure represents an astonishing 15 per cent of all able-bodied males, drawn from the militia or trained bands, or pressed into service by the lords lieutenant of the English counties.[11]

The fate of the anti-war stance taken earlier by Colet and his contemporaries needs to be considered in the context of these campaigns, and the subsequent, but less extensive, early Stuart contributions to the Thirty Years War. On the one hand, there was the empirical result of military activity, materially affecting the thousands called or forced to participate in the wars. Of these people a percentage would have witnessed the growing preoccupation with warfare in the plays of Shakespeare and his contemporaries. The effect of war on the population at large would, at any rate, have been a significant factor in the psychological make-up of the theatres' audiences during the period. On the other hand, there was the mass of publications devoted to the business of warfare, lamenting the disorganised state of the military apparatus and calling for reform and innovation. Woven into this body of work were the attitudes towards war and peace that were at least to qualify, and in most cases utterly traduce, the residual strand of the pacifism epitomised by Colet's remarks in 1513. Since the theoretical infrastructure behind these writers' concerns lay in Europe and in the so-called revolution in military affairs, it is worth pausing to take some account of this before returning to the issue of peace.

A range of influences can be seen as involved in the changing face of militarism in the period leading up to the proliferation of English plays concerning warfare in the late sixteenth and early seventeenth centuries. Changing economic conditions across Europe in the fifteenth and sixteenth centuries can be seen as both stimulating and facilitating new kinds of warfare. It is arguable that in many situations the declared cause of a particular conflict masks an underlying issue of resources. Certainly, increasing populations, the resulting transfer of forests and other sorts of formerly uncultivated land into agricultural use, and the desire to control land and sea communications across and between existing and newly productive areas, lay behind conflicts that have been recorded as dynastic, religious or chauvinist. The kinds of economically motivated military activity associated with colonialism beyond Europe can be identified in microcosm within it. Longstanding but periodically renewed disputes over trade routes to the east and, increasingly in the sixteenth century, over ports and communications with territory in Africa and across the Atlantic, replicated and extended a European phenomenon that can be traced back to the empires of the classical period and earlier. Issues of concern in the modern world, such as the relationship between warfare and resources, technology and the perpetuation of war, mutually assured destruction, and the morality of arms manufacture and distribution all have their equivalents in the late medieval and early modern periods. Territorial disputes were likely to be fought over mineral deposits that were processed and forged into weapons that facilitated further territorial disputes. Technical innovation motivated the establishment of specialised manufacturing (and a concomitant aesthetic of arms) that could operate across borders, stimulating new forms of capital exchange, and secure or destroy political alliances by proxy. And much of the gold and silver of the worlds beyond the Atlantic which repaid all the 'voyages of discovery', the energies of conquest and the fervour of piracy was absorbed by the increasing costs of European wars.

For many of its subjects and citizens the greatest impact of the European Renaissance must have been the consequences of their rulers' commitment to warfare. As the period went on, the scale and nature of those wars, their regularity and the economic conditions that they generated meant that even those not directly involved in the military institutions felt their impact. Non-combatants suffered increased taxation to finance wars, as well as disruptions to their livelihoods. They were caught up as citizens in the sieges that especially characterised the early part of the period, suffering looting or worse, and many succumbed to the various diseases that armies could be practically guaranteed to carry. The sixteenth and seventeenth centuries, according to Geoffrey Parker, saw:

> More belligerence than almost any other period of European history, registering a grand total of only ten years of total peace across the continent. During the sixteenth century, Spain and France were almost constantly at war; while during the seventeenth century, the Ottoman empire, the Austrian Habsburgs and Sweden were at war for two years out of every three, Spain for three years out of every four, and Poland and Russia for four years out of every five. 'This', as the Italian poet Fulvio Testi wrote in 1641, 'is the century of the soldier.'[12]

Most evident in the history of warfare leading up to the playwrights' representation of its ethics and practices in the theatres of the Tudors and early Stuarts is the accelerating scale of campaigns. Larger armies required more comprehensive forms of taxation and more sophisticated ways to train and deploy the participants: thus the machinery of war developed alongside the apparatus of the early modern state. Technical innovation made mass combat in the field a more skilled occupation and the sense of soldiering as a profession, rather than an obligation to a knight or monarch, clearly dates from this period. The most obvious technical advances are associated with the use in the West of gunpowder (a compound originally developed in China in the ninth century) for use in cannon and then smaller match- and later wheel-lock, artillery – the arquebus, musket and pistol. At the same time, increasingly reliable methods of forging metals and the development of alloys meant that swords, halberds and pikes were stronger and could be produced more efficiently. However sophisticated weapons became, and artillery made battles much more decisive, attention returns in the writing of the theorists and in government statutes, to the soldiers themselves.

Those writing of England in the Tudor and early Stuart periods about military matters were acutely aware of a sense of military history and there are scattered references throughout their works to the battles of the past and how they were won. Whilst disparaging remarks abound about the poor quality of the contemporary recruit, earlier soldiers were much celebrated. It is not unusual to find references to wars that were won through the energy and commitment of ordinary soldiers, whether they fought for the English Crown or not, and whatever the outcome. Recalling the wars in Scotland of the fourteenth century, Robert I's highly motivated army is celebrated as being drawn from a willing population and the skills of its foot soldiers acknowledged in the defeat of Edward II's knights at Bannockburn in 1314, despite the presence of over 20,000 English infantry. Similarly, the principal battles of the Hundred Years War – Crécy, Poitiers and Agincourt itself – are recalled for the skills of the ordinary soldiers rather than those of the knights. These histories acknowledge that unless mercenaries were used, the outcome of battles depended in the end on massed armies of ordinary people drawn away to war from their day-to-day lives. Although characterised as a period of military revolution by some modern historians in terms of technology and tactics, the concern of the Elizabethan writers looking back over 200 years of warfare was not only with innovations in weaponry and strategy. Rather, they were preoccupied with the social composition of armies and the motivation of their members. It was, in fact, an uneven period in terms of the various kinds of military organisation and personnel available. The tradition of armies of mounted knights continued in Italy long after it had been abandoned in any real sense elsewhere in Europe. French armies of the fifteenth century came closest to the idea of a recognisable standing army ahead of others, and the Spanish developed the mass use of guns at the same time as other armies continued to rely on the bow. During the sixteenth and seventeenth centuries the Swedish army became perhaps the most sophisticated in terms of a combination of advanced weaponry, tactics and the professionalism of its highly motivated soldiers: it was later to become, decisively, an example of good practice for Cromwell's military forces. Looking back at the wars of the past, and across at the various models abroad, Elizabethan military theorists were able to draw on a mass of evidence from which to develop their ideas about warfare. Yet however extensive their vision was of arrayed ranks of soldiers with up-to-date weapons and other equipment, that vision depended on an ideology of the soul of the individual soldier.

The military writing of the late sixteenth and early seventeenth centuries is an extensive genre which has held the attention of military historians for a number of years, especially since the publication of M. J. D. Cockle's important work, *A Bibliography of English Military Books up to 1642*.[13] Cockle listed in considerable detail and with extensive notes some 150 late fifteenth- to early seventeenth-century English language books devoted to issues of warfare. He extended his list to include what he described as 'contemporary foreign works', thereby embracing such influential European texts as Niccolò Machiavelli's *The Arte of Warre*, which first circulated in translation from 1560.[14] There are other familiar names, such as Christine de Pisan, whose *The Boke of the Faytes of Armes and of Chyvalreye* was printed by William Caxton in 1498. Of the Elizabethan English writers, Barnabe Rich is probably the best known. His polemical style is fairly typical of the Elizabethan militarists, urgently demanding the establishment of a standing army and describing its ideal composition and tactical approach.[15]

The issues at stake in this body of work are wide-ranging. Many writers were concerned with what might be called the practical detail of warfare, issues to do with weapons and equipment, soldiers' clothing and rations, or, say, the best method available for digging tunnels in order to undermine a fortress. Yet Henry Webb's summary of these issues hints at the links between such detail and wider ideological concerns – matters of organisation, responsibility, discipline, morale, training and expertise – and, above all, the theological basis on which warfare could be thought legitimate. These issues were the ideological materials of what we might call 'militarism', a set of propositions governing relations between the individual, the nation and the various forms of institution that were the equivalent of what a modern state would see as its armed forces. For Webb, the Elizabethan military writers were concerned with such matters as:

> What moral and physical qualities were requisite in officers and private soldiers, what training was necessary to achieve expertness in battle, what sorts or organisations could be formed and were best suited for different kinds of exploits, and what kinds of tactics might be most serviceable on the battlefield.[16]

It was hardly possible for early modern militarism to analyse issues of strategy, tactics and organisations, or even to address such matters as, say, the importance of keeping weapons in good order, without engaging in ethical, theological and ideological debate. I shall return to this body of writing in Chapter 4 in order to examine the range of issues it addresses. In the context of Colet's Good Friday sermon, however, it is of interest to note here the fate of the early Reformers' anti-war sentiment in relation to this significant and weighty canon of military texts. Over the course of the century and a half that followed the Dean's awkward encounter with Henry, those writing from within or on behalf of European militarism, some as soldiers or ex-soldiers but many simply as political commentators, advocated and finally secured a determined attitude towards warfare. This pro-war disposition, very different from that espoused by Colet and other Reformers, is arguably one that has lasted until the present day.

In simple terms, early modern militarism included a concern for the reinforcement of the idea that warfare could be justified in the name of Christianity. In the pursuit of this, the military writers depended on the presentation of a 'history' of warfare derived from biblical sources, carefully blended with accounts of warfare from the classical periods and the experience of Christian warfare in Europe and beyond in earlier centuries.[17] Little account is made of the kinds of uncertainties about warfare modern scholars have discovered in medieval literature and particularly that of the fourteenth century, such as *The Alliterative Morte Arthure* or *Wynnere and Wastoure*, which I shall return to in a later chapter.[18] Indeed, by 1619, the heroic figure of the earlier crusading knight had become for the early modern militarists the epitome of the Church Militant, renewed for service on behalf of the Reformation in the Low Counties, where the (Protestant) soldiers supplied:

> (a patterne for all Christendome) whose valor the Lord hath exceedingly blessed, in delivering them by force of Armes, from the tyrannie of the cruell Spaniards, to the great comfort of all true-hearted Protestants.[19]

By the time civil war had come again in the mid-seventeenth century, the ideal of the Christian soldier had been linked to that of divine determination of the outcome:

> Civil war makes that King who undertakes unjust wars against his subjects to repent him of his victory, when he truly sees what he hath done . . . for victory in war is neither got by multitude, nor strength, but by the ayd, assistance, and power of God. And therefore these military means must now be used.[20]

The early modern writers certainly did not, then, acknowledge positions in earlier literature, which arguably undermined 'commonplaces of chivalry and knightly warfare through inversion, irony and black humour'.[21] There is, instead, a studied and forceful repudiation of the kind of quasi-pacifism of some early Tudor theologians, and especially that of Erasmus and Thomas More.

Erasmus's position in *Moriae Encomium, Quera Pacis, Institutio Principis Christiani, Militaria* and other texts was clear enough:

> war is so monstrous a thing that it befits beasts and not men, so violently insane that poets represent it as an evil visitation of the Furies, so pestilential that it causes a general corruption of character, so criminal that it is best waged by the worst men, and so impious that it has no relation with Christ.[22]

Erasmus's arguments for pacifism can be traced across the considerable body of his writing and take a number of forms. The satirical *Quera Pacis* was published in 1517, a year after the influential *Institutio Principis Christiani*, which considered that 'the teachings of Christ apply to no one more than to the prince'. In terms of the proposed relationship between peace, Christianity and monarchy, John C. Olin has noted that:

> It is hardly necessary to point out that in these works, as in the whole moral approach, Erasmus stands in striking contrast to another contemporary scholar and observer Niccolò Machiavelli, whose own famous

book, *Il Principe* had been penned just a few years before. But if this contrast is exceedingly sharp, the similarity between the ideas of Erasmus and those expressed by Thomas More in Utopia, that supreme masterpiece of the Christian Renaissance, is very close. And 1516 is also the year of *Utopia*.[23]

Erasmus continued to publish widely circulated texts on the subject of human conflict and divine authority, including the *Colloquia*, produced from 1500 onwards, which included a variety of forthright attacks on soldiers and warfare. For example, in one of the colloquies, *Militaria* of 1522, the argument over warfare in general and plunder in particular, is delivered through an exchange between Hanno and Thrasymachus:

> *Hanno*: The old army spirit! . . . But you did refrain from sacrileges, I suppose?
> *Thras*: On the contrary. Nothing was sacred there; no building spared, sacred or profane.
> *Hanno*: How will you make amends for that?
> *Thras*: They say you don't have to make any amends for what's done in war; whatever it is, it's right.
> *Hanno*: The law of war, perhaps.
> *Thras*: Exactly.
> *Hanno*: Yet that law is the greatest wrong. It wasn't devotion to your country but hope of spoils that drew you to war.
> Thras: Granted; and in my opinion few men do there from any loftier motive.
> *Hanno*: To be mad with many is something!
> *Thras*: A preacher declared from the pulpit that war is just.
> *Hanno*: The pulpit doesn't often lie. But war might be just for a prince, not necessarily for you.
> *Thras*: I heard from professors that everyone has a right to live by his trade.
> *Hanno*: A splendid trade – burning houses, looting churches, violating nuns, robbing poor people, murdering harmless ones.[24]

Such a dialogue might question war, but if Erasmus's pacifism was an alternative position available to the Tudor monarch, then there is an irony in the fact that its usual formulation depended on a presentation of the Pauline paradox of the 'Christian Soldier'. The image is halfway towards a compromise with the prevailing religious rationale for the wars that dominated the period. Indeed, the nearer theologians came to actual debate with Tudor absolutism, the more flexible became the Christian ideal of pacifism in response to the counter-discourse of the just war: a concept that the military theorists either assume, or validate with further guarantees of divine justification.

Thomas More was in direct debate with Henry VIII over the subject of war. His Utopians had welcomed Swiss mercenaries to fight their battles for them and, in the last resort of war, had advocated training women so that 'in set field the wives do stand every one by their own husband's side'.[25] Anthony Kenny has noted of More's imagined state that:

> Unlike other nations, the Utopians do not regard war as anything glorious; but they are not pacifists either. . . . They prefer to win wars by stratagem and cunning than by battle and bloodshed. . . . When war is declared they cause posters to be set up secretly throughout enemy territory offering great rewards for the assassination of the enemy king, and smaller but still considerable sums for the deaths of other individuals [and] this spreads dissension and distrust among the enemy.[26]

The early modern militarists contested this kind of writing on all counts. Piecing together a selected representation of classical and medieval warfare they constructed a counter-thesis which insisted that war was manly, praised by most poets, dependent on character (and a dependable means by which to enhance character), waged by the best of men and blessed by God.

By the early years of the seventeenth century, the work of Erasmus, Colet and More was described as a matter of 'mere contemplation' by such early modern militarists as Thomas Digges, who noted that:

> to speak of peace perpetuall in this world of contention is but as ARISTOTLES FOELIX, XENOPHENS CYRUS, QUINTGIANS ORATOR, or sir Thomas Moors UTOPIA, a matter of mere contemplation, the warre being in this iron age so bien enracinée qu'il est impossible de l'en oster, si non avec la ruine de l'universe. So well ingrafted that it is impossible to take it away without a universal destruction.[27]

It is the world of Luther and Calvin rather than Aquinas, but the pacifism of some of the early Reformers remained important for the early modern militarists for three reasons. First, it acted as a conceptual link to the idealised period of the fourteenth century and before, when the politics of war expressed in theological terms stood more easily alongside the idea of chivalry. I shall show in the next chapter how sixteenth- and seventeenth-century military writers summoned images from the past to secure their vision of an ideal paradigm. Secondly, and ironically, Erasmus had written the influential *Enchiridion Militis Christiani* in 1516. With its set of rules governing the discipline and training of the 'Christian soldier', this text's formal links with the later military texts are more compelling than its existence as a pacifist antithesis to their polemic. It is as though the metaphorical (Pauline) association of Christianity with militarism becomes established as an equation, justifying the actual militarism espoused on behalf of the absolute state. Thirdly, early sixteenth-century pacifism can be held responsible, in part, for the decline (from much earlier paragons) in military discipline and 'character' that the militarists cite as both destructive of the nation and opening the door to the excesses of popular unrest. John Hale has remarked on the evolution of theories of Renaissance warfare thus:

> We could not, of course, expect to hear pacifist views expressed from Elizabethan, Jacobean or Caroline pulpits. Erasmian pacifism had faded away. . . . Catholic teaching, based on Aquinas, licensed the clergy to support a just war by every means in their power short of actual fighting. Luther had pointed out that 'war is as necessary as eating, drinking, or any other business' and that once war had been formally declared 'the hand that bears the sword is as such no longer man's but God's, and not man it is but God who hangs, breaks on the wheel, beheads, strangles.'[28]

According to Roland H. Bainton, Calvin 'repeatedly said no consideration would be paid to humanity when the honour of God was at stake'.[29] Clearly the problems that Colet had perceived in the application of Christian theology to war were largely irrelevant to the clergy, who increasingly addressed the issue during the reign of Elizabeth and the early Stuarts. Yet the discourse of theological justification for war had to be aimed continually at the mass of the population through the exhortations of the sermon – Hale considers them tantamount to an 'incitement to violence' – and especially much later, in the years of Puritanism leading up to the civil war.[30] There was, then, considerable urgency in the repudiation of what little Christian pacifism remained. This seems to indicate a residual reluctance on the part of those who heard the topic spoken of in many of the estimated 360,000 sermons preached to congregations in England and Wales, whose members were obliged by law to attend, in the years between 1600 and 1640.[31]

The last decade of the sixteenth century was characterised, then, in terms of military theory, by a proliferation of texts that combined specific recommendations concerning tactics and technology with a more general argument in favour of war, finally justified in the name of God. John Smythe's *Certain Discourses*, for example, begins with a wide-ranging polemic outlining the causes that had led to the ruin of the nation:

> Of which the first is long peace which ensuring after great wars to divers that have had notable militias and exercises military in great perfection, they by enjoying long peace have so much given themselves to covetousness, effeminacies, and superfluities that they have either in a great part or else utterly forgotten all orders and exercises military; in such sort that when they have been forced to enter into a war defensive for the defence of their dominions against any foreign nation or nations that have had a puissant and formed militia, they have been so void of the orders and exercises of war of their forefathers that either they have been conquered by their enemies invading, or at least have been in hazard of the loss of their estates and dominions.[32]

In common with a number of texts of this kind, Smythe raises the issue of effeminacy and related corruption in the state. He finds evidence for this weakness in the histories of the Egyptians, Greeks, Romans and Saxons, all of whom succumbed in one way or another to conquest through a neglect of militarism. Yet the principal history that provides evidence of such neglect is, for Smythe, the Bible itself since, 'if any of our such men of war be so obstinate that they will not believe such notable histories, let them resort to the Bible'.[33] God's hand can be seen in the history of warfare, and thus:

> That he be an emperor, a king, or a lieutenant general of an emperor or a king that doth command and govern an army: first of all things, that he do make God to be loved, feared, and served throughout his whole army.[34]

Many texts of the period, whilst justifying war in terms of Christianity in a general way, further cite the hand of God in support of particular features of the proposed model army. Smythe's text is concerned in part with promoting the longbow as a weapon requiring the kinds of skill that had been neglected during the long decline of England as a national power. This is a technical matter, but also one of national character in terms of the symbolism of the longbow, an issue that will be examined in more depth in Chapter 4. Yet even here, God's hand is imagined, justifying the re-adoption of the bow and directing the nation to renewed success. Abandoning the longbow is a symptom of the continuing decline, and:

> If through the negligence of the better sort of our nation, imitating and following the simple and ignorant opinions of our such unskilled men of war, [war] should come to pass it doth in mine opinion argue nothing more than that God hath withdrawn His hand and all right judgement in

matters military from us, and that in time to come, upon any great war either offensive or defensive, we shall, when it is too late, report the same, greatly to the hazard and peril of our prince, country and nation.[35]

The year after Smythe's *Certain Discourses* came Gyles Clayton's *The Approoved Order of Martiall Discipline* in which the arguments justifying war were extended in the name of a particular cause. The text links technical innovation to God's endorsement – God helps those who help themselves – and then includes a lengthy assertion that the desired and positive outcome of war was the cause of peace itself. The text issues the familiar warning about the danger of neglecting military matters:

> In laying aside the exercise of warlike weapons and Martiall discipline, how many kingdoms hathe beene overthrowne, how many Countries ruinated, and how many florishing Citties sacked and beaten downe flat to the ground.[36]

This text argues its own importance and purpose by noting that peace could only be guaranteed by war, a point that was easily forgotten in contemporary circumstances:

> Although (freendlie Readers) you thinke my labours might have beane verie well spared, in wryting any matters appertayning unto warres, for that every man is desirous to live in security of peace: but freendly Readers you are to understand, that this blessed peace cannot be maintayned and kept secure, without the use and practise of warlike weapons, and Martiall discipline. For we are to consider, the ambition of the world is such, that it is impossible for a Realme or Dominion, long to continue in quietnesse and safeguard, where the defence of the sword and Martiall featres of warre is not exercised and practised with discipline.[37]

Smythe's notion of war as a guarantee of peace becomes a familiar trope in the military writing. War is theologically and intellectually justified by its treatment in classical texts and in the Bible, which were 'forthright in prescribing of Lawes and Martiall discipline of Warres; the which in times past were appointed by the Almightie God himselfe'.[38] Texts such as this increasingly concerned themselves with somewhat oblique references to a potential internal threat that appear among the familiar accounts of external and international menace. Clayton refers to Elizabeth's foreign enemies, but also to her domestic ones: 'God confound her foes, and bring to light all traiterous Conspirators against her most excellent Majestie.'[39] This point appears during an argument concerning the best way to preserve peace, yet whether the force that is to disrupt this peace is internal or external is left vague. Clayton addresses the idea of internal threat by transferring the argument to the example of Rome:

> So if this worthy exercise of Martiall Discipline be used, and had in practise for the glory of God, and the defence of Christ hys Gospell, or for the defence of a Kingdom or Common-weale, no doubt there is, but that the GOD of Hostes is our chiefe Generall, and most worthy Capteine. . . . The exercising of warlike weapons, and the often using of them breedeth peace, but if warlike weapons should be layed aside, and Martiall discipline forgotten, then would it be with us, as it was with the Romans.[40]

The Roman Empire fell to foreign invasion, yet the internal weaknesses that led to its vulnerability cannot fully be explained here. Military decay was clearly involved, but the key factor is that, unlike the Romans, contemporary England has the support and involvement of God – but only if he is obeyed as the 'most worthy Capteine'.

Justifying war in the seventeenth century involved fewer abstract discussions of general ethical or theological points. The just war required definition, but in specific and increasingly topical and applied terms. The case for peace was pushed to the margins of argument and was replaced by the idea of war as a seemingly natural phenomenon. At the same time, specific wars in pursuit of specific objectives appear in the texts as evidence of war's continuing value. In the 1619 text *The Soldier Pleading His Own Cause*, war arises through the disorder of the multitude – an assumption given little qualification in the text, but an idea that served to blend classical pre-Christian examples of the benefits of war with late Roman Christian ideals. The text, in a sense, moves history on, from the origins of militarism to its maturity as the embodiment of Christian law:

> The fury of the rebellious, and disordered multitude of evill disposed persons hath increased Lawes Military, and was the origin of that honourable profession.[41]

Military power was, in fact, at the heart of early Christianity since:

> by Armes the Romanes enlarged their Empire over many nations, and brought many barbarous Countries to civility and prosperity [and] by the Armes and valour of the Emperour Constantine, the Lord redeemed his Church, and restored true religion among many nations.[42]

In the context of the Reformation, the parallel between military might, the Roman Empire and 'true religion' invites questions about the place of God in the conduct of warfare between Protestants and Catholics. Trussell notes that 'by Armes, the Spanish have got their power in the West Indies, and by Armes do they hold the same in obedience to their Sceptor'.[43] But clearly such Roman Catholic activity is not sanctioned by God if the soldiers in the Low Countries really are 'a patterne for all Christendome' and the 'great comfort of all truehearted Protestants'.[44]

War is justified in terms of both foreign and domestic threat, though emphasis is always placed on England's vulnerability to invasion from abroad, while the internal situation is analysed in terms of the justice that militarism fosters:

> The Lord our God, useth no occupation of men in his workes and proceedings, as he doth military men: for by them doth hee execute his wrathe upon the rebellious and faithlesse, and also by the same meanes it pleaseth him to deliver the righteous from oppression.[45]

Finally, though, internal and external threat are fused as equally threatening to the susceptible realm:

> The state that is not able to stand in Armes, and to vanquish the rage and power of intestine and forreine violence the same is sure to fall into the power of the spoylers, at one time or other, and then goeth things to havocke.[46]

The Soldier Pleading His Own Cause settles on the immediate situation of London itself, and although the focus is on foreign threat, presumably from the Spanish, there is a telling hint at the idea of domestic unrest as an important element in the argument in favour of militarism:

> French citizens [are] prepared. Citizens of Italy likewise. In the little Cittie of Geneva are 5,000 Citizens, in ordinary bands, sworne in Armes. STRASBOROUGH the same. In Amsterdam are weekly traynings of the wealthiest Citizens: and divers other Countries, and Citties the like. . . . And is London so secure, that it needeth not the knowledge of Armes? Why it is so careless, that it should despise the exercise, as a matter nothing pertaining to them? Certainly such security hath brought many a famous City of the world to ruine and misery: And London might oftentimes have been brought to the same praedicament, had not their Kings beene at hand to vanquish the insolency of Rebels by the force of Armes.[47]

The increasing preoccupation with specific historical examples of recent conflict in the argument for military preparedness allowed the military writers to present the Protestant cause as the principal rationale. 1623 saw the publication of *A Tongue Combat*, probably written by Thomas Scott, which takes the form of a long dialogue between two soldiers 'in a Tilte-Boat of Gravesend, the one going to serve the King of Spain, the other to serve the States Generall of the United Provinces'.[48] The two soldiers, Red-Scarfe, supporting the Catholic side, and Tawney-Scarfe, the Protestants, argue in front of an audience in the boat the terms of a dynamic debate over the status of the Gospel and the justification for armed struggle in pursuit of their respective causes. Scott notes that 'these twain gave each other their hand upon the conditions: and betweene them a Tongue-Combat, wherein neither of both were slaine or maimed'.[49] Tawney-Scarfe argues for the position Elizabeth had taken in the previous century on behalf of laws and liberties, and also in support of old friends, yet:

> the third motive and the greatest, which outwent matter of State, was the maintenance of the Gospel, and the peaceable state of the true reformed Church, which began there to inlarge itself; and whereof as shee was styled, so shee intended to proove her selfe (and performed what she intended) a true Defendress of the Faith.[50]

In this text any general theological justification of war is far outweighed by discussion of recent political events and the crisis over the state of the Reformation. Red-Scarfe offers a particularly vitriolic attack on the person and politics of Elizabeth, which is met by Tawney-Scarfe's account of the wickedness of Catholicism, with transubstantiation the principal doctrinal target and the Gunpowder Plot a manifestation of the political threat:

> and all the evidence which your eares have heard before the Judges on the Bench, and eyes have seen upon the Bridge, and tope of the Parliament house, can hardly persuade you to beleeve, that those Romane catholick crowes which now pearch above, did once plot and practise below to blow up the state.[51]

War is by this time thoroughly linked to the cause of Protestantism and texts such as this, moving from general theological debate to a pragmatic justification of war in terms of the battle for the Low Countries, begin to assume the notion of the 'Christian Soldier' as an armed combatant. The metaphor promoted by Erasmus has ultimately become literal – and the formerly spiritual campaigns tangible and deadly.

The Puritan essayist Richard Bernard was responsible in the 1620s for one of the most comprehensive texts justifying war in the name of religion. Bernard joined other clerics of the period in attacking the residual strand of pacifism associated at this time with Anabaptists, whom he considers 'but dreamers, for God is pleased to be called a man of Warre'.[52] *The Bible-Battels or the Sacred Art Military*, was published in 1629 and is respectfully dedicated to the king, yet the tone is revealingly one of grievance, urging Charles to become the 'Christian Soldier' that Protestantism required:

> That fortolde by Christ is now verified: a noise there is of warres, and a rumour of wars. Nation riseth against Nation, and Kingdome against Kingdome and now, as John saw in the vision, is the Holy Citty trodden under foote; but yet there is hope. Stand therefore (o King) in the Forefront of the Lords Battailes; though not in person, yet in the power of Your Might, to suppresse the insolence of high hearted Enemies. Our cause is just, though God please a while to afflick us, miraculous deliveries we have had. Who was it that delivered us from the intended Invasion; who it was that prevented the hellish Powder-plot, who it was that freed us from many Treacheries and Treasons practised against us?[53]

While recognising that some practicalities of military training require updating, Bernard's text insists that in broad terms the Bible offers a thorough description of the essential practicalities of training and military preparation for the seventeenth-century reader as well as a comprehensive theory of just war:

> Warre is the opposite to peace, and is by the prophet called evil; being the fruit of sinne, the punishment for sinne, yea so fearfull, as David once put to his choice, desired rather the pestilence, then the sword of an enemy. God hath warre with man, yea he hath some where sworne, that with some sorts, hee will have warre from generation to another for ever; there is no peace for the wicked.[54]

The sense of a fallen world constantly plagued by war not only 'naturalises' armed conflict but sanctions any war that is considered just since the instigator can claim the authority of God for the action that must follow. Bernard exhibits a consistent level of respect for Charles throughout the text, but there is also a curious insistence on authority and hierarchy that could be interpreted as recognition that Charles is somehow neglectful of his role. The long list of biblical wars cited include examples that indicate that war is justified when a certain kind of equilibrium has been lost, making a state ungovernable. The 'first moover' of all wars should be 'the supreme authority in the State, whether it be Monarchicall, Aristocraticall, or any of the rest, by which the people of a state is governed'.[55] There is something ironic about Charles being addressed in this way at a point when his authority was being challenged by groups within the state that were, within two decades, to establish a government that could only be described, in Bernard's words, as 'any of the rest'. Indeed, Bernard includes at one point a set of terms about the just war that might almost apply to the case made for the wars against Charles in the 1640s:

> Reproaches offered and injuries done to principall men in a State is just cause for war . . . for high authority is sacred, and the injuries, reproach or contempt offered thereto, is not to passe unpunished.[56]

When the crisis between Charles and his Parliament came to a head, the apocalyptic tone of texts such as *The Bible-Battels* was ratified and particularised by military writers concerned to lend their support to one side or the other. A text attributed to 'R. W.', and published in 1642 as hostilities began, allied the general concept of the just war with a theological validation of the current dispute in support of Parliament's cause.[57] The notion of the 'Christian Soldier' is by now an established literal one and the forces that were to be raised in aid of Parliament's cause were to be, in effect, the first concrete manifestation of much of what the military theorists had been advocating for decades.

> As Children through ignorance of the nature, and perill of Fire often times fall thereinto, and are burnt, so men not aquainted with the nature and danger of warre too often desire it, and too soone rush into it, to their owne ruin. And therefore we may see clearly, as in glasse, the true nature of this heavy plague of Warre, which now threatens our desolation, and the downfall of our Church and State. I have once againe stepte upon the Stage, and for the good of my Country, exposed myselfe to the fight, and censure of all eyes and tongues. Omitting wholly what I handled concerning Warre . . . in the Vindication of Parliament, and their proceedings; I will here lay down many things, concerning Warre in general and Civill Warre in particular. I. That Warre is not to be undertaken, but for just causes. II. That it belongs onely unto the Magistrate to make Warre, and not to private persons. III. That it is not to be moved, but repelled: not kindled but quenched: that is, rather for defence than offence: for the punishing of injuries, than the doing of wrong. All of which shows evidently the lawfulnesse of the Parliaments Warre, their Cause being Religion, and the Republic's good. Themselves the greatest Magistrates, and of the greatest power and this designe of theirs declined as long as possibly they could, with the safety of the state.[58]

'R. W.', then, offers a statement of theological justification for war that predicts the kind of ideological framework offered to members of the New Model Army itself. Ironically, this also hints at some of the (sub-magistrate) complaint that was to turn sections of Cromwell's army against him. Significantly, this late text places a validation of the notion of the Christian Soldier in the mouth of Christ himself:

> If Christianity should blame, or tax all warrs, then when the souldiers asked Christ what they should do for the salvation of their soules, he would undoubtedly have bidden them to cast away their weapons, and to give over Warre, which he dothe not, but only forbids them to wrong any, and bids them to be content with their wages, which showes plainely that some warrs are lawfull, and therefore not to be condemned.[59]

The military writing produced in the years between Colet's sermon at St Paul's and the outbreak of war between Charles Stuart and Parliament offered a complex theological, political and philosophical argument that secured the concept of the just war and pushed to the margins any residual notions of pacifism. The military texts are unremittingly imperative in their tone, and although pacifism remained an alternative, in the theology of the Anabaptists for example, the polarity between war and peace became meaningless. To the military theorists, for example, civil war could be the outcome of domestic quietude, but foreign war was a guarantee of internal peace. Christian war could help maintain 'true religion' abroad and also guard against decadence at home, and as we shall see, constant preparedness for war, whilst dependent on militarising civilian life, enhanced the concept of the ideal citizen. Above all, in the sixteenth and seventeenth centuries, war became a 'natural' condition of humanity, explained by the ambition associated with the Fall, but sanctioned by God's firm endorsement. The thread of Erasmus's general opposition to war and Colet's specific argument over the war in France had worn very thin by the time of the civil wars in the mid-seventeenth century. If it is to be glimpsed at all, it is within the theatrical performances that took place in the period between Colet and the Commonwealth.

On balance it might be argued that the Reformers' anti-war stance was, in the long history of Christian scriptural interpretation and exegesis, something of an anomaly, produced under the specific conditions of debate and revision at the time of the Reformation. Christopher Tyderman, taking account of the theological justification for the Crusades, has noted that 'the so-called Charity texts of the New Testament that preached pacifism and forgiveness, not retaliation, were firmly defined as applying to the beliefs and behaviour of the private person'.[60] He notes passages from the Gospels and St Paul that can be read as distinguishing the spiritual from the political. By the time Colet preached his sermon, Christianity had had 1,500 years to establish its attitude to war. Saint Augustine's fifth-century doctrine of the just war rehearsed Aristotle's notion in *The Politics* that a war should only be fought to secure peace and never as an end in itself. It is interesting to compare Aristotle's views on peace with those of the Renaissance military theorists. Like them, he saw the dangers of peace, but argued that the solution was for the lawgiver to organise leisure as actively as he organised war:

> And as for military training, the object in practising it regularly is not to bring into subjection those not deserving of such treatment, but to enable men (a) to save themselves from becoming subject to others, (b) to win a position of leadership, exercised for the benefit of the ruled, not with a view to being master of all, and (c) to exercise the rule of a master over those who deserve to be slaves. The lawgiver should make particularly sure that his aim in his legislation in general is to provide peace and leisure. And facts support theory here, for though most military states survive while they are fighting wars, they fall when they have established their rule. Like steel, they lose their fine temper when they are at peace; and the lawgiver who has not educated them to be able to employ their leisure is to blame.[61]

For Augustine, war originated in sin, but could be used to destroy sin. As Tyderman says:

> From Augustine's diffuse comments on war could be identified four essential characteristics of a just war that were to underpin most subsequent discussions of the subject. A just war requires a just cause; its aims must be defensive or for the recovery of rightful possessions; legitimate authority must sanction it: those who fight must be motivated by right intent. Thus war, by nature sinful, could be a vehicle for the promotion of righteousness; war that is violent could, as some later medieval apologists maintained, act as a form of charitable love, to help victims of injustice. From Augustine's categories developed the basis of Christian just war theory, as presented, for example, by Thomas Aquinas in the thirteenth century.[62]

That Aquinas, in his *Summa Theologica*, found it necessary to establish his more precise definition of the just war as a series of carefully honed responses to 'objections' to Christian warfare shows that the issue was one of considerable contention. Moreover, he plays on the distinction between the 'private' act of taking life versus the 'public' (state or Church) war, forbidding the former but sanctioning the latter, in a curious echo of the discussions about the biblical Charity texts. It is Aquinas, whose principles of the just war inform many modern examinations of the subject, whom Colet may have set out to contradict in his sermon for Henry VIII.

Whatever the case, the strident nature of the Elizabethan and Stuart military theorists' attack on residual Christian 'objections' admits the persistence of a strand of anti-war sentiment that they had to strive to overcome. As we shall see in the next chapter, their argument – extrapolated from the early notion of the 'Christian Soldier' by way of Augustine and Aquinas – expanded the issue to include a secular thesis concerning the benefits of militarism to the state. Militarism could not only condition and justify the theological and legal underpinning of the nation-state, but also guarantee a set of values associated with those individuals that would inhabit, and be identified as subjects of, the emerging form of state. As we shall also see, the theorists produced arguments concerning the relationship between civilian and military life, definitions of the militarised male as the epitome of masculinity, and above all a kind of ur-Orwellian blurring of distinctions between peace and war that are recognisable in the contemporary world.

Notes

1. The group I am thinking of includes John Fisher, William Grocyn, Thomas Linacre and Thomas More.
2. The charge of heresy was brought by Bishop Fitzjames of London, but was dismissed by Archbishop Warham.
3. This is not to say that Colet would have approved of Henry's subsequent argument with Rome, let alone the views of the secessionists.
4. This was not the first time that he preached against the wars in France.
5. See E. E. Reynolds (1965), *Thomas More and Erasmus*, London: Longman, p. 125, republished 2006 New York: Fordham University Press. Erasmus attacked the use of mercenaries in *Military Affairs*, *The Soldier and the Cathusian* and *Cyclops*. His account of Colet's anti-war stance and relationship with Henry can be found in P. S. Allen, H. M. Allen and H. W. Garrod (eds) (1906–47), *Opus Epistolarum Des. Erasmi Roterodami*, Oxford: Oxford University Press, Vol. IV, pp. 373–4 and 526.
6. F. Seebohm (1887), *The Oxford Reformers*, London: Longman, pp. 265–6. See also J. H. Lupton (1909), *Life of John Colet*, London: George Bell.

7. Seebohm, *Oxford Reformers*, p. 165.
8. Ian Roy, 'Towards the Standing Army', in David Chandler (ed.) (1994), *The Oxford Illustrated History of the British Army*, Oxford: Oxford University Press, quotes a Welsh soldier's view of the composition of one of these expeditions: 'so many depraved, brutish soldiers from all nations under the sun – Welsh, English, Cornish, Manx, Scots, Spaniards, Gascons, Portingales [Portuguese], Italians, Albanians, Greeks, Turks, Tartars, Almains, Germans, Burgandians, Flemings, who had come here . . . to have a good time under the king of England, who by nature was too hospitable to foreigners' (p. 30).
9. Tournai was temporarily held by Henry, and he seized Boulogne in 1544. Boulogne reverted to French sovereignty in the reign of Edward VI and Calais in the reign of Mary Tudor.
10. In fact, the French landed in the Isle of Wight in 1545, but were repulsed by local troops. Henry, meanwhile, was watching his flagship, the *Mary Rose*, sink in Portsmouth harbour.
11. Roy, in Chandler (ed.), *The Oxford Illustrated History of the British Army*, p. 39.
12. Geoffrey Parker (ed.) (1995), *Warfare*, Cambridge: Cambridge University Press, pp. 146–7.
13. M. J. D. Cockle (1900), *A Bibliography of English Military Books up to 1642 and Contemporary Foreign Works*, London: Simpkin, Marshal, Hamilton, Kent & Co.
14. Niccolò Machiavelli (1560), *The Arte of Warre, Written First in Italia by Niccolò Machiavelli and Set Forthe in English by Peter Whitehorne*, London. Machiavelli's thoughts on war seem to have found an audience. This volume was republished in 1574 and 1588. Versions of Machiavelli's *Libro dell'Arte della Guella* were also published in Italian in London in the last two decades of the sixteenth century, fictitiously imprinted with Piacenza or Palermo as their place of origin.
15. Christine de Pisan (1498), *The Boke of the Fayt of Armes and of Chyvalreye*, London.
16. Henry J. Webb (1955), 'Classical Histories and Elizabethan Soldiers', *Notes and Queries*, Vol. 200, November, pp. 468–9.
17. The best example is Richard Bernard (1629), *The Bible-Battels or the Sacred Art Military. For the rightly wageing of warre according to Holy Writ. Compiled for the use of all such valient Worthies, and vertuously Valerous Soutldiers, as upon all just occasions be ready to affront the Enemeies of God, our King, and Country*, London.
18. See K. H. Göller (ed.) (1981), *The Alliterative Morte Arthure: A Reassessment of the Poem*, Bury St Edmunds: D. S. Brewer; Juliet Vale, *Edward III and Chivalry*, Bury St Edmunds: Boydell Press; Richard W. Kaeuper (1988), *War, Justice and Public Order*, Oxford: Clarendon Press.

19. Thomas Trussell (1619), *The Soldier Pleading His Own Cause*, London.
20. R. W. [Richard Ward?] (1642), *The Anatomy of Warre*, London, p. 10.
21. Göller, *The Alliterative Morte Arthure*, p. 16.
22. Desiderius Erasmus [1511], *The Praise of Folly*, trans. Leonard F. Dean (1946), Chicago: Chicago University Press, pp. 112–13.
23. John C. Olin (ed.) (1965), *Christian Humanism and the Reformation: Selected Writings of Desiderius Erasmus*, New York: Harper & Row.
24. Desiderius Erasmus (1522), 'Military Affairs', in *The Colloquies of Erasmus* (1965), trans. Craig R. Thompson, Chicago: Chicago University Press, p. 14. See also 'The Soldier and the Carthusian', 'The Funeral', 'Chao' and 'Cyclops' in the same volume. For an account of Erasmus's pacificism, see John Huizinga (1957), *Erasmus and the Age of Reformation*, Princeton, NJ: Princeton University Press.
25. Thomas More [1516], *Utopia*, ed. Edward Surtz SJ (1964), New Haven, CT: Yale University Press, p. 125. For a comparison between Erasmus and More on warfare, see M. M. Philips (1965), *The Adages of Erasmus*, Cambridge: Cambridge University Press, pp. 114–16.
26. Anthony Kenny (1983), *Thomas More*, Oxford: Oxford University Press, pp. 34–5.
27. Thomas Digges (1604), *Four Paradoxes, or Politique Discourses concerning Militarie Discipline*, London, p. 109.
28. John Hale (1983), *Renaissance War Studies*, London: Hambledon Press, p. 487. See Martin Luther (1526), *Ob Kriegsleute Auch in Seligem Stande Sein Können*.
29. See Roland H. Bainton (1961), *Christian Attitudes to War and Peace*, New York: Abingdon Press, p. 145.
30. Hale, *Renaissance War Studies*, p. 490.
31. See H. Bender (1959), 'The Pacifism of the Sixteenth-Century Anabaptists', *Mennonite Quarterly Review*, Vol. XXX, pp. 7–9.
32. John Smythe (1590), *Certain Discourses, written by Sir John Smythe, Knight: Concerning the formers and effects of divers sorts of weapons, and other verie important matters Militarie, greatlie mistaken by divers of our men of warre in these days; and chielfly, of the Mosquet, the Caliver and the Long-bow; As also, of the great sufficiencie, excellencie, and wonderful effects of Archers: With many notable examples and other particularities, by him presented for the benefite of this his native Countrie of England*, London; ed. John Hale (1964), New York: Cornell University Press, p. 31.
33. Ibid.
34. Smythe, *Certain Discourses*, p. 34.
35. Ibid., p. 119.
36. Gyles Clayton (1591), *The Approoved Order of Martiall Discipline*, London, Sig. A. 3.

37. Gyles Clayton, *The Approoved Order*, Sig. A. 4.
38. Gyles Clayton, *The Approoved Order*, Sig. B. 1.
39. Gyles Clayton, *The Approoved Order*, Sig. B. 2.
40. Gyles Clayton, *The Approoved Order*, Sig. H. 2.
41. Thomas Trussell (1619), *The Soldier Pleading His Own Cause*, London. This text, as with many from the period, has varied systems of pagination. Trussell's book begins with signatures and then adopts page numbers. This quotation is from Sig A. 2.
42. Trussell, *The Soldier*, Sig. B. 4.
43. Ibid.
44. Trussell, *The Soldier*, Sig. C. 8.
45. Ibid.
46. Trussell, *The Soldier*, p. 21.
47. Ibid., p. 26.
48. Thomas Scott [?] (1623), *A Tongue-Combat Lately Happening Betweene Two Englishe Souldiers in the Tilt-Boat of Gravesend, the One Going to Serve the King of Spaine, the Other to Serve the States Generall of the United Provinces. Wherein the Cause, Course, and Continuance of those Warres, is Debated and Declared*, London.
49. Scott [?], *A Tongue-Combat*, dedication.
50. Ibid., p. 5.
51. Ibid., p. 47.
52. Richard Bernard (1629), *The Bible-Battels or the Sacred Art Military*, London, Epistle Dedicatorie. For a discussion of Bernard's treatment of the Anabaptists, see Hale, *Renaissance War Studies*, p. 494.
53. Ibid.
54. Bernard, *The Bible-Battels*, pp. 9–10. This volume's chapter titles reveal the way that the Bible offers illustrations of the practical concerns of military organisation and strategy: for example, 'Of Prest Men and Volunteers'; 'Of the Mustering and Choice of Souldier'; 'Of the Disciplining of an Armie and Orderly Government thereof'; 'Of the Evils to Bee Avoided in a Campe', etc.
55. Bernard, *The Bible-Battels*, p. 57.
56. Ibid., pp. 43–5.
57. 'R. W.' [Richard Ward?], *The Anatomy of Warre*.
58. Ibid., p. 1.
59. Ibid., p. 5.
60. Christopher Tyderman (2006), *God's War: A New History of the Crusades*, London: Allen Lane, pp. 29–30.
61. See Aristotle, *The Politics* (1962), trans. T. A. Sinclair, London: Penguin, pp. 435–6.
62. Tyderman (2006), *God's War*, p. 34.

4

'THE DOUBLE-ARMED MAN'

෧

This chapter has a fantasy hero. It appears in the form of the extraordinary figure of a foot soldier who features in a series of illustrations in William Neade's 1625 book of military theory and tactics, *The Double-Armed Man*.[1] I shall return to him later, along with his mounted counterpart, leaving him for the moment standing, somewhat awkwardly in his spurs and heavy-looking armour, with longbow drawn and steadied against his pike, a full quiver of arrows on one side of his waist, and an elegantly hilted sword at the other. Neade's text is one example from the wideranging canon of early modern documents that argued the case for an enhanced awareness of the military requirements of the developing late Tudor and early Stuart state, and the illustration is a perfect image of this canon's relentless idealism. One of my concerns is with the way that this idealism was guaranteed for the reader by means of a not altogether untroubled marshalling of representations of medieval militarism and chivalry, classical models and current military fads and fashions. The ideological assumptions underpinning the approach of those who theorised the optimum Renaissance army – and thus the subjectivities of the individual soldiers that were to be recruited to it – are best seen when the model becomes overdetermined by the relentlessness of its idealism.

Armies recruit individuals, yet notions of 'individuality' do not fit readily into the specialised human activity that is warfare: individual acts may be celebrated and rewarded, but in the 'theatre' of war their significance (as 'soliloquies' of war) depends on a collective 'troupe'. The controversy over sexuality and identity in modern military institutions is precisely predicated on the dialectical relationship between the individual body of the soldier as a human resource, and the larger, corporate organisation that shapes but also relies on that individual resource. Militarism in the modern world, as in the early modern period, defines and conditions a highly specialised form of subjectivity.

Some of the most resonant and decisive aspects of the unstable history of militarism and subjectivity are evident in late sixteenth- and early seventeenth-century England. If militarism can be thought of as a discourse governing the theory and practice of premeditated mass human conflict, then this was indeed a period of considerable transformation throughout Europe. It was not a period of all-consuming involvement by the English in warfare abroad, or indeed at home until the civil conflict that dominated the middle years of the seventeenth century. Yet neither could this period be regarded strictly as a time of peace, or one free from considerable military ambition. It was more a period of minor military adventures, many of them at sea, together with a steady commitment to military activity in France, Scotland, Ireland and the Low Countries. Yet it is precisely at this time of relative military inactivity that a widespread debate about the overall ideology of militarism was most determined. Indeed, it is possible to suggest that ideological debate in this period 'settled' a range of existing uncertainties to do with militarism that were transformed into a set of values and assumptions that have endured into the present century. They were certainly to underpin the more significant military establishment of the eighteenth and nineteenth centuries, thus facilitating the more or less constant engagement that characterised the growth and consolidation of the British Empire.

The early modern English debate over military matters, which led to the construction of what may be termed the 'gendered' military subject, was part of a far larger discourse. Militarism is obviously linked, both literally and symbolically, to important issues of political change. Yet it is also connected to matters of day-to-day organisation, identity and consent that seep from the walls of the institution (the military) into an ideally respectful civilian population. Examination of the paradigm that emerges of the ideal and specifically gendered soldier (and the terms of his subjection to an overall military machine) reinforces the importance of matters of subjectivity and power to the developing early modern notion of statehood. In the ideal emerging Renaissance proto-state the values of the military are seamlessly the values of the populace, hence the importance of military display to public ritual in succeeding centuries – a matter I shall come to later.

Much of this chapter is, then, concerned with the abundant English prose writing of early modern military theorists. It is in this that the ideal of the military subject is problematised and finally constructed (with an increasing determination) into a recognisable model for empire and for the individual. This was also a period rich in theatrical representations of warfare, ranging from depictions of classical military conflict, through narratives of English civil and dynastic warfare, to telling topical commentaries on late Tudor and early Stuart military activity. The public theatre can be said to have foregrounded the more unsettling aspects of the debate about gender and militarism that was being conducted in the military prose writing of the time. While the prose tended to 'contain' anxieties and discontinuities in the discourse of militarism, the theatre interrogated what some modern military historians have seen as a smooth 'progression' towards the settled, naturalised male soldier-subject during the period known as the English Renaissance. This effect is more to do with the dynamic of theatrical representation than with political resistance. It is fanciful to think that if the plays of Shakespeare and his contemporaries had offered a credible alternative to the inevitability of militarism – as a determining source of identity for the emerging state – warfare may have achieved less prominence and acceptance as part of the cultural condition of humanity. Yet the early modern theatre, like the agitprop political theatre of the late twentieth century, at least invites succeeding generations to glimpse a realm of difference and dissent.

Apart from a few exception, the military texts of the period are listed either in the *Short-Title Catalogue of Books Printed in England, Scotland and Ireland 1475–1640* or in M. J. D. Cockle's *Bibliography of English Military Books up to 1642*, already alluded to.[2] The reference I make to Cockle's body of some 150 texts is necessarily selective, but I have privileged those that best exemplify the preoccupation their writers had with theoretical issues, and excluded those that concentrate simply on practical issues. However, texts dealing exclusively with practical matters of, say, gunnery, tactics or field surgery are exceedingly rare. There is a clear impulse in the work of these writers to preface or frame their work by a justification of its importance in wider political and ideological terms. This feature is in itself evidence of the highly sensitive nature of warfare as a topic, and the urgency of their arguments concerning the relationship between militarism and the state. Many of the texts, from the slim volumes of tactics, to the larger treatises on the ethics of war, announce themselves discursively in grand terms, citing the 'art' or, interestingly, the 'science' of war. Another feature of the body of work overall is the complex system of interdependence. The writers 'borrowed' from each other, or from earlier classical or foreign works, or from the Bible, often without acknowledging their sources. It is sometimes difficult to ascertain the origin of a particular line of thinking and, as Cockle discovered, the dating of the texts is a science in itself. Cockle's list includes the significant number of foreign works that were either reprinted in London or circulated in their original form in England, one of which was particularly influential.

Niccolò Machiavelli's *L'arte Della Guerra* of 1519–21 was first translated into English by Peter Whitehorne, who published it with an extensive introduction and some additional material as *The Arte of Warre* in 1560.[3] Of the European texts, Machiavelli's commands a special place in the overall body of military writing available in early modern Britain, partly due to its wide circulation and frequent republication up to 1642. It can also be seen as 'silently' present in much of the work of the English military theorists, despite the fact that they disputed Machiavelli's disinclination towards the idea of standing armies. In what remains a critical text on the reception of Machiavelli in England, *The English Face of Machiavelli*, Felix Raab argued in 1964 that there was a considerable demand for Machiavelli's various writings in England during this period.[4] Although they had been banned in the first half of the sixteenth century, Italian and French language manuscripts of his work circulated illegally.[5] Towards the end of the century illicit Italian imprints of the *Il Principe*, the collected *Discorsi* and the original *L'arte Della Guerra* could be readily found in London, testifying to an impatience with the slow progress of translation following the lifting of the ban.[6]

The appeal of Machiavelli for English military theorists lay with his ideas on the establishment of an army that would be in constant readiness to defend, in Italian terms, the city-state, and could be deployed in pursuit of the Prince's foreign policy. *The Arte of Warre* also contained useful details on the training and disciplining of soldiers, and Whitehorne included illustrations of battle formations and military camps. Furthermore, Machiavelli's model chimed with developing English military theory in its firm opposition to the employment of mercenaries, a constant theme in the English works, which make frequent reference to the disastrous results of using such men in Henry VIII's French wars. Machiavelli notes that the Italian city-states had similarly depended on mercenaries, despite their anachronistic cultivation (late into the fourteenth century) of the figure of the knight, who had in effect become the leader in the field of foreign troops. Machiavelli's opposition to standing armies was derived from his celebration of the ideal of the 'citizen-soldier', and it is clear that certain elements of this ideal permeated early modern English military writing.

In Machiavelli's world the ideal male citizen would be physically strong and suitably trained and equipped to function when needed as a soldier: the 'arte' of war would complement the 'arte' of his trade or profession. This arrangement was informed by Machiavelli's elaborate conception of the code of 'virtù', which applied in wider terms to his ideal of the state's citizenry. But it also revealed an implied anxiety about professional soldiers in general, an anxiety that was subdued in English military theory, which mostly favoured professional soldiers in the pay of the Crown. J. G. A. Pocock has remarked that:

> The paradox developed in Machiavelli's argument is that only a part-time soldier can be trusted to process a full-time commitment to the war and its purposes. A citizen called to arms, with a home and an occupation (arte) of his own, will wish to end the war and go home, where a mercenary, glad rather than sorry if the war drags on indefinitely, will make no attempt to win it.[7]

Machiavelli takes the argument further by stating that the citizen-soldier system reinforces the authority of citizenship since military service, in this form, can in itself develop a sense of 'virtù' when the values associated with military 'arte' combine with a civilian professional 'arte'. Pocock notes:

> The contention that only the soldier can be a good citizen is also made, but less explicitly. The thought implementing it is complex, but rests in part on some assertions made in the preface.[8]

The preface (or 'proem') celebrates the pagan gods of ancient Rome for their civic function in that society, yet the monotheism of contemporary Italy can also be accommodated since Machivelli's 'virtù' reconciles military consciousness with theological integrity:

> In whome ought there to bee more feare of God, than in him, which every daie committyng himself to infintie perilles, hath moste neede of his helpe.[9]

This is something of a gesture towards Christianity however, as Machiavelli soon returns, in the dialogue form adopted by some of the English military theorists, to the classical form of militarised 'virtù':

> *Cosimo*: What thyngs are those, that you would induce like unto the antiquitie?
> *Fabrica*: To honour, and to reward vertue, not to despise povertie, to esteeme the maners and orders of warfare, to constrain the citezeins to

love one an other, to live without sects, to esteme the private, than the publicke, and other like things . . .[10]

Where the English writers take issue with Machiavelli is with his notion of that all citizens should be soldiers, but although they preferred the idea of the professional soldier, they did acknowledge the benefits that the experienced soldier could bring to civilian life. In his introduction to *The Arte of Warre*, Whitehorne notes:

> It is to bee thought (that for the defence, maintenaunce, and advancemente of a Kyngome, or Common weale, or for the good and due observacion of peace, and administration of Justice in the same) no one thing to be more profitable, necessarie, or more honourable, then the knowledge of service in warre, and dedes of armes.[11]

Indeed, Whitehorne exaggerates Machivalli's views about the relationship between war and the state to set out an argument that is to become a central component of English military theory: that military activity guarantees or even enhances both prosperity and peace itself, since in the past:

> when through long and continued peace [societies] began to bee altogether given to pleasure and delicatenesse, little regardyng Martiall featres, nor suche as were expert in the practise thereof . . . [t]heir dominians and estates, did not so moche before increase and propere, as then by soche meanes and oversight, thei sodainly fell into decaie and utter ruine.[12]

Whitehorne establishes the overall proposal that peace is guaranteed only by a warlike spirit and constant preparation for war, concluding that 'even Lady Peace her selfe, doeth in maner from these crave her chief defence and preservacion'.[13]

CLASSICS

Classical writing on war gave a strategic weight to early modern military theory. Roman texts in particular were marshalled in a highly selective way or carefully reworked to show their relevance to contemporary England.[14] Few works in the overall body of military writing espoused total commitment to classic models. Those that did include *The Pathwaie to Martial Discipline*, in which Thomas Styward recommended the reader to 'prosecute the auncient order of the Romans', right down to the adoption of Roman weaponry and equipment.[15] However, the main emphasis was on adjusting the theory to take account of modern ballistics and other forms of technology. In his introduction to Bernadino de Mendoza's *Theorique and Practise of Warre*, Sir Edward Hoby noted that the general theory of warfare had been:

> from the first creation of the worlde until nowe the verie same, the disposition of the people onely varying in the difference of weapons, engines, and instruments, which have bin invented.[16]

Thus the classic writers were part of a continuum and could reveal universal values and timeless truths about military matters. Sir Clement Edmondes observed in his *Observations upon the Five First Books of Caesar's Commentaries* that there was a disparity between classical theory and contemporary experience and argued for a synthesis, since:

> It is not only experience and practice which maken a soldier worthie of his name, but the knowledge of the manifold accidents which arise from the variety of humane actions and this knowledge is onely to be learned in the registers of antiquitie and in histories, recoding the motions of former ages.[17]

Few texts argued for a complete detachment from classical theories of war. Those that did invited their readers to contrast reports of recent wars with the elevated scholasticism of contemporary texts that derived their rhetoric from the classics. Thomas Digges noted that 'the Time was changed, the Warres were altered, and the furie of Ordinaunces such as those Roman Orders, were mere toyes'.[18]

MILITARY HISTORY

From the earliest fifteenth-century accounts of chivalry to the late Caroline propaganda, there is a preoccupation with setting the contemporary and accelerating decay in military structures, and therefore the ill-preparedness of the state, against an idealised history. The common concern is with the urgent necessity for the state to maintain a powerful and efficient body of prepared and well-equipped men in order to deter invaders or to pursue just wars abroad on behalf of the monarchy. The writers discuss moral and religious justifications for warfare, the importance of classical models, foreign armies, model military leaders and contemporary attitudes to militarism. Most lament the decay of the medieval *fief* system through which the aristocracy could raise local men through feudal obligatory systems. Most call for the establishment of a standing army, or at least some action to prevent the seemingly terminal decline in the various militia systems that had evolved from the *fief*.

It is worth noting how some military historians have responded to Tudor and Stuart military writing. For the last hundred years or so the view has been expressed in some quarters that it is evidence of an 'enlightenment' – substantiated by the recognition in the early writing that militarism was a 'science'. Contradictions and hesitations in the canon of writing as a whole have been smoothed over in order to represent it as a homogeneous genre synchronically and one situated diachronically in a military continuum essentially unaffected by political change. It is a canon that embraces everything from Flavius Vegetius to the Falklands and beyond.[19] Writing in 1926, Eric Sheppard was able to compensate for the fact that the Tudor and Stuart years saw little military activity by the English, and some decline in standards of military preparedness, by noting that:

> individual Englishmen were gaining experience in the armies of foreign powers and proving in Holland, France and Germany that the war-like virtues of the race had not been lost.[20]

A particularly influential historian called Robert Higham ignored an example of early seventeenth-century nostalgia in William Barriffe's *Military Discipline*. Writing in 1939 Higham could only note a slight anachronism, since 'it must be confessed that at one point Barriffe provides for the "beneficial use of bow and pike" and it may therefore be argued that his line, although modern and scientific, is less enlightened than it might be'.[21]

These are extreme and distant examples, but in fact the sense of contrast between the medieval and the early modern which is so central to the exhortations of the military writers was also disregarded by some post-war historians. The clear sense of crisis that underpinned the earlier writing is obscured by an optimistic comparison between the Tudor period and modern times by influential modern military historians such as Correlli Barnett. For Barnett, the militia system, based on levying men from the shires, proves by its very continuation during a time of social mobility that the Elizabethan period was one of unusual homogeneity:

> Elizabethan England was in social flux, some men (and families) rising and some falling. Perhaps for this reason stress was laid on the distinction of rank, yet this was a distinction of degree, rather than the absolute barrier of a distinction of kind. The society of an English shire was therefore homogeneous despite its differing social levels.[22]

The state of the Elizabethan militia system is considered not in comparison with the medieval but with modern engagements. Barnett notes that during five months in 1591 the 3,500 men sent to France to participate in the Protestant cause were reduced to 800 by neglect and disease. Yet the Elizabethan resistance to foreign service simply compares unfavourably with the more decisive national response of recent times so that 'the ordinary people of Elizabethan England did not therefore spring to volunteer like their descendants of 1914'.[23] The military climate of Elizabethan England was poor, but the social cohesion of this early period was to mature into a twentieth-century society enhanced by military awareness and responsibility. For other late twentieth-century commentators, the call to arms of the early modern military writers is uncritically explained as out of line with contemporary policy. John Hale has written that 'whilst almost constant wars were absorbing the other European powers, England, from the security of her island position, was relatively unaffected'.[24]

These responses to Tudor and Stuart militarism do not acknowledge the clear sense of historical difference that is evident in the canon of military writing. Such Elizabethan and early Stuart nostalgia, something we might call 'medievalism', sought to evaluate the decay in contemporary military consciousness (and to qualify the resultant decline in standards) by reference to an earlier epoch – often unspecified temporally, unless particular battles were invoked – but one defined as history by three principal contingencies. It was the national history of 'the English', despite the involvement of the Welsh as historically instrumental to the victories which shaped the ideal. Secondly, it was a history which spoke of the homogeneity of the society which had forged it – an important aspect of a 'medievalism' which further revealed an anxiety over matters of social order in the present. Thirdly, it was a history that could be regained by attention to both the details and the philosophy of the new militarism.

The substance and imperative form of this writing, and especially its preoccupation with revivals of the symbolic order and chivalric codes of the past, is partly explained by the absolutist project advanced during the late Tudor and early Stuart years. Such an explanation would also acknowledge a fear of popular unrest that is never far from the business of military order. Seen in this context, the latter day historiography that chooses to regard the military texts as expressive of some form of military 'enlightenment' is reductive and reactionary, especially when a rhetorical link is made with the present through the notion of a military continuum, as is often the case with those responsible, say, for the guardianship of regimental history and military museums.

RESISTANCE

Certainly, the imposition of military training and the recruitment or pressing of men into active service was proving a source of considerable discontent among those subject to such activities in the late sixteenth and early seventeenth centuries. It often resulted in disturbances that may have fuelled Shakespeare's interest in military matters as he set about recording the very history that the military theorists allude to. Evidence of popular disturbances in the period has proved a contentious area of investigation among scholars. For some, acts of unrest have been exaggerated in order to represent them as determining an early class consciousness which is not justified by examination of their sporadic form and the fact that they were both disorganised and lacking an objective. Others have resisted this marginalisation and emphasised the widespread nature of the disturbances, regarding them as reconditioning later, trade-based combinations and popular political movements.

Whatever the case it seems clear that the persistent pattern of disturbances which resulted in the use of the repressive Riot Act of 1411 and Tudor Statutes can be seen in the context of the quasi-absolutism being attempted by the Tudor and early Stuart governments. Certainly the Privy Council saw fit to record the instances and significance of many acts of 'rebellion'. In the county of Essex alone, for which records are particularly detailed, anti-enclosure violence was reported in various areas before 1563, and there were repeated disturbances from 1567 to 1570 in Walthamstow.[25] Note was made of 'certain lewd persons' who thought 'to move some rebellion' in the county in 1576, and there were riots in 1577 at South Weald and Brentwood, between 1582 and 1588 at Revenhall, at Burnham in 1584, Finchingfield in 1585, Halstead in 1586, 1587 and 1588, at Burnham (again) in 1589, at Waltham Abby in 1592, and so on until the failure of the harvests in 1595–7 led to more extensive rioting in London and the seizure of food along the grain roads of Somerset, Wiltshire and Kent in 1596.[26] Edward Cheyney describes one particularly highly organised 'rebellion' in Oxfordshire from this troubled year. Three hundred men assembled, and:

their plan was to attack the houses of six or eight of the neighbouring gentry, most of whom were known to be away at the time, and seize their horses, armour and victuals. There was some talk of cutting off gentlemen's heads and tearing down the hedges that enclosed the old open fields and cut off the old cross-country road ways. They would go to the house of Lord Norris, Lord Lieutenant of Oxfordshire, where they could get weapons for 100 men. If they found themselves still weak, they would march to London where they believed the apprentices would join them.[27]

The so-called Midlands Rising of 1607 involved co-ordinated unrest throughout Warwickshire, Leicestershire and Nottinghamshire, and the Western Rising of 1626–32 spread from the Forest of Dean across the counties of south-west England following extensive food rioting in Somerset, Wiltshire, Hampshire, Berkshire, Sussex, Hertfordshire and Suffolk over the previous two years.[28] The leading participants in the Western Rising were accused in Star Chamber of having 'in Contempt of all Authority combined together and resolved to pull down all the present and ancient Inclosures'.[29]

Records of rioting in the period seem to suggest three principal but related areas of grievance: shortage of food, land enclosure (and the draining of the fens) and the imposition of military training. It is the last reason that establishes a link with the military writing of the period, produced in support of the state, but also as a critique of the state's absolutist experiments. As the records of the Privy Council show, these continuing riots considerably preoccupied the offices of central government. Buchanan Sharp's survey of the evidence concludes that 'fear of riot, and of riot's accompanying potential for overturning the established order, is a constant theme in Tudor and Stuart political pronouncements'.[30] And where military training combined with other grievances, as was the case in the Forest of Dean disturbances, a major irony appeared in the relationship between public order and militarism. The late Tudor and early Stuart state had insufficient means with which to suppress popular unrest. And it also discovered that attempts to reconstitute the medieval *fief* system in order to raise men for foreign expeditions and to institute a disciplined internal police force (including the 'trained bands' of the larger towns) led in itself to further discontent. Thus Keith Wrightson's account of the potentially more violent of these events concludes that the armed rioters were 'simply employing the methods learned (and the equipment employed) at musters of the militia'.[31]

Wrightson is of the opinion that the early modern riot was 'more in the nature of a controlled and remarkably disciplined demonstration than an abandonment of restraint on the part of the people'.[32] Whatever the nature of these disturbances, it is clear that the system of raising and training men for domestic and foreign military duty had decayed at the opening of the seventeenth century. Not only was it a cause of riots, but it was a system too ineffectual to raise reliable forces in order to police the troubled state in the first place. Sharp continues:

> the tenacious resistance of such people to the Crown's will made it impera-
> tive that all the police and judicial authority of the state be brought to bear
> for the punishment of the rioters and the prevention of further outbreaks;
> otherwise, politically dangerous and socially destabilising consequences
> were feared. But it became obvious in the course of this work that in the
> court of Star Chamber, commisions of the oyer and terminar, the *posse*, and
> the militia, the Stuart state lacked efficient or effectual means of repression.[33]

As far as overseas service was concerned, mutinies had not been uncommon during the last years of Elizabeth's reign. Edward Cheyney reports that in 1595:

> there had been a serious mutiny of the drafted men of Norfolk, Suffolk
> and Essex at Ipswich . . . the men 'utterly refusinge to goe beyond the
> seas', disembarking after they had been put aboard, threatening to march
> on London, and stirring up the discontented masses of that old rebellious
> district.[34]

The pressing of soldiers – 17,800 for the wars in Europe and 2,292 for duty in Ireland between 1589 and 1596 – had resulted in the dual problems of potential mutiny and local resentment at the pressure of concentrated groups of ill-disciplined soldiers travelling to and from the wars.[35] Furthermore, pragmatic attempts to introduce some order into the procedures for raising armies met resistance from members of the gentry, who were forced to fund and organise musters and supplies. Many questioned the legality of such impositions just as Parliament itself was to do in the Petition of Right over billeting in 1628, and over forced taxation (Ship Money) in 1634.

Popular unrest in the early modern period never proved a material threat to the monarchy until it became allied to the more coherent causes of the mid-seventeenth century. Yet its continued re-emergence in the years during which these causes gathered momentum troubled an increasingly centralised state that was experimenting with a form of absolute government which, in marked contrast to similar endeavours in Europe, lacked the vital ingredient of a trained and disciplined standing army. Without the ability to impose its will by force, English quasi-absolutism relied on an expensive display of power in order to flood any channels through which discontent might flow towards the heart of the state. The limitation placed on the project of absolutism in England by an absence of the very military apparatus and medieval ideal espoused by the military writers had effects well beyond an inability to suppress the continual acts of unrest that plagued successive administrations. The crucial display of sovereign power was an expensive spectacle that required a concerted and coherent foreign policy (including a commitment to the Reformation) which would be seen to be effective. This necessitated the raising of an army and therefore consultation with a series of Stuart parliaments as increasingly unwilling to finance what proved to be a series of mismanaged adventures as they were to finance domestic extravagance. The English attempt to conjure a sense of absolutism led to a situation in which, lacking a repressive apparatus for internal policing (and thus the enforcing of consent), it nonetheless attempted a foreign policy which in itself required parliamentary approval. This highlights the importance of the relationship between domestic stability and foreign policy – a point discussed at length in the contemporary military writing.

In terms of both technique and employment, the armies of England and the leading European states underwent considerable transformation during the sixteenth and seventeenth centuries when various forms of absolutism were being consolidated. Spain and France, with their large populations and constant military engagements, developed massive and sophisticated armies. England, meanwhile, could no longer participate in such extensive operations from across the Channel. The smaller (and lighter) medieval cross-Channel expeditions, which had characterised English rule and influence in northern France and beyond, could no longer be realised, and Henry VIII's calamitous adventures in France, using levied armies, were the last serious attempts at major interventions on a scale to match the European rivals. Had he listened to Colet, he might have saved considerable face since these experiments both drained the exchequer and limited the prestige of the Tudors. When the later Tudor militarists sought to correct the mistakes of the recent past and to speculate on the qualities of an ideal military state, it is unsurprising that they had to draw on sources that included images of the feudal past. Thus they created a picture that was in sharp contrast to the realities of the recent situation. The raising of mass armies had produced no gain and still less acclaim, and even if naval power assured insular security, that in itself had led to the atrophy of the military body so essential to the absolutist project and the policing of the state. As to the remnants of the noble class whose celebrated ancestry was incorporated into the contemporary image of previous centuries, Perry Anderson has noted that:

> in the isolationist context of the island kingdom there was an exceptionally early demilitarisation of the noble class itself. In 1500 every English peer bore arms; by Elizabeth's time, it has been calculated, only half the aristocracy had any fighting experience. On the eve of the Civil War in the 17th century, very few nobles had any military background.[36]

Demilitarisation of the aristocracy fuelled the polemic of the early modern militarists. It has to be reckoned against the inability, or refusal, of the Tudor and Stuart states to keep up with many facets of the technical revolution in weaponry which occurred in Europe from the mid-fourteenth century onwards. Whilst there was a considerable decline in the use of heavy cavalry, this was not compensated for by a widespread development in the use of gunpowder as a propellant. There is evidence of early enthusiasm, such as the English use of 'crakys of war' (gunshot) in action against the Scots in 1327, and 'gonnes' at Berwick in 1333, and Henry V had depended to some extent on artillery at the siege of Harfleur. Yet the rapid adoption of the cannon as a standard battlefield weapon in fifteenth-century Europe seems to have been ignored by the English military strategists. Despite Henry VIII's interest in the manufacture of cannon and the importation of the latest types, this was in the end a limited initiative. R. C. Smail notes that 'in the use of firearms by the infantry the English were even more hesitant. Their victories in France had made the archer and the longbow into objects of national pride, and they were reluctant to abandon them.'[37] At the same time, English (and perhaps more damagingly Welsh) proficiency with the longbow declined to the point where it could no longer be relied on, as it had been at Crécy, Poitiers and Agincourt where bows had been perhaps more instrumental in victory than the vanguard of knights.

It was against this background of military decline that some of the early modern militarists formulated a discourse that might be described as one of 'medievalism' – a nostalgia for an idealised chivalric order. In the climate of popular disorder, itself partly a result of the chaotic military structures which so poorly imitated those of the idealised past, these writers were impelled to construct a militarism that could combine the values of the past with a contemporary and innovative sense of what would constitute the relationship between the individual and the military institution, and between that institution and the state.

DISCIPLINE, PURPOSE AND KNOWLEDGE

It was a concern for the matters of character and discipline, a knowledge of arms and the ethics, and ultimately for the relationship between the soldier and the state which led the early modern militarists to speculate on the present decay that so clearly contrasted with an idealised past. As with many of these arguments, the medieval pattern that they glorify had to be tempered by modern conditions and politics. For the purposes of late sixteenth- and early seventeenth-century polemic, the past was a place of clear military objectives and success, substantiated by the reputation of knights at home and abroad; thus images of the chivalric past are never summoned without indignation at the present decay. And there was a distinct agenda to do with masculinity in all this. Barnabe Rich, writing in 1578, accused the 'carping cavillers' of the court of having distilled and corrupted the English tradition of a militaristic nobility, by growing 'lazy and greedy, wallowing in vice and wickednesse' and by:

> Neglecting those disciplines which made them both honourable and worshipful – whose magnamitie in the times of warres hath made them famous in forrain countries, and whose nobleness and vertues . . . in times of peace, doe shine coequal with the best.[38]

Rich's *Allarme to England* laments the passing of an age of nobility and virtue when the tournament (as in the *Pas d'Armes*) was actually a display of martial discipline, and scorns its transformation into the courtly jousting games and 'soft and silken wars' which Glynne Wickham confirms as having 'lingered as a Court prerogative . . . conducted in the tiltyard by day and in the banquet hall as a climax to a masquerade by night' into the early years of the seventeenth century.[39] At stake in this lament is a sense of sexual difference, since in England:

> Gentlemen that are descended of honourable families in these days give themselves rather to become Battalus Knights [effeminate men] than Martiall Knights, and have better desire to be practised in Carpet trade than in that kind of virtue. To be shorte . . . in Englande, Gentlemen have robbed our women of their minds, and our women have bereved us of half our apparell.[40]

It would be a mistake, however, to conclude that such texts are simply conservative, recommending a wholesale return to the values of the 'Martiall Knightes'. Rather, these values are to be renegotiated in important ways, almost with an awareness of the problems modern historians have associated with the dispersal of power inherent in a chivalric code that had legitimised private feuding instead of maintaining public order.[41]

The ideological project was to derive an image from the past of chivalric integrity, moral purpose and military discipline, which would be appropriate to the creation of a modern army. The aim of this was not only to represent abroad an increasingly centralised state, but also to provide an internal police force in order to forestall possible popular unrest, a threat which the early modern writers refer to throughout the canon of military texts. The ideal military structure would have to overcome the problems associated with the unpopularity of the militia system and its lack of quality as a fighting force. Barnabe Rich cites the case of London where:

> when they set forth soldiers, either they scoure their prisons of thives, or their streets of rogues and vagabonds . . . the name of a soldier is become so odious to the common people . . . God grant us that we never be given to trie the service of such people.[42]

By paying close attention to the recommendations of the military theorists, the status of the soldier in society would be fundamentally changed, since, according to Geoffrey Gates, the English in recent times:

> hath had that fault of being unnatural and unthankful to soldiers, for if England were not an island but stood in the continent of the world environed with mightie nations . . . then it should know the value of a soldier, and lick the dust off the feete of her men of prowesse: then would the lawyer and the merchant humble themselves to the warriers.[43]

Furthermore, there are a great many examples of the early modern militarists revealing that an established army would allow warfare abroad, which in turn would establish internal peace. For Peter Whitehorne, peace is guaranteed only by war, since earlier societies:

> when through long and continued peace, began to bee altogether given to pleasure and delicateness, little regardyng Martiall feates, nor such as were expert in the practise thereof: Their dominians and estates did not so moche before increase and prospere as then by soche meanes and oversight, thei sodainly fell into decaie and utter ruine.[44]

For Thomas Digges war was 'sometimes lesse hurtfull, and more to be wisht in a well governed State than peace' since peace promoted 'ease and pleasure, two seducing Syrens in whose beastly servitude too many are intralled past recoveries'. And he recommends 'forreine warre, a sovereigne medicine for domestical inconveniences. Desire warre rather than quietnesse, and therefore fall out at home if forreine foes the wanting'.[45] In *The Politicke and Militarie Discourses* the idea of war as an insurance against civil unrest is expressed quite openly, since the ideal:

> Great estate replenished with warlike people, ought still to have some foreine warre wherewith to keepe it occupied, lest being at quiet they convert their weapons against each other.[46]

According to texts like this, the 'warlike people' would be inspired by displays of militarism presented in 'publicke places of Exercise', as had been the case in earlier times.[47] An additional demand was that the modern military formation would consist of soldiers who had a clear knowledge of their own worth in the social formation and the worth of their cause. This knowledge, equivalent to that held individually by the idealised medieval knight, would, in the early modern ideal army, be held by each and every private soldier:

> In would seem requisite and necessarie that great regarde shoulde be used in the appointing of lawes, discipline, and orders, the which not only among themselves, but also to their utter enemies ought inviolaby to be kepte according to the iustice and equite of the cause for which they entred into armes.[48]

The militarist theorists are nostalgic for a concept of the knight, but aware also that if a parallel were to be made between the military formation and the social formation, then the modern soldier was to be a citizen rather than a king in miniature. The private, knowing soldier would submit himself willingly to the overall body of the army institution, know his weapons and his cause, and be self-motivated and active; he would be at the same time both the autonomous knight and the anonymous figure lost within the disciplined ranks of advancing soldiers, so that:

> He may well be called a trained soldier that knows by the sound of drum and trumpet, without any voice, when to march, fight, retire, etc.; that is able in marching, embattling and fighting; that has some sight in the mathematicals and in geometrical instruments, for the conveying of mines under the ground, to plant and manage great ordnance, to batter or beat

down the walles of any towne or castle; that can measure altitude, latti-
tudes and longitudes, etc. Such a one may be termed in my opinion an
expert soldier.[49]

In this way the early modern militarists forged an ideal of the soldier-
as-citizen, an expert and an example to others, able to police his
fellow citizens and fight abroad, to know himself and his cause, and
to strengthen his body so that it could strengthen the overall body of
the army.[50] Listing the qualities and skills which the public should
expect in the soldiers they were to observe in the 'publicke places of
Exercise', *The Soldier Pleading His Own Cause* includes 'Obedient'
behaviour, 'Secrecie', 'Sobriety', 'Courage', 'Loyalty'. The public
was also to be able to assume that the soldiers were 'Free from
Bribes', 'Wise and Politicke' and practised in such 'Artes of Warre'
as 'Arithmetick' and 'Geometry', as well as having 'Knowledge in
Histories' and the ability 'to speak divers Languages'.[51]
    That each soldier should have a 'Knowledge in Histories' is the key
to early modern military idealism. It is a condition which makes sense
of the disparate forces which underpin the demands of the writers: the
chaotic militia system; the threat of popular discontent; the require-
ment for a national military identity; and the vulnerability of the
absolutist state at the end of the sixteenth century. Early modern militarism, pragmatic, innovative and with a close awareness of technical advance, nonetheless proposed an ordering of the past which
we might speak of as a form of 'medievalism'. If the past could be
regained, refashioned and revalued, then the future was assured.
Typical of this process and, I want to suggest, representing an encod-
ing of the whole sense of early modern 'medievalism', is the treatment
of weaponry in the military texts where military idealism, linking
images of the past with contemporary discontents, most closely
reveals the ideological work of these texts.

WEAPONS AND SYMBOLS

Whilst acknowledging the considerable impact made on the military
scene in Europe by the use of gunpowder, the early modern militarists
were, in line with their 'medievalism', often reluctant to relinquish
weapons which they thought of as symbolic of England's triumphant
military past. Humfrey Barwick's insistence in 1594 that munitions
should be adopted in order to restore the status England had enjoyed
in history due to the use of the longbow, brought a swift response

from a number of writers.[52] In 1596, the writer known as 'R. S.', whose treatise was 'abstracted out of ancient and modern writers', promoted the particular effectiveness and 'Englishness' of the longbow and lamented its recent decline.[53] Most texts, however, advocated a synthesis of the old and the new so that the bow could still yield its symbolic national significance, its 'medievalism', alongside such modern weapons as the musket. Just such a compromise had been suggested in Thomas Styward's *The Pathwaie to Martiall Discipline*, a book which, in 1581, 'entreateth of sundrie proportions and training of Calavers, and how to bring Bowes to a great perfection of service'.[54]

It is with the argument for a synthesis of old and new that I return to two of the best examples of this kind of 'medievalism', significantly taken from books which appeared towards the end of the long period of early modern military writing. These may be considered mature examples of the form and are characterised by a sense of overdetermination or fantasy in the presentation of the ideal soldier, totally removed from the conditions from which he has been recruited. William Neade's *The Double-Armed Man: By the New Invention: Briefly Shewing some Famous Exploits atchieved by our Brittish Bowmen* was printed in 1625 at the 'signe of the Gun in Pauls Alley'. It includes a series of illustrations of a soldier, described as a 'pikeman', in various attitudes, each displaying the use of one of his several weapons. In the frontispiece we see him standing with his bow steadied against his pike, and in a later illustration he is 'croucht and charged for the horse with his sword drawne', with his pike aimed at the advancing enemy:

> This Portraiture of charging for horse, is to shew that the Bow is very materiall for this service; for the five or six first ranks standing coucht at this charge, the middle and the reare may shoote their volleys of arrowes, and therewith both gaule, wound, disorder, and kill the enemy, both man and horse.[55]

This is the experienced, valued, expert soldier and in many ways the figure represents everything that could be desired in the contemporary ideal. The figure is strong in body, for how else could he maintain the unnatural crouch with one knee bent towards the enemy, his long pike set against his rear foot and extending through his left hand, his other leg stretched out behind him, and his sword raised above his head? Alert and ready, he is, in fact, with his sword, pike and bow, 'triple-armed'. This is also the ideal masculine figure, embodying a sense of strength and diligence, which proves that training has distanced him from some more primitive state. The figure also contains an imprint of the ideal of earlier times since he is, in an odd way, also a medieval knight. His helmet is plumed, his armour is heavy and extends to the knee, and he is wearing spurs.

In the actual battles of the late sixteenth and early seventeen centuries, a figure 'of new invention' is more likely to have been a musketeer. The accompanying 'words of command' for advancing ranks alternatively to 'crouch low' and 'come up to your order, and shoot your arrows' are those which apply to guns.[56] Yet the 'Double-Armed Man' exactly encodes the 'medievalism' of the period, his bow and arrow aimed with the symbolic force of history. He is resonant with the values of both the old and the new: a restored masculinity, a modernised chivalry and the beard and ruff of the contemporary gentleman. This was an appealing image, since in his introduction to a facsimile of the text, Stephen V. Grancsay notes:

> A year before the publication of his work, Neade had presented the manuscript to Charles I who commanded that the author should exhibit his new weapon in St. James' Park in his presence. The new exercise combining the use of the bow with the pike was performed before the King. Neade thereupon petitioned the King to make use of his new invention compulsory by law, and he and his son were shortly after authorized by Proclamation to instruct all those who are fit to exercise arms in the use of the weapon, 'specially the chiefe officers and all others of our Trayned Bands'.[57]

Still more bizarre is an illustration from John Cruso's *Military Instructions for the Cavalerie*.[58] This text was produced only a decade or so before the engagements on English soil which motivated the actual introduction of many of the more workable recommendations concerning discipline, knowledge and expertise found in the texts – ironically enough, not on the side of absolutism but against it. The Knight illustrated in Cruso's text would have fared badly against the New Model Army, but in 1632 he represents perfectly the medieval aspect of early modern militarism.

He appears in twelve sequential illustrations, each labelled with the 'words of command', which will help the instructor discipline his cavalry as they mount their horses and prepare their weapons for an advance on the enemy. At first glance the elaborate armour, plumed helmet, high saddle and elegant, heavy horse (which trots through the sequence with dressaged discipline equal to that of its rider) are entirely medieval. It is not difficult to imagine him, like Peraldus's Knight, with a shield of faith and an accompanying flight of doves representing the gifts of the Holy Spirit.[59] Yet Cruso's Knight is modern: he has no sword, shield or lance, and the 'instructions for the Cavallerie' are to 'draw your pistoll', 'order your pistoll', 'lode your pistoll', and so on.

The medieval images that appeared in early modern military texts are witness to a crisis in the politics of a state determined on an absolutism which was never furnished with the essential component of a disciplined, equipped and motivated standing army. As a result of this absence, early modern English militarism steered an uneasy path between pursuing a revolution in military thinking (towards a modern, technically sophisticated army supplied with knowing 'citizen soldiers') and the retention of an iconography derived from a particular reading of history. The uncertainty of this 'medievalism' in the face of the chaos of actual attempts to participate in campaigns is the source of much examination and parody in early modern literature, particularly that produced for the contemporary stage. Romantic portrayals of medieval chivalry were to survive the upheavals of the mid-seventeenth century, of course, and have been cultivated ever since; but on the actual battlefield the 'Double-Armed Man' would have found his arrows had little effect against Cromwell's Ironsides.

If we are in any doubt about what all this anxiety was about, there is another text that shows that the masculinity espoused in the idealism of the military theorists was balanced by the feminine nature of the lands and peoples that were to be subdued. The gendering of military and geopolitical concerns in this writing is nowhere more shockingly supplied than in an account of Ireland produced in the 1620s by the retired soldier, Luke Gernon:

This Nymph of Ireland is at all points like a young wench that hath the green sickness for want of occupying. She is very fair of visage and hath a smooth skin of tender grass. Indeed, she is somewhat freckled (as the Irish are) – some parts darker than others. Her flesh is of a soft and delicate mold of earth, and her blue veins trailing through every part of her like rivulets. She hath one master vein called the Shannon, which passeth quite through her, and if it were not for one knot (one main rock), it were navigable from head to foot. She hath three other veins called the sisters – the Suir, the Nore, and the Barrow, which, rising at one spring, trail through her middle parts and join together in their going out. Her bones are of polished marble, the grey houses show like colleges, and being polished is most embellished. Her breasts are round hillocks of milk-yielding grass and that so fertile that they contend with the valleys. And betwixt her legs (for Ireland is full of havens) she hath an open harbor, but not much frequented. It is now since she was drawn out of rebellion some sixteen years and yet she wants a husband: she is not embraced; she is not hedged and ditched; there is no quickset put into her.[60]

Such erotic descriptions were calculated to reinforce the masculinity of the colonial project and to seduce the post-rebellion colonisers who were to be 'planted' in Ireland. Yet they also guaranteed the masculinity of the military enterprise that was to secure that project. In texts like this it is also possible to read that the soldier-subject was to be drawn away from any tendency towards domestic 'rebellion' at home as well as to the business of maintaining and planting post-rebellion Ireland. The threat of unrest at home was altogether associated with the process of raising troops for the quasi-absolutist regimes of the late Tudors and early Stuarts. But state documents from the period are also full of embarrassed accounts of colonisers adopting the supposedly feminine trappings and language of the colonised. Edmund Spenser's *A View of the Present State of Ireland*, written in the last decade of the sixteenth century, reported on this phenomenon among those populations 'planted' in Ireland in order to introduce Protestant politics and values, but who succumbed to the 'feminine' Irish language and the social mores of the culture they were supposed to eradicate.[61]

'PUBLICKE PLACES OF EXERCISE'

Despite Charles's interest in staging a public performance of Neade's 'new invention' it was adopted neither by the trained bands nor anyone else. But the idea of a display of armed men that would simultaneously celebrate the past and guarantee the future is suggestive in terms of the outcome of all this writing about matters of military discipline and the relationship between the army and the state. Many of the technical and organisational models advanced by the theorists of the sixteenth and early seventeenth centuries were adopted by both sides during the English civil wars but were particularly practised by Cromwell's New Model Army. Cromwell's activities in Scotland and Ireland during the years of the Commonwealth might also be said to epitomise the military theorists' recommendations for soldiers who were theologically certain of their cause. Despite evidence of extensive demonstrations against the wars, many led by women, and

Thomas Hobbes's note that 'there were very few of the common people that cared much for either of the causes', the conflict established new military structures and within them, more ideologically committed soldiers than ever before.[62] These structures also, of course, contained layers of discontent and bred institutional dissent, ranging from demands for back pay to the more politically charged discussions that took place in Putney in 1647. The Levellers' demands for abolition of the monarchy, elections and an end to conscription were allied to the cause of the common soldier, even if their origins lay in the City of London. The Putney Debates raise a general point about the possible consequences of the kinds of military training and discipline advocated by the military theorists. On the one hand, armies of knowledgeable, articulate, literate and disciplined soldiers were more likely to produce victories, partly through their enhanced skills but also through their high level of motivation. At the same time such trained soldiers, had they the collective will, could also commit themselves to an alternative cause, demanding their rights or becoming subject only to their own commanders, as in the case of the *coup d'état*. The potential a state's military wing has to separate itself off, act independently or threaten the populace which is supposed to serve is necessarily increased by educating its personnel. And improved communication between members of an army, whilst facilitating military activities, simultaneously provides channels for dissent.

The structures of military organisation that grew from the demands of the military theorists, and were implemented by those in charge of latterday armies in Britain and elsewhere, perhaps reflect this tension between autonomy and integration as far as the relations between army and state are concerned. Soldiers have to remain special kinds of subject, convinced of the morality of the just war and willing to kill: yet they must not be special enough to become divorced from the state and the people for whom they are asked to do this particular kind of work. For this reason, early modern military training and organisation evolved intricate systems of performance, codes of identity and notions of cultural heritage that constantly reinforce the delicate balance between the state and the soldier to this day.

One aspect of this can be found early on in Charles's wish that Neade display his 'new invention' in public in St. James' Park. Like many other countries, but perhaps with an exaggerated sense of its own heritage, modern Britain continually puts its armed services on display in the public realm: on a day-to-day basis, at recurring moments of celebration or political moment, or on special occasions.

Soldiers in uniforms redolent of the long history of the British Army guard Buckingham Palace and establishments in nearby Whitehall. They escort the monarch at such events as the opening of Parliament, and parade at the annual 'Trooping of the Colour', representing the long tradition of royal command of the armed forces. Most of the leading members of the royal family are nominally members of one branch or other of the services and appear in uniform as part of these displays. Royal weddings, state funerals, jubilees and similar moments of national importance are all conducted against a background of military pomp. This traditional 'presence' is important for a number of reasons: a demonstration of authority; a reinforcing of the status and longevity of the monarchy; an underpinning of national pride. But it also shows the military to be linked to the state and to be somehow 'available' to the people. The military is not separated from the public, and in theory, almost anyone can enlist.

Yet at the same time the armed services are special and separate. Their work involves the legitimate killing of others in pursuit of the (more or less) secular just war, and the very particular skills needed to perform such activity. The military is trained, equipped, housed and variously catered for in a discrete way that shows that even though its members are drawn from the public, they become something different from that public. What becomes apparent when one crosses the line that separates the civilian from the military subject is that the latter is a kind of exaggerated or ideal version of the former according to a whole range of qualifications, scales, values and judgements. Military life in Britain is organised according to rank, and rank still reflects and reinforces to a large degree the class formation of civilian society. It is also organised with little respect for privacy, the joke among new recruits being that this is the first thing a 'private' soldier loses. Military establishments ideally reproduce civilian life, with the trappings of the domestic: shops, places of entertainment, different types of housing for different ranks or according to marital status. Garrison towns are like towns on the outside world, but tidier, more efficient and better regulated. Military and naval bases, like ships, run according to strict timetables, and a sense of constant preparedness is reinforced by the fact that they are themselves defended by guards. The services have their own police forces and judicial systems, their own health care and catering corps. And within these miniature towns the inhabitants are ideally fit and strong, are clean, have 'military' bearing, practical haircuts and wear uniforms. They label their spaces with acronyms, salute each other, give and receive orders, and, like many professions, have special jokes and exclusive vocabularies. In a sense, this is all a performance, and one that is hard to be without on the outside world.[63] What is being performed is a kind of ideal or at least heightened sense of how society is organised in civilian life, with all hesitations, weakness and inefficiency eliminated. The idea of military life as a model has not escaped those in the world outside. Some still occasionally recommend a return to conscription in Britain as a cure for juvenile delinquency and many endorsed the 'boot camp' training of young offenders that was particularly in vogue in Britain under John Major's administration of the early 1990s. This was the period of Cabinet minister Michael Portillo's 'Don't mess with the SAS speech' and his plans as Secretary of State for Defence to extend the cadet corps in schools to allow every child over the age of thirteen an opportunity to join the ranks. A newspaper reported in January 1997:

> In line with Mr Major's classless society, the popular image of the cadets as a coterie of public-school patriots would change, as Mr Portillo said yesterday, to mean 'excellent opportunities for all young people . . . to play a marvellous role on our society [sic]. They help young people towards the good values of life, towards self-esteem, self-discipline, team work and respect for others'.[64]

What such exhortations miss is not so much the flaws in the ideal of military life itself, which I shall return to in the last chapter, but the fact that recruits to the forces experience not just the immediate security (or severity) of the service life. In Britain and elsewhere, they are also asked to entertain a seductive and comprehensive set of historical traditions. Such traditions are scrupulously upheld. In the army, for example, the history of the regiment, its colours, uniforms and earlier campaigns are celebrated and held in considerable regard, not only through rituals and commemorations but also in regimental museums, libraries and galleries. Regiments often compete with each other, resist amalgamation with other regiments, and offer a determined focus of identity for the new recruit. History for modern service personnel is arguably as important as chivalry or the symbolism of the bow was for the early modern militarists, and the older the regiment, the deeper the significance. 'Monck's Regiment of Foot', for example, was commissioned in 1650 as part of the New Model Army. Instrumental in the restoration of the monarchy in 1660, Monck's men avoided the general disbanding of the army, finding favour with Charles II by quelling a revolt in January 1661. In February they paraded at Tower Hill and symbolically laid down their arms, renouncing their association with the New Model Army and becoming part of the New Standing Army. They were renamed the 'Coldstream' Regiment of Guards after the Scottish village from which they had marched to London to prepare the way for the king's return from France.

All regiments have their histories, but the Coldstream Guards have a special significance since they evolved from the New Model Army which was based on models from abroad and disciplines derived from the pages of the Elizabethan and early Stuart military theorists. In their present role, as a 'household regiment' protecting the queen, or on active, often peacekeeping, service around the world, they carry with them the force of that theory mediated by their own campaigning history. What their history does not admit is its basis in ideas that draw largely on a constructed image of masculinity, a marshalling of God's sanction in the pursuit of war and a marked hostility to peace – a concept greeted in various texts with nothing more than a sneer.

Notes

1. William Neade (1625), *The Double-Armed Man: By the New Invention: Briefly Shewing some Famous Exploits atchieved by our Brittish Bowmen*, London, reproduced in facsimile with an introduction by Stephen V. Grancsay (1971), York, PA: George Shumway.
2. A. W. Pollard and R. R. Redgrave (1926), *A Short-Title Catalogue of Books Printed in England, Scotland and Ireland 1475–1640*, London: The Bibliographical Society; and M. J. D. Cockle (1900), *A Bibliography of English Military Books up to 1642 and Contemporary Foreign Works*, London: Simpkin, Marshall, Hamilton, Kent & Co.
3. Niccolò Machiavelli (1560), *The Arte of Warre, written first in Italia by Nicolas Machiavelli and set for the in Englishe by Peter Whitehorne, studient of Graies Inne: with an additio of other Marcialle featres and experiments*, London. This translation was reprinted in 1563, 1573 and 1588. It was edited by Henry Curt (1905) as *Niccolò Machiavelli – 'The Arte of Warre' and 'The Prince'*, London. My references are to this edition.
4. Felix Raab (1964), *The English Face of Machiavelli: A Changing Interpretation 1500–1700*, London: Routledge & Kegan Paul.
5. For an account of this demand see ibid., pp. 30–76.
6. *I Discorsi* and *Il Principe* were printed as pirated editions in London by John Wolfe in 1584 with the fictitious imprint 'Palermo'. Wolfe was also responsible for illicit Italian editions of *Istorie Fiorentine* (imprinted 'Piacenza') and *Il Libro dell'Arte della Guerra* (imprinted 'Palermo') in 1587.

7. J. G. A. Pocock (1975), *The Machiavellian Moment*, Princeton, NJ: Princeton University Press, p. 200.
8. Ibid., p. 201.
9. Machiavelli, *The Arte of Warre*, p. 14.
10. Ibid., p. 31.
11. Ibid., pp. 3–4.
12. Ibid. p. 6.
13. Ibid.
14. The work of the classical military writers Ælian, Modestus, Sextus Julius Frontius and Publius Flavius Vegetius Renatus were often bound together in one volume from the late fifteenth century. The writings of Xenophon, Orbicius, Apsyrtus, Leo, Constantine, Polyænus and Polybius, all with military themes, appeared during the sixteenth century. See Cockle, *English Military Books*, p. xvii.
15. Thomas Styward (1581), *The Pathwaie to Martial Discipline, devided into two Bookes, verie necessarie for yong Souldiers, or for all such as loveth the profession of Armes*, London, Sig. A. iv. R.
16. Bernadino de Mendoza (1597), *Theorique and Practise of Warre, Written to Don Philip Prince of Castil, by Mendoza. Translated out of the Castilian Tonge into Englishe, by Sr. Edwarde Hoby Knight*, London, Sig, A. 4r.
17. Sir Clement Edmondes (1581), *Observations upon the five first bookes of Caesars Commentaries, setting forth the practise on the art military, in the time of the Roman Empire. Wherein are handled all the chiefest points of their discipline, with the true reasons of every part, together with such instructions as may be drawne from their proceedings, for the better direction of our moderne wars*, London, Sig. *ijr.
18. Thomas Digges (1590), *An Arithmeticall warlike Treatise named Stratiotics . . . As well concerning the Science or Art of great Artillerie, as the Offices of the Sergeant Major Generall, the Coronall Generall, and Lord Marshall, with a conference of the English, French and Spanish Disciplines, beside sundry other Militarie Discourses of no small importance*, London, title-page.
19. The most productive period for this kind of writing was the end of the nineteenth century, and some of the best examples are: Sir Sibbald Scott (1868), *The British Army: Origin, Programme and Equipment*, London: Cassell; Clifford Walton (1894), *History of the British Standing Army*, London: Harrison & Sons; C. M. Clode (1869), *The Military Forces of the Crown*, London: John Murray.
20. Eric Shepperd (1926), *A Short History of the British Army to 1914*, London: Constable.
21. Robin Higham (1972), *A Guide to the Sources of British Military History*, London: Routledge & Kegan Paul, p. 1.

22. Correlli Barnett (1970), *Britain and Her Army, 1509–1970: A Military, Political and Social Survey*, New York: William Morrow, pp. 31–2.
23. Ibid., p. 41.
24. John Hale (1961), *The Art of War and Renaissance England*, Washington: Folger Library.
25. *Acts of the Privy Council*, VIII, 137.
26. Ibid., IX, 182, 187–8, 263 and 373.
27. Edward P. Cheyney (1926), *A History of England*, 2 vols, London: Longman, Vol. II, Pt v, p. 33.
28. The events which occurred in the Forest of Dean were highly organised, when 'some 500 men "did wilt two drums, two coulers and one fife in a warlike and outragious manner assemble themselves together armed with gunnes, pykes, halberds and other weapons" and set off to cast down enclosure'. See Keith Wrightson (1982), *English Society, 1580–1680*, London: Hutchinson, pp. 150–1.
29. *Acts of the Privy Council*, X, 12, 16, 34, 141, and XXII, 537 and 557.
30. Buchanan Sharp (1980), *In Contempt of All Authority*, Berkeley, CA: California University Press, pp. 3–4; Wrightson, *English Society, 1580–1680*, pp. 6–7.
31. Wrightson, *English Society, 1580–1680*, pp. 6–7.
32. Ibid.
33. Sharp, *In Contempt of All Authority*, pp. 6–7.
34. Cheyney, *A History of England*, Vol. II, p. 28.
35. In the spring of 1596 fewer than 200 men returned to Essex from the 2,000 pressed for military service abroad that year, a statistic that led Sir John Smythe to attempt a rebellion during the muster of a further 1,000 men destined for a similar fate – an act of disloyalty explained by Lord Burghley as 'by reason of his drinking in the morning of a great deal of white wine and sack' in the White Hart, Colchester. Smythe was in fact a leading military theorist of his time who 'had discussed the legality of sending pressed men for service overseas with Manwood, Lord chief Baron', according to his editor, John Hale. See his edition (1964) of Smythe's *Certain Discourses*, New York: Cornell University Press. Smythe's book was originally published in 1590.
36. Perry Anderson (1974), *Lineages of the Absolutist State*, London: Verso, p. 125. See also Lawrence Stone (1967), *The Crisis of the Aristocracy*, London: Oxford University Press, pp. 199–270.
37. R. C. Smail (1958), 'The Art of War', in Austin Lane Poole (ed.), *Medieval England*, Oxford: Clarendon Press, pp. 128–67, esp. pp. 162–3.
38. Barnabe Rich (1578), *Allarme to England, foreshewing what perilles are procured when people live without regarde to Martiall Lawe*, London, sig. C.iii.

39. Glynne Wickham (1974), *The Medieval Theatre*, Cambridge: Cambridge University Press, p. 155.

40. Rich, *Allarme to England*, sig. H.

41. See Richard W. Kaepaur (1988), *War, Justice and Public Order*, Oxford: Clarendon Press.

42. Rich, *Allarme to England*, sig. K iiii.

43. Geoffrey Gates (1579), *The Defence of Militarie Profession*, London, pp. 9–10.

44. Henry Curt (ed.) (1905), *Niccolò Machiavelli: 'The Arte of Warre' and 'The Prince'* . . . *Englished by P. Whitehorne*, London, p. 6.

45. Digges, *Four Paradoxes*, p. 104.

46. François De La Noue (1587), *The Politicke and Militarie Discourses*, London, p. 124.

47. Digges, *Four Paradoxes*, p. 51.

48. Rich, *Allarme to England*, sig. I.

49. Thomas Smith (1616), *The Arte of Gunnerie*, London, sigs. Aii. R–v.

50. These qualities, combined in the individual soldier bound to the larger institution, are increasingly referred to through the metaphor of the body. The best example is James Achesome (1629), *The Military Garden, Or Instructions For All Young Soldiers*, London.

51. Trussell, *The Soldier Pleading His Own Cause*, Introduction.

52. Humfrey Barwick (1594), *A Briefe Discourse, Concerning the force and effect of all manuell weapons of fire and the disability of the Long Bowe of Archery, in respect of other of greater force now in use*, London.

53. R. S. (1696), *A Briefe Treatise, To Proove the necessitie and excellance of the use of archerie*, London.

54. Thomas Styward (1581), *The Pathwaie to Martiall Discipline, devided into two Bookes, rerie necessarie for yong Souldiers or for all such as loreth the profession of Armes*, London, title-page.

55. William Neade (1625), *The Double-Armed Man*, reproduced in facsimile with an introduction by Stephen V. Grancsay (1971), York, PA: George Shumway.

56. Ibid., p. 48.

57. Ibid., p. 6. See 'A Proclamation for the use of the Bowe & the Pike together in Militarie Discipline', London, 1633, in Francis Grose (1801), *Military Antiquities*, Vol. 2, London, pp. 173–4.

58. John Cruso (1632), *Military Instructions for the Cavallerie*, London.

59. Gulielmus Peraldus (*c.* 1236), *Summa de Vitiis*.

60. Luke Gernon (1620), *A Discourse of Ireland*, London, p. 15.

61. Edmund Spenser [written *c.* 1596, published 1633] (1970), *A View of the Present State of Ireland*, Oxford: Oxford University Press.

62. For evidence of popular opposition to the civil conflict of the mid-seventeenth century, see Charles Carlton (1992), *Going to the Wars: The Experience of the English Civil Wars 1638–1651*, London and

New York: Routledge. For an account of Hobbes on the war, see B. Manning (1957), 'Neutrals and Neutralism in the English Civil War', PhD thesis, Oxford University.

63. I am thinking here of the difficulties service personnel sometimes have in adjusting to civilian life after long periods in the forces, whether or not they have been actively engaged in fighting.

64. *The Independent*, 24 January 1997, p. 3.

Part III

Shakespeare and the Wars

5

'WE BAND OF BROTHERS'

❧

Richard's is the most fulsome sneer of all. Tudor pro-war polemic managed its sustained attack on any remaining vestiges of Christian pacifism by means of a steady and usually high-minded appeal to its readers' sense of history, logic and common sense. Yet, as we have seen, the rhetoric involved in these treatises occasionally descended into simple invective, especially in the work of Barnabe Rich and particularly around issues of nationality and masculinity. Men were, it seems, becoming 'effeminate' and thus, somehow, 'forgetting themselves' and contributing to the trends that had led to the increasing vulnerability of their country. These writers considered the lack of a military apparatus as a fissure in the nation's defences, despite the coastal fortifications and naval might, and they also saw the absence of war as a threat to internal stability. While they were busy lamenting the decadence that accompanied peace, a figure stepped onto the English stage that apparently thought much the same as they did about the relationship between war, gender and nation. The opening lines of *The Tragedy of Richard the Third* are so familiar that we perhaps hear them without listening to the binary between gender and war, one that would have been very familiar to anyone in the audience even casually versed in the military writing of the immediate period:

Now is the winter of our discontent
Made glorious summer by this son of York;
And all the clouds that loured upon our house
In the deep bosom of the ocean buried.
Now are our brows bound with victorious wreaths,
Our bruisèd arms hung up for monuments,
Our stern alarums changed to merry meetings,
Our dreadful marches to delightful measures.
Grim-visaged war hath smoothed his wrinkled front,
And now – instead of mounting barbèd steeds
To fright the souls of fearful adversaries –

He capers nimbly in a lady's chamber
To the lascivious pleasing of a lute.[1]

(I.i.1–13)

No figure in the theatre of the time speaks more contemptuously of the decadence of peace or so clearly defines a discourse of masculine militarism. In his 1981 edition of *Richard III* Antony Hammond points out that the opening two lines recall, among other earlier texts, Sir Philip Sidney's *Astrophel and Stella*, published as a pirated edition in 1591, a year before Shakespeare's play: 'Gone is the winter of my miserie, / My spring appears . . .'[2] Hammond claims that the line is 'almost proverbial', which is rather appropriate in the context of Shakespeare's dramatisation of the Tudor chroniclers' history of the Plantagenets.[3] Now that Edward IV has been restored to the throne, Richard is repeating here something like the official post-war line. Shakespeare swaps 'summer' for spring to allow the 'sun/son' pun in connection with Edward, who had the sun as a heraldic device, and the extra syllable in the line invites the actor to emphasise 'glorious' in a sarcastic way if so desired. The seasonal allusion sets up the content and tone of the speech that it begins, with its determined sense of barren winter followed by fertile spring and summer. As with much of what Shakespeare gives his Richard to say, there is strong sense of irony here, given the carnage to come and the fact that the promising 'son' of York will soon be on his deathbed.

The imagery continues with two lines that form an oddly implausible sequence: 'clouds that loured' are 'buried' in the 'deep bosom of the ocean'. It is as if Shakespeare fabricates what sounds like a brittle kind of cliché in order to reinforce the fragility of the peace that has seemingly been assured by recent events. As it was to those arguing against peace while Shakespeare was writing and staging the play, the absence of war is associated here with pleasure, and, by implication, with sensual activities relating to women. As soon as war gives way to mere celebration ('our brows bound with victorious wreaths') and remembrance ('Our bruisèd arms hung up for monuments') a space is opened that will be filled by casual delights and, specifically, sexual distractions. Clearly there are continuities in the realm of metaphor and imagery between courtship and warfare, war and dance, but for Richard, 'merry meetings' and 'delightful measures' are what we succumb to when peace is restored, potentially seducing even War (himself) into capering in a lady's chamber. Shakespeare seems to have borrowed the association from Christopher Marlowe's Tamburlaine, whose sons strike him at the beginning of the second part of *Tamburlaine the Great*, printed in 1590, as far 'too dainty for the wars':

> Their fingers made to quaver on a lute,
> Their arms to hang about a lady's neck,
> Their legs to dance and caper in the air
> Would make me think them bastards, not my sons.[4]
> (I.iii.29–32)

Richard may adapt lines from the earlier play, but Tamburlaine, as we shall see in a later chapter, is not really a suitable alter-ego for Shakespeare's warlike usurper. Richard's menace, in this play at least, is demonstrated by his verbal dexterity, the acquisitive nature (and gullibility) of those around him – and his repeated use of private assassination and the public axe as the means by which to clear a way to the throne.

Interestingly, two of the better-known film adaptations of *Richard III* have presented Richard as a kind of fascist figure, with the Second World War very much in mind as a context in which to make the play intelligible to modern audiences. Laurence Olivier's version, inspired by his many wartime performances of the role of Richard, was released in April 1955. Although set in a colourfully designed medieval (but clearly not Merrie) England, it was received as a kind of meditation on the capacity for individual evil so recently embodied in the figure of Adolf Hitler.[5] Olivier had hoped to boost wartime morale with his film of *Henry V*, released in November 1944 and famously dedicated to 'the Commandos and Airborne Troops of Great Britain'. With *Richard III* he again wanted to reach a popular audience, this time implying parallels between Shakespeare's representation of a figure from the Tudor chronicles and the twentieth century's own superlative demon. Shakespeare offered mid-twentieth-century audiences both the inspiration for anti-fascist resistance and a study of the kind of psychology that had seduced and misled the German people.

Olivier was not the first to see the possibilities of associating Richard with Hitler. Bertolt Brecht's 1941 play *Der Aufhaltsame Aufstieg des Arturo Ui* (*The Resistible Rise of Arturo Ui*) was a 'parable' for the theatre.[6] It had apparently been developed from an earlier prose work set in classical Italy, which Walter Benjamin described as 'a satire on Hitler in the style of a Renaissance historian'.[7] The American setting for Brecht's play provided a structure of analogy that traced the rise of a petty gangster, Arturo Ui, from street-corner bully to military dictator. Brecht's episodic scene structure, his use of a Prologue, an Epilogue and other devices, owed much to classical theatrical models as well as to the plays of Shakespeare and his contemporaries. The first appearance of the figure of Arturo Ui/Adolf Hitler is accompanied by an Announcer's remark:

> Doesn't he make you think of Richard the Third?
> Has anybody ever heard
> Of blood so ghoulishly and lavishly shed
> Since wars were fought for roses white and red?
>   (Prologue, 38–41)

Arturo Ui raises questions concerning the status and effect of Shakespeare's language that are central to Brecht's exploration of political persuasion and militarist rhetoric.[8] In a later scene (scene 6) Mark Antony's speech from Act III of *Julius Caesar* is evoked. A world-weary actor is summoned to coach Ui, the Richard-like gangster, to walk, talk and persuade a crowd in a way that recalls the filmed images and commentators' accounts of Hitler at work. The actor is keen to impress upon Ui that Shakespeare offers 'the grand style' that will suit Ui's sense of domination over his listeners. This is usually very humorous in performance. And although we should heed Brecht's remark that 'it is risky to encourage a people to laugh at a potentate after once failing to take him seriously', there is something enormously suggestive about Brecht's appropriation of Shakespeare's Richard for the purposes of his overtly political epic theatre.[9]

The ageing actor's choice of Mark Antony's speech clearly contains an irony for an audience that knows Shakespeare's play; and the figure of the actor is itself a joke at the expense of an outmoded tradition of English classical acting. Yet notwithstanding this, the idea of Shakespearean verse as an epitome of rhetoric, and the ease with which Ui masters it, open up the structures of power and language in both Shakespeare's plays and *Arturo Ui*. Brecht's play uses the speech from *Julius Caesar* in a seemingly unmediated way (in terms of the qualities of rhetoric) that depends on a range of assumptions about Shakespeare's language. At one level there is the customary elevation of Shakespeare to a symbol of cultural worth. The actor is keen to impress upon Ui that, although he has himself been 'ruined by Shakespeare', the Bard offers much that will suit Ui's sense of domination over his listeners. It is an aesthetic that knows no history, since the actor claims that 'Art knows no calendar'. Yet Arturo Ui and his gang have little idea about what Shakespeare means in these terms, so that at another level the focus is on the sheer power, the theatricality, of Shakespearean language. In Brecht's play this is clearly very accessible. Its transforming power can be apprehended in minutes as Ui takes over the speech and begins to deliver it with a menace that presages his later militaristic speeches. It is a kind of sleight-of-hand that will empower the individual who learns the trick. As Ui remarks, he is 'not trying to convince professors / And smart-alecks. My object is the little / man's image of his master'. It matters little what a professor (or a smart aleck) thinks but it does matter what the little man's image of his master is, and this gives Shakespeare a highly charged and peculiarly compelling symbolic role in Brecht's play. The point is clearly one of form over content as Ui's remark about professors makes clear, and the force of the speech lies in the audience's recognising it as a medium for persuasion, an index of mastery and the appropriate register for war.

The makers of another screen version of *Richard III* were aware of Brecht's allusions to Shakespeare's play. Richard Eyre's innovative production for the Royal National Theatre inspired a popular 1995 film directed by Richard Loncraine. Ian McKellen played Richard, as he had done for Eyre in the theatre, and with Loncraine's help, he was responsible for writing the film's imaginative screenplay. In a fascinating introduction to his annotated text of this heavily cut but beautifully crafted adaptation of Shakespeare's play, McKellen describes the way that Eyre's interpretation had been 'translated' for the cinema, fixing it on celluloid for all time:

> Previous Richard IIIs, like David Garrick and Henry Irving, even my contemporaries like Al Pacino and Antony Sher, still trail glory, but despite prints and photographs, memoirs and memorabilia, their success is no longer tangible.[10]

McKellen notes that in transferring a production from stage to screen, he and Loncraine were following the precedent set by Olivier. Despite the subtlety of the allusion in Olivier's case, the result is that both major screen versions of the play from the second half of the twentieth century invoked an association between Richard and Hitler. The Loncraine film, following the theme established by the stage production, set Shakespeare's play in a decadent 1930s England, a stylishly and superficially attractive art deco world, but one that has clearly 'fallen' as a result of its inhabitants' vast appetites for power and position. The 'piping peace' that Richard evokes in the second half of his opening speech has produced a world of enormous excess, lubricated by alcohol and drugs, and defined in part by the allure of sexual desire. Richard still consolidates his position and gains the crown through the means described by Shakespeare and his chronicle sources. Yet at the same time, this Richard is seen to secure that position by creating a popular militaristic party. As he does this the film summons images that recall the German Nazis or the Italian Partito Nazionale Fascista, chillingly spliced with an evocation of Oswald Mosley's British Union of Fascists.[11] Writing about this feature of the film, McKellen draws a parallel between the 1930s setting, in relation to the 1990s, and Shakespeare's distance from the events he relates in his early history plays. He also acknowledges the commonplace of the 'Tudor myth' which Shakespeare is seen to have been dramatising:

> The historical events of the play had occurred just a couple of generations before the first audience saw them dramatised. The comparable period for us would be the 1930s, close enough for no-one to think we were identifying the plot of the play with actual events, any more than Shakespeare was writing about the real King Richard. He was creating history-which-never-happened. Our production was properly in the realm of 'what might have been'. Also, the 30s were appropriately a decade of tyranny throughout Europe, the most recent time when a dictatorship like Richard III's might have overtaken the United Kingdom, as it had done Germany, Italy, Spain and the empire of the Soviet Union.[12]

McKellen raises an important issue about the relationship between the focus of a piece of theatre and the generalities of association that can be aroused in particular audiences in terms of the political environment from within which they view the action. This observation comes close to the sort of the ideological project that Brecht aspired to in his epic theatre. Brecht's *Arturo Ui* was clearly a study of Hitler's rise to power and very particular in the parallels that it offered between power and persuasion, as well as the aesthetics of military violence. Each episode in Ui's advance is juxtaposed with projected inscriptions recalling Hitler's eradication of opponents within Germany and his occupation of neighbouring territories. In this way Brecht sought to 'make strange' the manner and matter of Hitler's violent acquisition of power in terms of the dramatic theory of *Verfremdungseffekt*, or alienation effect. *Arturo Ui* is, however, also about the general, transhistorical relationship between rhetoric and dictatorship. Hitler is not the only potentate, and certainly not the last. Thus, just as *Mother Courage*, set in the Thirty Years War, is concerned to encourage its audiences to consider universal ideas about the condition of warfare, Brecht recognises a paradox that McKellen saw at work when he and Eyre toured with the 1930s stage version of *Richard III*:

> Audiences across the world took the point and revealed a paradox: the more specific a production, the more general its relevance. Although our story was obviously an English one, audiences took the message personally wherever we toured. In Hamburg, Richard's blackshirt troops seemed like a commentary on the Third Reich. In Bucharest, when Richard was slain, the Romanians stopped the show with heartfelt cheers, in memory of their recent freedom from Ceaucescu's regime. In Cairo, as the Gulf War was hotting up, it all seemed like a new play about Saddam Hussein. One critic lambasted me for poor taste when I ruffled the young prince's hair, before imprisoning him, as Hussein had just been seen doing to a little English boy he had taken hostage. My stage business, of course, had been devised six months previously – life was imitating art. It was reminiscent of the scene in *Arturo Ui*, where Bertolt Brecht's seedy greengrocer learns the art of dictatorship by studying *Richard III* with a ham actor.[13]

In fact, Brecht's Arturo Ui studies lines from *Julius Caesar*, but McKellen's slip is understandable because of the way that Brecht's Announcer invites the audience to think of the figure of Richard III at the beginning of the play. The point about the political connections an audience makes between the stage and its own context is an important one, as in the wartime productions such as Olivier's or those of G. R. Wilson Knight, noted in Chapter 2. And the use of Shakespeare in teaching and performance to offer a critique of the state in Eastern European countries during the years of communism is well documented.[14] In *Arturo Ui*, Brecht established a chain of association between Hitler, the 'parable' of an American mobster (itself enriched by the popularity of the contemporary Hollywood gangster movie) and his generalised philosophy of the relationship between dictatorship and rhetoric, and between war and business.

The image that unifies these parallels and leads us back to speculation on the relationship between sixteenth-century productions of *Richard III* and their reception by audiences attuned to war is that of Richard as a soldier. *Arturo Ui* ends with the Ui figure merging with Hitler in a direct address to the audience about his military ambitions. Swastikas unfurl as the analogy dissolves into a single point of historical reference. The end of the play is the starting point for an international military campaign. Brecht invites us to consider military aggression as the governing rationale of dictatorship – and clearly history supports this. This aspect of modernity might have been established according to the theories of Renaissance militarists, especially in terms of their ideas concerning the necessity of foreign wars as a guarantee of domestic stability.

Richard III ends with the king as a soldier on the battlefield. He famously calls six times for a horse and then, in a kind of dumb show, he and Richmond fight hand to hand, Richard is slain and his body is carried off stage. Richmond re-enters with Lord Stanley and other lords to be proclaimed king. This is, of course, a profoundly compelling moment in the play and in the overall sequence of Shakespeare's history plays in terms of the chronicles from which they were adapted. It is the founding moment of the Tudors' ruling dynasty and, as McKellen reminds us, one that represents an episode that was just a couple of generations away from the lives of Shakespeare's audiences. The view of critics such as E. M. W. Tillyard, that Shakespeare uncritically rehearses a 'Tudor myth' over the course of the history plays, came under scrutiny almost as soon as he expressed it and has been the subject of a range of critiques over the last half-century.[15] It is the case, however, that in a rudimentary way, Shakespeare secures the happy origins of the Tudors. Richard is destroyed and Richmond is established as Henry VII, the grandfather of Shakespeare's own monarch. And thus, with the ideologically optimistic *All is True* (or *The Famous History of the Life of King Henry the Eighth*) to come, the gap is closed between the civil war and present peace that looks very much like historiographical closure.[16]

Predicting the alternative title for that late addition to the overall historical sequence of Shakespeare's chronicle plays, Elizabethan audiences witnessing the end of *Richard III* might have said 'all is true' as far as Tudor reputations were concerned. However, just as those attending modern productions of the play (or watching the films) are either directed to or submit their own contexts and parallels, Shakespeare's audience might have introduced a range of associations that resist, or at least complicate, a seamless response to Richard's demise. Richard has a range of identities in the play. Some he assumes himself, such as when he pretends to be a victim of unrequited love in his early 'merry meeting' with Lady Anne and blames her beauty for his earlier 'effect', the killing of Henry and Edward:

Your beauty was the cause of that effect –
Your beauty that did haunt me in my sleep
To undermine the death of all the world
So I might live one hour in your sweet bosom.
(I.ii.21–4)

And later, in order to win over the mayor and other citizens, he pretends religious zeal and a reluctance to ascend to the throne. Buckingham directs the action as Richard appears with two bishops:

Two props of virtue for a Christian prince,
To stay him from the fall of vanity;
And see, a book of prayer in his hand –
True ornaments to know a holy man.
Famous Plantagenet, most gracious prince,
Lend favourable ear to our request,
And pardon us the interruption
Of thy devotion and right Christian zeal.
(III.vii.96–103)

Other images for Richard, some of which have been picked out of the text by directors as governing styles for their interpretations of the figure, come from those around him. For Antony Sher, Richard was the 'bottled spider' in the Royal Shakespeare Company's production of 1984. Simon Russell Beale played him as a kind of toad in Sam Mendes' production of 1992 at The Other Place in Stratford. Although in such productions the emphasis is on a single developed characteristic, Richard emerges as a figure assembled from a range of complementary identities: Machiavellian politician, misogynist manipulator, artful assassin, beguiling uncle to his doomed nephews. Above all, he recalls the Vice of a slightly earlier form of popular theatre, drawing on a Morality Play tradition that would have been familiar to many in Shakespeare's audience. The Richard figure has a strong degree of credibility in terms of this tradition which, in performance, has the potential to obscure an audience's more historically sanctioned view of him as purely venal. Despite the infanticide and other killings, and his place within the chain of events that hasten the near-spiritual ascendancy of the Tudors, Richard-as-Vice receives a mixed response in many audiences.

The unsettling truth of the matter is that, at least until Act IV when his command of the situations he has created begins to fail and his followers begin to desert him, Richard presides over the action in a manner that seems designed to charm, or even implicate, the audience. No response is ever guaranteed in the theatre, but the odds in this play are stacked heavily in favour of something approaching respect for this grotesquely attractive figure. Antony Hammond's stimulating introduction to the play quotes the work of Peter Happé in explaining how Shakespeare's presentation of Richard played upon the qualities of the Vice:

> Of the sixty-odd characteristics of the 'formal Vice' listed by Happé, the following can be recognised in the Richard of Shakespeare's play: the use of an alias, strange appearance, use of asides, discussion of plans with the audience, disguise, long avoidance, but ultimate suffering of punishment, moral commentary, importance of name, and reluctance concerning it, self explanation in soliloquy, satirical functions which include an attack on women, and various signs of depravity such as boasting and conceit, enjoyment of power, immoral sexuality.[17]

Shakespeare connects his Richard to the tail end of a Morality Play tradition that had lately isolated the Vice figure from its former symbolic function as an embodiment of evil and given it a secularised and somewhat aesthetically pleasing role on the English stage.[18] The Richard of modern productions at least usually has charisma and appeal, and his steady engagement with the audience often seems almost to draw its members into the unfolding action. Despite the accumulating evidence provided in the sequence of murders and betrayals of his private immorality and public abuse of power, there is something potentially seductive about the sheer forcefulness of the figure in the theatre, relentlessly on course, 'if not to Heaven, then hand in hand to Hell' (V.vi.43).

Much of this appeal is bound up with Richard's humour, again drawn from the Morality tradition, but not entirely so. We might feel that some of the audience laughter witnessed at most twenty-first-century productions of *Richard III* is due to modern sensibilities – or even a degree of insensitivity to the historical circumstances it dramatises. Yet in this respect Shakespeare was only reproducing the tone adopted by at least one of the chroniclers from whom Elizabethan audiences could have drawn their history of the fifteenth century. The relationship between Sir Thomas More's *History of King Richard III* and Shakespeare's play is complex and rather indirect. Yet More's text was an available history of Richard and one that, despite its origins at the heart of Tudor historiography, cannot help but give Richard an ironic if sinister appeal.[19] While it may have been that Shakespeare's audience observed a disrespectful silence as Richard reinforced the validity of the Tudor ascendancy over the former tyrant, it is hard to think of proceedings being quite that sonorous. Or perhaps Shakespeare's Richard, like Brecht's Arturo Ui, produced laughter only so that the audience is forced to reflect (even as it laughs) on how easy it was to be seduced by a devilish tyrant.[20] Brecht was clearly influenced by Shakespeare, but Shakespeare had been dead for over 300 years before he fell under the influence of Brecht.

Whatever the case, there are other elements in the figure of Richard beyond his sheer theatricality and humour that may have contributed to his potential attractiveness to Elizabethan audiences. In addition to the immediacy and consistency of his engagement with those observing, and the sheer cleverness of the multiple identities we have already mentioned, Richard has other appealing qualities. The figure represents wider ethical and theological concerns that are drawn from the chronicle sources and consolidated, in his favour, by the theatrical form through which they are mediated. It is not unusual to see theatre programmes which allude to Richard's 'deformity' by reminding modern audiences of the less enlightened times in which Shakespeare, apparently without reservation, reproduced a popular equation between physical disability and unnatural evil. Whatever the prejudices of a sixteenth-century audience, the Richard they are shown seems uninhibited by his physical condition. He blames it on 'dissembling nature' in the opening speech of the play and later uses it to his advantage.

Thus, although the figure of Richard is at one level permanently 'fixed' as the 'bottled spider' (a medieval specimen of depravity), he is at the same time a multivalent instrument in the contemporary moral laboratory of the Renaissance theatre. The connection between Richard's physical disability (or at some points, his ugliness) and his evil nature is continually remarked upon by those around him. At the same time, however, he steadily proves that in the dramatic world that evolved from the *Henry VI* trilogy, he is by no means the only source of evil. It becomes clear that it is in the interests of those around him to promote the sub-humanity of Richard because in many ways he is representative of a collective malaise that they wish to conceal. The three parts of *Henry VI* may be a cumbersome and unwieldy apparatus, but it is a necessary one if an audience for *Richard III* is fully to realise, in viewing the play's particular fictional world, the extent of the general complicity in helping to make that world come about.[21] What some critics have seen as Shakespeare's difficulty in containing his sources in the trilogy might alternatively be seen as a tribute to Shakespeare's integrity in constructing the background for the events that are played out in *Richard III*.[22] The trilogy may seem overdetermined, its detail occasionally threatening its performance values, but it provides an encyclopedic guide to the fallen world of the play that it precedes. This allows Richard to be somewhat redeemed in *Richard III* itself as, in the popular formulation, a 'Scourge of God', operating at once in violation of God's laws but also as a kind of powerful disinfectant in the diseased environment of the play. The recuperation afforded by this further identity does not invite sympathy, but it might just encourage pity.

Richard remains the embodiment of evil (just as the captive princes embody innocence), yet this is a useful quality in the hands of both God and the Tudor chroniclers if the historical stage is going to be cleared for the anointing of Henry VII. Moreover, the perplexing issue of the play's generic credentials, and therefore those of its hero, complicates the matter further. In using the variant title *The Tragedy of Richard the Third* the modern *Oxford Shakespeare* edition of the play reminds us of a difficulty faced by some critics in their assessment of the work. Richard's intolerable behaviour ought to be incompatible with the sense of loss that is often experienced by modern audiences and, for all we know, by sixteenth-century ones. If there is a concomitant sense of tragedy, then what are the qualities that might invite us to pity his downfall? Hammond raises the point by positioning (or universalising) the figure of Richard within a chain of similarly driven figures:

> To be sure, he is no conventional Aristotelian hero 'much like ourselves'; not at all a Macbeth. In *Richard III* we do not participate in the agony of a man's loss of his soul; Richard, true to his dramatic origins, is committed to evil at the beginning of the play. Whatever was potentially good in him is already subverted to the drive of will and power, the Machiavel's immense belief in his *virtù*, his superiority to the rest of mankind – that belief in power and ability which later finds re-expression in Raskolnikov's theories, or in Nietzsche's *Übermensch*.[23]

He also points to Richard's almost Christ-like agony at Bosworth after the visit of the ghosts of those he has eliminated along the way. This is a credible enough reading, reinforcing the almost irresistible power that Shakespeare's Richard has to provoke comparisons with other studies in power, as with the Hitler parallel of modern productions. But almost tucked away within this account of what makes Richard a potentially tragic figure is another remark, one that should be given more significance in the context of the military texts against which *Richard III* can be situated. Hammond notes that:

> Nothing becomes Richard in the play so well as his death, as he dares an opposite to every danger, and seeks Richmond (the doubtless wisely, but

unheroically, disguised Richmond) in the throat of death. It is the only action in the play which reminds us of Richard's early achievements as a warrior.[24]

This seems a profound but understated point. In a Vice-like way, Richard has assumed (or acted out) an impressive range of identities throughout the play, with the audience, unlike the other characters, privileged to see them all. He has scourged the fallen kingdom on behalf of God (without having to adopt the seriousness we expect of Him) and delivered all into the hands of the Tudors. Towards the end, he is visited by ghostly manifestations of his conscience, sufficient perhaps to draw (from a generous Aristotelian audience at least) a modicum of pity:

> I shall despair. There is no creature loves me,
> And if I die, no soul will pity me.
> Nay, wherefore should they? – since that I myself
> Find in myself no pity to myself.
>
> (V.v.154–7)

Given the multiplicity of identities he has taken on, this may seem like just another one, played out for the benefit of the genre. By this stage there is really little left in the way of redemption, since in his dream 'every tale condemns me for a villain' (V.v.149). His former subjectivity, ironically composed of a range of played-out parts, is now played out, leaving him with the singular and straightforwardly villainous reputation the chroniclers fixed him with.

Yet this is not quite the end. There is more acting and more 'action' (as Hammond puts it) to come, and it is what happens next that makes *Richard III* such a provocative play in the light of the Elizabethan discourse of militarism. Richmond and Richard address their troops and the battle takes place, offstage except for the appearance of Catesby calling out to Norfolk and his soldiers to attempt the king's rescue:

> Rescue, my lord of Norfolk! Rescue, rescue!
> [*To a soldier*] The King enacts more wonders than a man,
> Daring an opposite to every danger.
> His horse is slain, and all on foot he fights,
> Seeking for Richmond in the throat of death.
> [*Calling*] Rescue, fair lord, or else the day is lost!
>
> (V.vii.1–6)

Richard, however, refuses rescue and is killed by the almost saintly Richmond. Richard is fixed immutably for all time as a villain, but it is not simply a question of the response to Richard as a figure in the history of the theatre, or within Tudor historiography. Despite the efforts of members of the Richard the Third Society, the Society of Friends of Richard III and other Ricardians, there seems little hope for Richard's overall historical reputation, and although the figure of Richard was inspired by the Tudor chronicles, this legacy is largely Shakespeare's doing. But these closing scenes are disturbing precisely because of the way that Shakespeare has, to this point, so carefully invested his Richard with a degree of attractiveness, positioned him as the necessary Scourge of God in a fallen world, and even given him tragic potential. This treatment altogether bolsters an additional identity (really a reversion to the earlier plays) which emerges at the end: Richard as soldier.

The contorted nature of the *Henry VI* trilogy may well be due to Shakespeare's difficulty in managing the complexity of the sources against the demands of dramatic structure and narrative. The result, however, is a veritable catalogue of the various kinds of warfare that Shakespeare and his audiences would have known about. It may be that some of Shakespeare's chronological infelicities are not simply due to problems he had with structuring the narrative. Given the importance of war to his audiences, there may have been a desire to accommodate within the trilogy an impressive range of battles of different types, various military conditions and the effect of these on those subject to them – a kind of compendium of conflict. He may also have wanted, while establishing the pre-history of *Richard III*, to provide an elaborate military and historical context for a statement about the relationship between war and the state which we can observe at the heart of the trilogy. The *Henry VI* trilogy deals with the association between foreign campaigns and civil war, the susceptibility of an internally divided state to insurrection, the vulnerability of military alliances and the volatile nature of war itself. It raises more specific issues to do with the relationship between warfare and superstition, a questioning of war as a purely masculine endeavour (in the portrayal of Joan of Arc) and the difficulty of the 'weak' king as military leader. It also invites speculation on the way that the pathos of war is presented – in terms of the figure of Talbot in Part I, but also in the extraordinary scene in Part III (*Richard Duke of York*) where the identity of two soldiers' victims are revealed to the audience. Henry, isolated from the battle proper, has been speculating on kingship and dreaming of life as a shepherd, when he is suddenly interrupted:

Alarum. Enter [at one door] a Soldier with a dead
man in his arms. King Henry stands apart.
SOLDIER
Ill blows the wind that profits nobody.
This man, whom hand to hand I slew in fight,
May be possessèd with some store of crowns;
And I, that haply take them from him now,
May yet ere night yield both my life and them
To some man else, as this dead man doth me.
[He removes the dead man's helmet]
Who's this? O God! It is my father's face
Whom in this conflict I, unwares, have killed.
O heavy times, begetting such events!
From London by the King was I pressed forth;
My father, being the Earl of Warwick's man,
Came on the part of York, pressed by his master;
And I, who at his hands received my life,
Have by my hands of life bereavèd him.

(II.v.55–68)

Henry recoils from this revelation, speaking of a 'piteous spectacle', 'harmless lambs' and joining in with the soldier's grief, saying, 'I'll aid thee tear for tear'. At this point another soldier enters with a dead man in his arms:

SECOND SOLDIER
Thou that so stoutly hath resisted me,
Give me thy gold, if thou hast any gold
For I have bought it with an hundred blows.
[He removes the dead man's helmet]
But let me see; is this our foeman's face?
Ah, no, no, no – it is mine only son!

(II.v.79–83)

The 'artificial' symmetry of the scene and its careful symbolism – two fathers and sons juxtaposed with the 'fatherly' presence of the shepherd king – give it a special place in the play. The linear action is held up for a moment of contemplation and reflection, and while the pity of this war lies in its civil nature pitting son against father and father against son, Shakespeare introduces a number of more general issues on the practice of warfare. First, there is the repeated point about the connection between war and gold, each soldier recognising the profit that can be made, but each claiming that it has been earned. This recalls the dialogue between Hanno and Thrasymachus in the colloquy *Militaria* where Erasmus condemned this feature of warfare. Secondly, there is the first soldier's explanation of how he and his father were pressed into the wars according to their positions in service to a lord. This rehearses those arguments in the contemporary military theory about the virtues of a standing army and the inadequacies of earlier feudal arrangements. But more striking than these is how this little tableau is dismantled and the action resumed. Henry and the two soldiers weep over the bodies of the dead, and although Henry insensitively claims a hierarchy of sorrow, 'Was ever king so grieved for subjects' woe? / Much is your sorrow, mine ten times so much' (II.v.111–12), the scene remains poignant and reflective. There are elements here that recall the formal devices of tragedy: the contrived situation that foregrounds wasteful death, the figure of authority standing over the bodies, the proclamations of grief and sorrow, and the overarching sense of pity. It is as if the second soldier senses this. His next lines contain all the ingredients of the final scene of a tragedy: 'a winding sheet', 'a sepulchre', 'funeral bells' and 'obsequious' regard for the loss of a hero – all reckoned against the evocation of Priam, a figure from classical history. But the formula that applies to tragedy is reversed in a subtle but charged way. Instead of the dead son being gloriously entombed, the funeral bell tolling to draw attention to his fate, these emblems of public grief and remembrance are summoned, but reconfigured as part of the private world of the father:

SECOND SOLDIER (*to his son's body*)
These arms of mine shall be thy winding sheet;
My heart, sweet boy, shall be thy sepulchre,
For from my heart thine image ne'er shall go.
My sighing breast shall be thy funeral bell,
And so obsequious will thy father be,
E'en for the loss of thee, having no more,
As Priam was for all his valiant sons.
(II.v.114–20)

The second soldier's command of the formulaic imagery of tragic death undermines its potential to smooth over and institutionalise wasteful death. It pre-empts the ritual of an imagined military funeral and amplifies the father's powerful and bitterly subversive final couplet: 'I'll bear thee hence, and let them fight that will – / For I have murdered where I should not kill'. Henry, meanwhile, can only repeat his earlier thought: 'Sad-hearted men, much overgone with care, / Here sits a king more woeful than you are.'

From this earlier showcase of failed enterprises, poor judgements, 'feminised' warfare and general pathos emerges Richard, Duke of Gloucester, who declares that he can 'set the murderous Machiavel to school' (III.ii.193). He is already doomed in terms of his historical legacy, but he is a figure bolstered by his military reputation and dramatic appeal. As we have seen, Richard, at the beginning of his own play, scorns the feminising of the state in much the same terms as those of the contemporary writers of military theory. For them, 'Piping peace' had indeed led to 'merry meetings' and 'delightful measures', threatening the fabric of the state's ascendancy. Richard's denunciation of the feminising of the state has overtones of other writers' appeal for a reinvigoration of masculine norms that were slipping away from the Elizabethans' vision of national identity. Yet *Richard III* invites its audiences to regard Richard's ambition (recorded in terms that are simultaneously military and misogynist) as the very essence of the world which the Tudors had swept aside. This is an extremely unsettling ideological stance when viewed in the context of the way in which Richard mimics the very position adopted by those contemporary advocates of English remilitarisation.

Towards the end of a performance the audience watches a very simple but highly stylised opposition between two military camps. On the Elizabethan stage, as with most modern productions, two tents would probably have represented the two armies. The symmetry invites comparison and judgement, as does the action that unfolds. Each army's leader sleeps and dreams, each rises for battle and delivers what might in modern parlance be called a 'motivational' oration to his troops concerning the justice of the campaign. Richmond's speech is a model of justification for war and the cause. It is the abstract discourse of the just war, which speaks of God's involvement and protection, and of a future inscribed in the present outcome. The speech sounds like a passage from one of the more conservative military theorists:

> Much that I could say, loving countrymen,
> The leisure and enforcement of the time
> Forbids to dwell on. Yet remember this:
> God, and our good cause fight upon our side.
> The prayers of holy saints and wrongèd souls,
> Like high-reared bulwarks, stand before our forces.
> Richard except, those whom we fight against
> Had rather have us win than him they follow.
> For what is he they follow? Truly gentlemen,

A bloody tyrant and homicide;
One raised in blood, and one in blood established;
One that made means to come by what he hath,
And slaughtered those that were the means to help him;
A base, foul stone, made precious by the foil
Of England's chair, where he is falsely set;
One that hath ever been God's enemy.
Then if you fight against God's enemy,
God will, in justice, ward you as his soldiers.
If you do sweat to put a tyrant down,
You sleep in peace, the tyrant being slain.
If you do fight against your country's foes,
Your country's foison shall pay your pains the hire;
If you do fight in safeguard of your wives,
Your wives shall welcome home the conquerors.
If you free your children from the sword,
Your children's children quites it in your age.
Then in the name of God and all these rights,
Advance your standards! Draw your willing swords!
For me, the ransom of this bold attempt
Shall be this cold corpse on the earth's cold face;
But if I thrive, the gain of my attempt,
The least of you shall share his part thereof.
Sound, drums, and trumpets, boldly and cheerfully!
God, and Saint George! Richmond and victory!

                                              (V.v.191–224)

This ornate and thoroughly principled oration is also exactly in line with the ideological position Richmond is given in the Tudor histories: God and right are on his side and will give him certain victory. Yet read in the context of the more fervent and popular theorists, Richard's oration, which in many matters of form mirrors Richmond's, might be considered the more competitive and attractive speech. Just as Richard (as Vice figure) is often seen as more compelling than the bland Richmond, his speech chimes more completely with the extremes of nationalist and militarist rhetoric found in some of the contemporary theory:

What shall I say, more than I have inferred?
Remember whom you are to cope withal:
A sort of vagabonds, rascals and runaways,
A scum of Bretons and base lackey peasants,
Whom their o'ercloyèd country vomits forth
To desperate ventures and assured destruction.

You sleeping safe, they bring you to unrest;
You having lands and blessed with beauteous wives,
They would distrain the one, distain the other.
And who doth lead them, but a paltry fellow?
Long kept in Bretagne at our mother's cost;
A milksop; one that never in his life
Felt so much cold as over shoes in snow.
Let's whip these stragglers o'er the seas again,
Lash hence these overweening rags of France,
These famished beggars, weary of their lives,
Who – but for dreaming on this fond exploit –
For want of means, poor rats, had hanged themselves.
If we be conquered, let *men* conquer us,
And not these bastard Bretons, whom our fathers
Have in their own land beaten, bobbed, and thumped,
And in record left them the heirs of shame.
Shall these enjoy our lands? Lie with our wives?
Ravish our daughters?
Drum afar off
            Hark, I hear their drum.
Fight, gentlemen of England! Fight, bold yeomen!
Draw, archers, draw your arrows to the head!
Spur your proud horses hard, and rise in blood!
Amaze the welkin with your broken staves.
                                    (V.vi.44–71)

At this point a messenger arrives to tell Richard that Lord Stanley's
men will not be joining the battle on Richard's behalf:

A thousand hearts are great within my bosom.
Advance our standards! Set upon our foes!
Our ancient word of courage, fair Saint George,
Inspire us with the spleen of fiery dragons.
Upon them! Victory sits on our helms.
                                    (V.vi.77–81)

Richard's speech expands on the idea of nation that the military
theorists calculated as the most important reason for the introduction
of a standing army. Richmond's army lacks credibility in terms of a
national ideal since it is composed of Bretons, thought of here as
French and therefore reminiscent of the traditional sixteenth-century
enemy. It also consists of 'vagabonds, rascals and runaways' – a key
complaint for those theorists who were disgusted by the composition
of Elizabethan armies. Moreover, Richard can appeal to the 'yeoman'
of England to fight against foreign peasants, resurrecting an old adage

about the centrality of a certain class of citizen to a military and national ideal. Richard also speaks in a way that is both informal and colloquial, just as the theorists recommend. Comparing the two attitudes to the forthcoming battle and in the context of the late sixteenth and early seventeenth centuries, Richard's xenophobia might have been read as the more potent discourse. Richmond, though victorious (as history dictates), gives the formal or theoretical justification for war, while Richard evokes a discourse which was to underlie the justification offered in the contemporary world. Comparing the two speeches, Richmond's rhetoric is arguably a sanitised and lukewarm version of the just war ethic, set against the emerging 'realism' of the theorists. The fact that Richard and Richmond both appeal to the duality of God and Saint George unsettles these authorities in an ironic way, but Richard's assertion of masculine, class-oriented and nationalistic fervour positions his oration much more clearly in the pragmatic and popular canons of the Elizabethan military theorists. Furthermore, his description of Richmond as a 'milksop' has a curiously authentic ring in terms of Richard's later assertion that 'I think there be six Richmonds in the field: / Five I have slain today instead of him' (V.iv.10–11). Despite his overall valorisation of Richmond as the coming Henry VII, Shakespeare's hint that Richmond has somehow broken the codes of chivalry by concealing his identity adds some weight to Richard's military reputation. Hammond notes:

> This surprising information is Shakespeare's invention. In Hall, Richard actively seeks single combat with Richmond who is nothing loth to encounter him. The idea of a king thus protecting himself was not uncommon (it occurs again in 1 Henry IV, V.iii). But the stratagem, while suitable enough for the sly Henry IV, hardly seems appropriate in the heroic Richmond.[25]

The end of the play comes quickly with the death of Richard and what seems the conventional post-conflict assessment of what has transpired. Henry VII calls for a list of the 'men of name . . . slain on on either side' (V.viii.12), and ensures their interment 'as becomes their births' (V.viii.15). Civil strife will now give way to 'smooth-faced peace' (V.viii.33) personified in the last line of the play as feminine (V.viii.41), echoing Richard's soliloquy at the start of the play. Shakespeare has fulfilled an historical task in dramatising the chronicles of Holinshed, Hall and More, reinforcing the claim of Henry to the throne, and securing the reputation of the Tudor dynasty. As Jean Howard and Phyllis Rackin have noted:

Looking back to the preceding plays and forward to the Elizabethan present, *Richard III* imposes a tidy ending on the first tetralogy: old crimes are punished, every chicken comes home to roost, and the moral account books are neatly balanced to provide a providential warrant for the accession of Henry VII.[26]

Yet there remains the paradox that has troubled critics over the centuries – the sheer dramatic appeal of the figure of Richard. And in the context of the parallel appeal of the contemporary military theorists – and the ideological proximity between Richard's military reputation and the sentiments of those theorists – Shakespeare could be said to have created a critique of their views. Members of twentieth- and twenty-first-century audiences may be asked see Richard as a kind of early Adolf Hitler, but sixteenth-century ones might have registered him among the prescriptive ideal model soldiers of the military writers. What emerges from this process – the contradictory aesthetic of the doomed usurper and child-killer as authentic military leader – is the tendency of militarism to form itself into an independent discourse, isolated from, and inherently superior to, the particular dramatic or historic conditions from which it arises and from conventional morals.

If there is indeed a sense of autonomy in this discourse, established in the *Henry VI* trilogy and played out in *Richard III*, then it is of interest to see how this phenomenon fares in Shakespeare's later plays. The first tetralogy was written and staged in the period when the contemporary military writing was gaining ground in terms of its voice and volume, and we may suppose, given the many references to its concerns in the plays, in terms of its influence. Shakespeare's grounding of the figure of Richard in the matter of this writing may be entirely coincidental. Yet his eye for topical historical reference points and the unavoidable presence of a military apparatus, however ramshackle, in London itself, would seem to suggest that any dramatisation of military values would have been a sensitive matter. Shakespeare's sustained interest in the history play as a genre would make such an engagement inescapable, and it is worth noting the dates of composition of these plays since they correspond to the most prolific period of military theory. These dates are the subject of considerable critical attention and debate, but an approximate scheme, following Stanley Wells and Gary Taylor (but using the Folio titles) would be:

The Second Part of King Henry the Sixth (1590)
The Third Part of King Henry the Sixth (1590)

The First Part of King Henry the Sixth (1592)
The Life and Death of Richard the Third (1592–93)
The Life and Death of Richard the Second (1595–96)
The Life and Death of King John (1596–97)
The First Part of Henry the Fourth (1597)
The Second part of Henry the Fourth (1598)
The Life of King Henry the Fifth (1598)
The Life of King Henry the Eighth (1613)[27]

In this compositional sequence *Richard II* is of particular importance since it provides a critique of a waning chivalric code of militarism. One level of the play is in its analysis of the discontinuities that arise between the figure that inherits the crown and the role of king which that figure has to act out. In this it has something in common with the *Henry VI* trilogy and much in common with Christopher Marlowe's contemporaneous *Edward II*. Like Marlowe's play (but unlike *Richard III*), the sense of tragedy is clearly defined, bound up with issues of 'weakness', the abuse of position and the detrimental influence of 'favourites' whose encroachments on the throne are couched in terms of their subordinate social class as much their sexual threat. In its dramatisation of war, *Richard II* articulates the 'personal' antithesis between the figures of Richard and Bolingbroke with their distinctive approaches to armed conflict. The play proceeds from the confusions arising from an attempt to implement chivalric law by means of the (interrupted) single combat, through a war in Ireland, to an invasion launched from France. It ends with an 'atoning' crusade to the Holy Land by the new king following the convenient liquidation of Richard. The play's topicality for Elizabethan audiences has often been discussed by critics in terms of its depiction of a monarchy diluted by the influence of favourites. A set of associations is derived from Queen Elizabeth's apparent reaction to a performance of the play (in which she saw parallels with her own situation) and the idea that it was revived for performance at the time of the Essex rebellion shortly before her death.[28] Of wider significance in view of the concerns expressed by the military theorists would have been the relationship between war and prestige. Bolingbroke returns to England at the head of an army in order to reclaim land and inheritance, but departs on a crusade in order to redeem a reputation marred by the consequences of this military act. Richard's earlier decision to go to war against the rebellious Irish is set against his scornful dismissal of Bolingbroke's treacherous and demeaning appeal to his 'craftsmen' countrymen (I.iv.27). Richard's determination to attend to the Irish at the head of his army is an act of prestige recalling Elizabethan histories of earlier kings. But it would also have struck a topical note at the time of the play's first staging in terms of the economic effects of such displays of majesty:

> We will in person to this war,
> And for our coffers with too great a court
> And liberal largess are grown somewhat light,
> We are enforced to farm our royal realm,
> The revenue whereof shall furnish us
> For our affairs in hand. If that come short,
> Our substitutes at home shall have blank charters,
> Whereto, when they shall know what men are rich,
> They shall subscribe them for large sums of gold,
> And send them after to supply our wants;
> For we will make for Ireland presently.
> (I.iv.41–51)

Moreover, in the context of texts by Shakespeare's contemporaries and successors Richard's juxtaposition of his Irish campaign – a source of prestige – with the domesticity of the 'poor craftsmen' seemingly beguiled by Bolingbroke, seems highly portentous since, as we shall see later, some early modern craftsmen had very particular and uncompromising attitudes to war.

Shakespeare's next history play was probably *King John*, one that critics have often addressed by speculating on its date of composition, its relationship with the anonymous *The Troublesome Reign of John, King of England* (1591) and, indeed, its authorship. In terms of the compositional sequence of Shakespeare's histories it is usually ascribed to the years 1596–7, placing it between the first and second tetralogies, with *The Troublesome Reign* as one of its sources. *King John* has proved troublesome in itself due to a perception that it is aesthetically inferior to Shakespeare's other history plays. Critics point to its cumbersome episodic structure, inconsistencies in the development of character (especially with regard to John and the Bastard) and an over-reliance on battle scenes. It is, in the words of one critic, 'bogged down in armies on the march, sieges, and turgid speeches'.[29] Yet *King John* seems absolutely fit for purpose in terms of the development of Shakespeare's history cycle as a moment of hesitation or uncertainty over many of the military issues that are being discussed beyond the theatre. Its very awkwardness may reflect the overdetermined nature of the 'Tudor myth' and the attendant military theory that together sought to underpin the developing Protestant state. It is as if the theatre cannot quite match the ideological texture of these stories of the past and the military models for the future. Howard and Rackin contrast *King John* with *Richard III* by noting that:

> Separated from the temporal and genealogical chain that unites the two tetralogies, *King John* moves farthest back into the past, and the entire action seems designed to foreground every kind of moral and political and historiographic ambiguity. The providential justice that determines the outcome in *Richard III* is nowhere to be seen, and every attempt to resolve the action or make sense of it is immediately frustrated by the moral ambiguities of an episodic plot where success and failure ride on the shifting winds of chance.[30]

This is an astute summary from two critics who, unlike many more traditional commentators, have taken *King John* very seriously, especially for the way that authority in the play is expressed through patriarchy and issues of familial legitimacy. In the context of the military theory of the time, its confidence boosted by the defeat of the Armada (where Providence took the form of shifting winds to create an immediate myth), it is right to see more coherence in the plays that came before and after *King John*. Yet it might be said that the strength of *King John* in relation to an understanding of the power of militarism lies in its excessive display of war's moral ambiguity and susceptibility to fortune. These are matters that are indeed relatively better contained and smoothed over in the adjacent plays, even if they remain hardly more coherent in those plays. In terms of the value placed on individual components of Shakespeare's canon of history plays, it is perhaps those that have traditionally been judged the poorest, such as the *Henry VI* plays and *King John*, that have most to reveal about the ideological underpinnings of the whole set. *King John* stands as a revealing index to some of the military issues played out in the other history plays, and the episodic structure allows an isolation of some of the terms of the debate that was continuing in the period's military prose.

An example of this is apparent in the figure of King John himself, seen as inconsistently developed by critics who dislike, or perhaps distrust, the play. Shakespeare departs from the probable source in *The Troublesome Reign* to present a John who goes from villainous strength to weakness, brought down by a war that offers such patriotic and nation-defining opportunities in other plays. Moreover, Shakespeare has to dramatise a peace settlement brokered by a cardinal in a way that might be construed as mischievous, if I may be forgiven a slightly intentionalist note. He certainly removes the virulent anti-Catholicism so evident in the source, allowing the play's concerns to sit suggestively alongside those of his Elizabethan audience attuned as it would have been to wars with Catholic states. It is thus a play that works against the formulas established in the earlier histories and developed in the later ones. Here, war weakens the state rather than strengthens it and it is a weakened king who brings the kind of peace that, according to the theorists, could only be achieved by a warlike strong leader. And at the end Shakespeare allows the Bastard, who in another shift in characterisation mutates from sceptical observer to extravagant patriot, to utter a sentiment reminiscent of the military theorists' prescription of the relationship between internal peace and external conflict:

Oh, let us pay the time but needful woe,
Since it hath been beforehand with our griefs.
This England never did, nor ever shall,
Lie at the proud foot of a conqueror,
But when it first did help to wound itself.
Now these her princes are come home again,
Come the three corners of the world in arms
And we shall shock them. Naught shall make us rue
If England to itself do rest but true.
(V.vii.110–18)

The Bastard's conversion to warlike nationalism, his cultivation of the grandeur of war itself earlier in the play and the play's overall preoccupation with ideas of legitimacy distinguish it from others in the sequence of Shakespeare's history plays. It could be seen as a kind of pastiche. The thematic concerns of the other plays are drawn together – too awkwardly for many critics and directors – in a way that leaves them open to scrutiny as component parts. A common response to *King John* has been to dismiss it altogether, or to write in its margin 'could do better': yet this sense of alienation is a useful critical mode to bring to an examination of Shakespeare's most celebrated play about warfare.

BEING HARD IN HARFLEUR

In the modern era critics have viewed Shakespeare's portrait of the face of warfare in *The Life of Henry the Fifth* as a triptych. On the left have clustered interpretations that regard the play's bellicose speeches and unjustified killings as evidence of Shakespeare's hostility to the excesses of war, with Henry himself their apologist as he embarks on a nationalist endeavour based on the flimsy justification for the war allowed by his advisers. Ranged to the right are those who harness the play to an earlier tradition, consolidated by the chroniclers, celebrating Henry's achievement at Agincourt. For these observers the play is Shakespeare's account of a triumphant, against-the-odds victory with the power to inspire subsequent generations, especially at times of national emergency, but along the way as a constant reminder of English pride and fortitude. Between these extremes is the familiar narrative of Shakespeare's 'even-handedness': his acknowledgement of the chaos of war and its innocent victims, but also his awareness of war's potential for a demonstration of the determination and resilience of the human spirit. War may be brutal and often haphazard, but it distils human nature and produces some memorable lines. This central, liberal account allows the critic to analyse the play's speeches as rhetorically overblown, but at the same time to recognise the necessity of hyperbole in times of danger. In a sense this was the spirit of Laurence Olivier's wartime vision of the play, closely allied to Churchill's speeches from the same period of national vulnerability. It is a position made morally acceptable when mediated through an understanding that Shakespeare registers war as encouraging pity as well as terror. War is a terrifying aspect of human behaviour, but at least we retain sufficient humanity to pity its victims.

However, it might also be said that Shakespeare invites as much scepticism about heroic militarism in *Henry V* as in earlier plays. If the figure of Henry has traditionally been regarded as an embodiment of heroic militarism, or at worst a pragmatic leader, it has taken the earlier plays to get him to either position. In the *Henry IV* plays Prince Harry was more bound to codes of drinking and civilian licence than warlike pursuits. The Harry of the Boar's Head is defined against Shakespeare's distinctly anti-heroic characterisation of militarism in the form of Sir John Falstaff whose receipt of brides by men resisting service and his creation of rolls of imaginary soldiers (for whom he can claim pay) has been explored by Paul Jorgensen.[31] Falstaff may play on a sense of his lineage, but his practices, as Jorgensen notes, were all too familiar as those of the kind of military man responsible for raising troops in Elizabethan England. Harry's long progress towards repentance, military distinction (newly defined against the figure of Hotspur) and finally kingship itself requires him to enter into a realm of idealism based on his rejection of the allure of civilian life and its codes. In short, in order to become more 'like himself', as he says to his father in the first part of *Henry IV*, he will have to assume the mantle of military, and therefore filial, duty. In doing this, a prince who has been 'a truant' to 'chivalry' might have done worst than pay attention to the urgings of the Elizabeth military theorists in the anachronistic fashion that, as we shall see in a later chapter, Christopher Marlowe's Tamburlaine had already managed to do:

> I will redeem all this on Percy's head,
> And in the closing of some glorious day
> Be bold to tell you that I am your son;
> When I will wear a garment all of blood,
> And stain my favours in a bloody mask,
> Which washed away, shall scour my shame with it.
>   (III.ii.132–7)

Harry becomes Henry by giving up drinking at the Boar's Head, a resolve that immediately allows him to speak in poetry as well as prose; and he also gives up on Sir John Falstaff. When he goes to war as king in *Henry V*, Shakespeare questions the righteousness of warlike pursuits through their juxtaposition with the world the prince has left behind. This is partly represented by the 'absent-presence' of Falstaff, and partly by the hangover of sentiments from the Boar's Head, embodied by the ordinary soldiers he met there and whom he takes to France. The war is won through divine support, the power of rhetoric and the threat of material brutality rather than simply through the idealistic codes of chivalry recommended by the contemporary military theorists. A central scene in *Henry V* interrogates the heroic masculinity, which has removed him from the condition of the inn. 'May I with right and conscience make this claim?' he had asked the Archbishop of Canterbury in the debate about the Salic law at the beginning of the play. Yet it is with 'conscience wide as hell' that he signals the consequences for the citizens of Harfleur if they refuse to give in to his siege:

> How yet resolves the Governor of the town?
> This is the latest parle we will admit.
> Therefore to our best mercy give yourselves,
> Or like to men proud of destruction
> Defy us to our worst. For as I am a soldier,
> A name that in my thoughts becomes me best,
> If I begin the batt'ry once again

I will not leave the half-achievèd Harfleur
Till in her ashes she lie burièd.
The gates of mercy shall be all shut up,
And the fleshed soldier, rough and hard of heart,
In liberty of bloody hand shall range
With conscience wide as hell, mowing like grass
Your fresh fair virgins and your flow'ring infants.
What is it then to me if impious war
Arrayed in flames like to the prince of fiends
Do with his smirched complexion all fell feats
Enlinked to waste and desolation?
What is't to me, when you yourselves are cause,
If your pure maidens fall into the hand
Of hot and forcing violation?
What rein can hold licentious wickedness
When down the hill he holds his fierce career?
We may as bootless spend our vain command
Upon th' enragèd soldiers in their spoil
As send precepts to the leviathan
To come ashore. Therefore, you men of Harfleur,
Take pity of your town and of your people
Whiles yet my soldiers are in my command,
Whiles yet the cool and temperate wind of grace
O'verblows the filthy and contagious clouds
Of heady murder, spoil, and villainy.
If not – why, in a moment look to see
The blind and bloody soldier with foul hand
Defile the locks of your shrill-shrieking beards,
Your fathers taken by the silver beards,
And their most reverend heads dashed to the walls;
Your naked infants spitted upon pikes,
Whiles the mad mothers with their howls confused
Do break the clouds, as did the wives of Jewry
At Herod's bloody-hunting slaughtermen.
What say you? Will you yield, and this avoid?
Or guilty in defence, by thus destroyed?

(III.iii.84–124)

This is of course, a speech that was understandably excised from Olivier's wartime adaptation of the play for the screen. The film was, after all, supposed to evoke the liberation of Europe rather than summon images of wartime atrocities. Other disturbing parts of Shakespeare's play were also excluded, such as Henry's repeated order that the French prisoners should be slaughtered.

Here Shakespeare is following his source in Holinshed rather than embellishing the story. But the scene at the siege of Harfleur is the one that has troubled critics intent on characterising Henry simply as the heroic warrior of such earlier speeches as this one in Act III:

> In peace there's nothing so becomes a man
> As modest stillness and humility,
> But when the blast of war blows in our ears,
> Then imitate the action of the tiger.
> Stiffen the sinews, conjure up the blood,
> Disguise fair nature with hard-favoured rage.
> (III.i.3–8)

Harfleur invites us to consider the real distance between military conflict and civilian ethics: the mantle of war, with its intricate weave of discipline, logistics, restraint, national pride and divine authority cannot cover the real business of the battlefield. The idea that in his thoughts Henry is a soldier mirrors the recommendations of the military writers: that a soldier should have knowledge of his status and purpose. But the outcome is an anti-civic mayhem in which the unrestrained behaviour of his soldiers will show the contradiction between their cause and their 'nature'. Henry's threats amount to a catalogue of images and allusions that come close to contravening a majority of both the seven deadly sins and the Ten Commandments. Moreover, his notion that the consequences that will befall the citizens of Harfleur will be somehow their own fault is a piece of logic-chopping worthy of Richard of Gloucester himself. Unlike the killing of the prisoners, these threats are not derived from Holinshed, who does not describe the aftermath of the taking of Harfleur. This expansive and all-consuming vision of hell seems to be Shakespeare's own invention.

Despite this it is tempting for some to excuse Henry's threats as simply the excesses of medieval or Renaissance warfare. Certainly there is one Elizabethan military theorist who acknowledges that the despoiling of a city might follow its capture, recommending an 'orderly' and fairly distributed seizure of booty. This is William Garrard, whose *The Arte of Warre* was published in London in 1591 not long after the Armada and almost a decade before *Henry V* was first performed. Like many of the theorists, Garrard assembled his book from a range of other people's work: but as a model of good practice, his ideas on sieges are as besmirched as the face of

Shakespeare's personification of war at Harfleur. We learn from the subtitle that they were supposedly:

> *drawne out of all our late and forreine services, by William Garrard Gentleman, who served the King of Spayne in his warres foutenn yeeres, and died Anno Domino 1587. Which may be called, the true steppes of warre, the perfect path of knowledge, and the playne plot of warlike exercises; as the reeder hereof shall plainly see expressed.*

Garrard, a mercenary who had fought for the King of Spain but fortunately, perhaps, died a year before the Spanish Armada, seems to lack distinction as an authority for Henry's ambitions on behalf of English history.

Whatever we make of Harfleur we are left with Henry's considerable reputation, based mainly on his success at Agincourt and reinforced by his prediction that the battle's date, the festival of Saint Crispin, will always be remembered for its association with the victory:

> This story shall the good man teach his son,
> And Crispin Crispian shall ne'er go by
> From this day to the ending of the world
> But we in it shall be rememberèd,
> We few, we happy few, we band of brothers.
>   (IV.iii.56–60)

We shall see in a later chapter that alternative associations came to exist for 25 October, involving other kinds of bands of brothers, but Shakespeare's play clearly contributed to a mythology surrounding Henry V that can be seen as developing during the seventeenth century. In the early years of the conflict between Charles I and Parliament, for example, Prince Rupert, the king's nephew, in many ways a substitute for the king on the field of battle, achieved considerable notoriety for his acts of cruelty and theft.[32] Having been created Duke of Cumberland by his uncle, he was nicknamed 'Prince Robber, Duke of Plunderland' by his own troops, such was the ruthlessness of his approach to the acquisition of goods and property from his own countrymen. But he also cultivated an image derived from the figure of Henry V as stories circulated of his going among his troops in disguise on the eve of battle. As Charles Carlton has remarked:

> In the English civil war these tales focused not upon the king but on the prince, who took over much of the mystique of the heroic leader that traditionally belonged to the sovereign.[33]

Carlton also notes that Charles himself 'ordered a soldier to be hanged on a signpost for stealing a chalice from a church' and it is interesting to speculate on whether the king was consciously imitating Henry's endorsement of the punishment of Bardolph in Shakespeare's play (III.vi.98–114).

Shakespeare seems to leave the Henry of Harfleur at a considerable distance from the ideal warrior-king. Henry identifies himself as a soldier first and foremost and then speaks of his own soldiers as being like Herod's 'slaughtermen', the pursuers of the infant Christ. Not only will soldiers become merciless infanticides, but they will behave like the agents of a demonic biblical figure with a long history on the English stage.[34] It is a shocking allusion that sits uncomfortably with a rationale that contrasts the figure of 'Harry' (of the undisciplined, feminised realm of the Boar's Head) with an idealised 'Henry' of the manly battlefields of France. Over the course of Shakespeare's histories we are thus presented with an odd set of bookends. At one end is the grotesquely villainous Richard of Gloucester who, despite everything, is ennobled by the field of battle. At the other end the saintly Henry/Herod, elevated but ultimately tarnished by his military role, stands like a method actor who cannot disengage from his part. Interestingly, another 'soldier' in another play evokes the figure of Herod as a traditionally noisy character likely to 'split the ears of the groundlings' and finally emptied of meaning by overacting. The soldier in question is also a prince who would be king, and the occasional is his advice to the Players in Act III of *Hamlet*.

Notes

1. Quotations from the plays of William Shakespeare are taken from the three-volume edition of *The Oxford Shakespeare* (1987), ed. Stanley Wells and Gary Taylor with John Jowett and William Montgomery, Oxford: Oxford University Press. I use their titles for the first citation of each play but where appropriate revert to the more commonly used (shorter) titles thereafter.
2. Sir Philip Sidney [1591], 'Astrophel and Stella', in *The Poems of Sir Philip Sidney*, ed. W. A. Ringler Jr (1962), Oxford: Oxford University Press, 69, l. 7ff.
3. I use the term 'Plantagenet' to include the houses of Lancaster and York.
4. References are to Christopher Marlowe [1590], *Tamburlaine the Great*, ed. John D. Jump (1967), London: Edward Arnold.
5. Laurence Olivier played Richard III on stage a number of times during the war, most notably at the Old Vic in 1944.

6. Brecht's play was developed over the years from 1941 and first performed after the war. See Bertolt Brecht (1965), *Der aufhaltsame Aufstieg des Arturo Ui*, Berlin: Suhrkamp Verlag. References here are to Bertolt Brecht, *The Resistible Rise of Arturo Ui*, ed. John Willet and Ralph Manheim (1981), London: Methuen.

7. Walter Benjamin (1967), *Versuche über Brecht: Herausgegeben und mit einem Nachwort versehen von Rolf Tiedemann*, Berlin, p. 125. I am grateful to Elisabeth Rother for her help with translating material from German.

8. This literary link with *Richard III* is reinforced by Ui's wooing of Dullfleet's widow (scene 13), recalling Richard's wooing of Anne in the second scene of Shakespeare's play, and again by the appearance to Ui, in a nightmare, of the ghost of the murdered Roma/Röhm in scene 14. *Richard III* is a reference point in Brecht's play since its protagonist is a recognisable authority in the business of persuasion and 'theatricality' as well as a memorably bloodthirsty source of civil war.

9. Quoted in Brecht, *The Resistible Rise of Arturo Ui*, ed. Willet and Manheim, p. 107. For a longer analysis of Brecht's play and its relation to the rhetoric of *Julius Caesar*, see Simon Barker (2005) ' "It's an actor, boss. Unarmed": the Rhetoric of Julius Caesar', in *Julius Caesar: New Critical Essays*, ed. Horst Zander, New York and Abingdon: Routledge, pp. 227–39.

10. Ian McKellen (1996), *William Shakespeare's Richard III*, Woodstock, NY: The Overlook Press, p. 7.

11. The equation works both ways as Fascism itself depended on precisely choreographed theatrical display. In Britain, Oswald Mosely devoted much time to the development of uniforms and other iconography, as well as to his own rhetorical skills. See Stephen Dorril (2006), *Blackshirt: Sir Oswald Mosely and British Fascism*, London: Penguin.

12. McKellen, *William Shakespeare's Richard III*, p. 13.

13. Ibid.

14. See especially Jan Kott (1965), *Shakespeare our Contemporary*, London: Methuen; and Wilheim Hortman (2002), 'Shakespeare on the Political Stage in the Twentieth Century', in Stanley Wells and Sarah Stanton (eds), *The Cambridge Companion to Shakespeare on Stage*, Cambridge: Cambridge University Press, pp. 212–29.

15. See E. M. W. Tillyard (1944), *Shakespeare's History Plays*, London: Chatto & Windus. Tillyard explains in the book that one source for *Richard III* was Edward Hall's 1548 *The Union of the Two Noble and Illustrate Famelies of Lancastre and York*. He notes that 'in the total sequence of his plays dealing with the subject matter of Hall [Shakespeare] expressed successfully a universally held and still comprehensible scheme of history: a scheme fundamentally religious, by which events evolve under a law of justice and under the ruling of God's

Providence, and of which Elizabeth's England was the acknowledged outcome' (pp. 320–1).

16. Wells and Taylor use the title *All is True* for the play written by Shakespeare in collaboration with John Fletcher that saw the destruction of the Globe Theatre by fire on 29 June 1613 by the use of a cannon during the performance. *The Famous History of the Life of King Henry the Eighth* is the title used in the 1623 folio.

17. William Shakespeare. *King Richard III* (1981), ed. Antony Hammond, London: Methuen, pp. 100–1. Hammond cites Peter Happé (1966), 'The Vice 1350–1605', PhD thesis, London University.

18. Ibid., p. 100.

19. Shakespeare, *King Richard III*, ed. Hammond, p. 79.

20. I have seen productions of *Arturo Ui* in which the audience is duped into voting for Ui.

21. In these terms it is clear to see the sense of Brecht's interest in *Richard III* as providing a parallel with the success of Hitler: the idea that fascism was constructed in the tainted politics created by an earlier war.

22. See, for example, James E. Ruoff (1975), *Macmillan's Handbook of Elizabethan and Stuart Literature*, London and Basingstoke: Macmillan. He notes that the 'real problems in the *Henry VI* plays do not, however, pertain to historical authenticity – a matter of as little concern to Shakespeare's audience as to a modern one – but to the great difficulty he experienced in harnessing the chaotic events of his sources in the English chronicles. In the Wars of the Roses he found what he hoped was a single, controlling saga, and to this subject he brought a single theme that was both palatable to his audience and consistent with his personal view of English institutions and history: that divisive factions motivated by ambition and vanity are the principal threat to a commonwealth, and that these factions must be curbed by a powerful central authority sanctioned by hereditary right, justice and wisdom. But neither subject matter nor theme proved sufficient to give dramatic unity to the bewildering variety of characters and episodes in the chronicles. This failure is especially evident in Part I, where the "noble-minded Talbot" emerges as the hero out of a vague mass of unrelated episodes' (pp. 195–6).

23. Shakespeare, *King Richard III*, ed. Hammond, p. 106.

24. Ibid.

25. Ibid., p. 329, n.

26. Jean E. Howard and Phyllis Rackin (1997), *Engendering a Nation: A Feminist Account of Shakespeare's English Histories*, London: Routledge, p. 119.

27. The sequence historically, with approximate dates of composition, is: *The Life and Death of King John* (1596–97); *The Life and Death of Richard the Second* (1595–96); *The First Part of Henry the Fourth* (1597); *The Second Part of Henry the Fourth* (1598); *The Life of King*

Henry the Fifth (1598); *The First Part of King Henry the Sixth* (1589–90); *The Second Part of King Henry the Sixth* (1590); *The Third Part of King Henry the Sixth* (1590); *The Life and Death of Richard the Third* (1592–93) and *The Life of King Henry the Eighth* (1613).

28. See Wells and Taylor's introduction to the play, p. 107.
29. Ruoff, *Macmillan's Handbook of Elizabethan and Stuart Literature*, p. 241.
30. Howard and Rackin, *Engendering a Nation*, p. 119.
31. See Paul A. Jorgensen (1956), *Shakespeare's Military World*, Berkeley, CA: University of California Press, pp. 64–71 and 130–43.
32. Pamphlets decribing this behaviour include the anonymous *A True Relation of Prince Rupert's Barbarous Cruelty against the Town of Birmingham*, London; and *Prince Rupert's Burning Love to England Discovered in Birmingham's Flames*, London, both of 1643.
33. Charles Carlton (1992), *Going to the Wars: The Experience of the English Civil Wars 1638–1651*, London and New York: Routledge.
34. Of the extant Mysteries, Herod's massacre is most graphically played out in the surviving York Cycle, performed until 1572. The fragment allotted to the Girdlers and Nailers has Herod's reaction to the news of the birth of Christ, but also the anguish of the mothers whose children are murdered by his knights.

6

THE EXIT STRATEGY

༜

The Tragedy of Hamlet, Prince of Denmark, together with *The Tragedy of Othello, the Moor of Venice, The History of King Lear* (or *The Tragedy of King Lear*) and *The Tragedy of Macbeth* are much concerned with warfare, despite their preoccupation with matters of seemingly personal or familial disquiet.[1] Located mainly within courts, palaces or castles, each of their protagonists struggles variously across the sequence of plays with the ethics and theology of revenge, social caste and private jealousy, loyalty and love, and in the case of *Macbeth*, the relationship between fate and ambition. *Macbeth* simultaneously has to play its part in an ordering of Scottish history that unsurprisingly becomes central to the concerns of audiences in London with the succession of James VI of Scotland to the English throne. Yet in all these plays there is war: the tragedy is set against a background of war in the case of *Hamlet* and *Othello*, or results in warlike activity in the case of *Macbeth* and *King Lear*.

Of the four plays, I want to concentrate on *Hamlet*, which includes what some audience members in the years leading up to the death of Elizabethan may have considered one of the most astonishing representations of warfare in the whole of the unfolding Shakespeare canon. They may still have been absorbed by the threat of a new Armada and were certainly able to witness the effects of Elizabeth's Irish campaigns in the form of musters and the spectacle of gangs of returned soldiers in the streets of London. Had they the mind they could also have read of war in the many treatises available from the printers established in the area around St Paul's. Those who had studied or heard of this material would know of its insistence on the appropriate qualities that defined the soldier, the ideal relationship between the military and the sovereign, and the way that warfare could be justified in the name of God and the state. Some attending early productions of *Hamlet* may thus have experienced something of an intellectual shock at the end of this new play. *Hamlet* begins with soldiers, contains many images and analogies pertaining to war, and includes news of battles that take place, as it were, just off-stage. At the end of the play these diverse allusions are united in a particularly acute visual and verbal evocation of the virtues of militarism.

It is entirely possible to overlook or forget the very end of *Hamlet*. Such is the burden of the play's tragic dimension, centred on the figure of Hamlet himself, that the question 'what happens at the end of *Hamlet*?' may well produce answers from those remembering productions which focus on other aspects of the play's final moments. There is certainly plenty of memorable business from which to choose: the series of lethal physical exchanges, summaries of previous events and speeches about the future. Characters whom we hardly know take up important positions and what they have to say is critical in terms of bringing some order to the chaos of the scene. These are celebrated elements in the play and present many challenges for modern actors and directors. Elements of the speeches are well known, and there is always a high level of expectation from the audience. If nothing else, these interlocking exchanges signal the end, both of the play and of the high levels of concentration it has demanded all round. In performance there is often a discernible sense of release from the high level of commitment necessarily given to the play by actors, technicians and audience.

So what do we remember from the end of Hamlet? It may be his final words, which, leaving aside the 'O, O, O, O' that persists in many editions, offer a convenient and moving point of closure, supported by Horatio's memorably affecting:

Now cracks a noble heart. Good night sweet prince.
Flights of angels sing thee to thy rest.

(V.ii.12–13)

Alternatively, people often recall the sheer number of poisoned and lacerated bodies left on the stage, the result of the narrative of 'carnal, bloody, and unnatural acts', the 'accidental judgements' and the 'casual slaughters' that Horatio promises to record as a tale for posterity. For many, this extremely high level of carnage undoubtedly characterises the play, just as it should seem a source of horror for those who come on the scene from elsewhere. These figures, ambassadors and soldiers, should be used to human frailty and bloodletting, yet they recoil with horror from what they find at Elsinore.

Yet the manner in which the dead are addressed and physically removed from the stage makes for a curious reflection on the attitudes to war that run through the play. It starts with an odd kind of competition which seems momentarily to arise between Horatio and the newly arrived Fortinbras over what to do with the bodies. It is not entirely a question of ownership, but it has something to do with the men's positions in the hierarchy of those who are left alive to reflect on the slaughter and consider Denmark's future. Horatio is the local man and has his story to tell. He is protective of those who will feature in it, even though they are now dead. Fortinbras is the outsider, and we cannot be entirely sure of his motives and plans. What to do with the bodies certainly has much to do with the purpose and meaning of remembrance – with stories of the dead. Horatio wants to get the record straight and is ever loyal to the memory of the dead. First of all he firmly denies the Ambassador's claim that Claudius (or is it Hamlet?) commanded the death of Rosencrantz and Guildenstern, an important correction since someone's reputation is at stake. He then advises a public display of the bodies:

> He never gave commandment for their death.
> But since so jump upon this bloody question
> You from the Polack wars, and you from England,
> Are here arrived, give order that these bodies
> High on a stage be placèd to the view;
> And let me speak to th' yet unknowing world
> How these things came about.
>
> (V.ii.328–34)

Horatio's suggestion that the loss of so many may be in part mitigated by their serving some didactic purpose, the bodies displayed as an exemplification of past wrongs, seems to correspond with the highest ideals of the tragic form. The use of the word 'unknowing' acknowledges the fact that there is an audience within Denmark ready to learn of the particular circumstances and events of the story. Horatio invites the idea that the whole sequence of the action, once properly told, will serve as a parable of human behaviour that will add to the common good. For a moment one feels the playhouse charged with the moral force of Greek tragedy, the action reaching out from the *orchestra* to embrace a civic audience in a conditioning or corrective way. At the very least this promise of further analysis means that the ending of this play corresponds with other tragedies from the period.[2] The story will begin when the play ends. Fortinbras seems to have read about the poetics of tragedy and says of Horatio's promised account, 'Let us haste to hear it': the business of tragedy is to evoke pity and terror from which we learn to reform our ways. The play will start again, but this time with Horatio's interpretation of events and the wisdom of hindsight. Yet the bodies remain, and what happens to them arrests the flow of the tragic formula.

RITES OF PASSAGE

Fortinbras agrees that Hamlet's body (if not the others) should be borne to the stage just as Horatio has suggested. Yet this order, the first he gives with his new authority within Denmark (his 'new order'), seems quite extraordinary in terms of the ceremony that is to accompany the elevation and display of Hamlet's corpse:

> Let four captains
> Bear Hamlet like a soldier to the stage,
> For he was likely, had he been put on,
> To have proved most royally; and for his passage,
> The soldiers' music and the rites of war
> Speak loudly for him.
> Take up the body. Such a sight as this
> Becomes the field, but here shows much amiss.
> Go, bid the soldiers shoot.
>
> (V.ii.349–57)

If we were to be less than critical about the proceedings here it is perfectly possibly to see this elaborate ritual as a practical way of removing the bodies from the open playing area of an Elizabethan playhouse. As Nick de Somogyi has noted in his convincing discussion of the textual variants of the play, the Q2 text has 'bodies', so it may be that all the corpses are carried off.[3] This would have been an understandable piece of stage business in an Elizabethan theatre, a kind of exit strategy that avoids leaving so many 'dead' actors on stage in full view of the audience, awaiting their 'resurrection', and already anxious for refreshment at the Mermaid Inn. In many tragedies directions of some kind are given for the removal of bodies. So, in *Hamlet* either all the bodies are carried from the stage, or simply Hamlet's. Yet only Hamlet's is going to receive the extraordinary accolade of a military escort, with officers as bearers and the soldiers' music, the volley of shots; and perhaps there are other unspecified 'rites of war' that would have been familiar to Elizabethan audiences. The soldiers present may offer some kind of salute or a lowering of their arms in tribute.

The question arises as to quite why Hamlet receives this treatment, and it is one worth exploring in some detail given the nature of the play, the times and the atmosphere of war in Shakespeare's London. One explanation may be that since, as Fortinbras observes, the whole scene looks like a battlefield, its victims should be treated appropriately as some species of paramilitary. Perhaps Fortinbras, who tells of his sorrow, treats everyone he feels sorry for as though they had been soldiers. Yet if this were the case, then such dignity in death would have been extended to other parties in the casual slaughter of which he has yet to hear detail. In matters of degree, the corpses include royalty, and a soldier is supposed to honour even his enemy's dead. Yet Hamlet is singled out for special treatment. Perhaps it is because he is a prince who has died young and wastefully and this is Norway's version of the state funeral.[4] What seems more likely from what he says is that Fortinbras really considers Hamlet to be a quasi-soldier. If this is the case, then a number of issues arise that reflect on the figures of Fortinbras and Hamlet, and on the presentation of militarism in the whole play.

Fortinbras himself constitutes a kind of 'exit strategy' in his own right: his appearance on the scene facilitates the end of the play and allows a channelling of all that has happened through his person and into the future. Like everyone else, he will hear Horatio's story, but what is more important is that he will assert his 'rights of memory' in Denmark. Someone needs to get a grip in Denmark and, if the military theorists believe in their own approach to statesmanship and their own values about the desired military leader, then Fortinbras fits the bill. He seems a disciplined military leader with a good degree of knowledge, which will be enhanced when Horatio gets to tell his tale. Fortinbras has a number of victories to his credit, and a good sense of what he sees as appropriate protocol when it comes to dealing with the unexpected, such as coming upon the corpse of a prince. Yet in terms of how the play has proceeded, Fortinbras is an unknown figure, his reputation depends almost entirely on an identity derived from his military background, bearing and purposefulness in the field, a point I shall return to. The fact that he orders military rites for Hamlet's 'passage' to the stage invites the audience to consider that Fortinbras may well be about to establish a new order in Demark, but it may be one framed by his own line of work. Fortinbras obviously links royalty with militarism. He states that Hamlet, had he 'been put on' would have 'prov'd' most royal', and would, presumably, then more distinctly have absorbed the values associated with a soldier.

All this hardly seems credible when Hamlet is measured against the list of qualities that the contemporary military theorists saw as a requisite in the 'true' soldier. If anything, Hamlet lacks a uniform identity, let alone an identity that would be set off by donning a uniform. He is a figure dispersed across a range of sometimes complementary but often rather discontinuous identities. Many of these have been formulated for him by criticism, editorial decisions and at the hands of countless actors and directors. Hamlet was a point of identification for the Romantics, a case study for Freudians, a Renaissance man for humanists. In the theatre and on the screen he has been played as a rebel, a conservative, an atheist, a believer, a dissolute student, a philosopher, a hippie, a masochist, a misogynist, though rarely all these things in a single production. One fixed point about the figure of Hamlet is the difficulty we have in fixing him. Another is that he exhibits absolutely no potential in terms of a life in the armed forces (he cannot fight very well), although had they been around at the time he might have made a passable suicide bomber given his tendency to kill the innocent. Oddly, the only moment at which we see Hamlet securely fixed with a single identity is when Fortinbras practically declares him to have been a soldier all along. Fortinbras may be complimenting Hamlet by offering him the very best treatment according to his own militarised values, and the audience may miss its significance, but in fixing Hamlet thus he potentially seals off the prince from his own (or Horatio's) story: thus militarism usurps the tragic form.

DELICATE AND TENDER PRINCES

Fortinbras's military credentials correspond neatly with some of the ideals expressed by the military theorists, although the audience only has a glimpse of these in Act IV and the evidence comes from a single Norwegian Captain and is at once interpreted for us by Hamlet himself. Coming across Fortinbras's army en route to engage the Poles, Hamlet asks of the Captain the nature of the land that is to be fought over. The Captain replies:

> Truly to speak, and with no addition,
> We go to gain a little patch of ground
> That hath in it no profit but the name.
> To pay five ducats, five, I would not farm it,
> Nor will it yield to Norway or the Pole
> A ranker rate, should it be sold in fee.
>   (IV.iv.8–13)

For the military theorists such a campaign may have seemed as justified and impressive as Hamlet deems it to be. The accent is on 'name'
and prestige, and one can speculate whether the action is called for in
order to boost the reputation of Fortinbras and his uncle in Norway.
Hamlet considers this a turning point in his quest for revenge and is
spurred on:

> Witness this army of such mass and charge,
> Led by a delicate and tender prince,
> Whose spirit with divine ambition puffed
> Makes mouths at the invisible event,
> Exposing what is mortal and unsure
> To all that fortune, death and danger dare,
> Even for an eggshell.
>
> (IV.iv.38–44)

Given the atmosphere in London at the time of Hamlet's first performances this image of a military paradigm may have invited some
scepticism. Hamlet's aesthetics may have been appealing to the military writers of time: the talk is of divinity in arms and of a military
spirit, but it is an abstraction that must have seemed a long way from
the actual experience of war for some members of Shakespeare's audience. Yet this is a play and there is room for idealism. What is more
telling is the seamless and circular relationship between Hamlet and
Fortinbras. Hamlet recognises Fortinbras as a 'delicate and tender
prince'. Given the way that the campaign is such a source of inspiration in terms of his own stalled pursuit of Claudius, the Norwegian
instantly becomes an embodiment of his own better self which has
hitherto been obscured by doubt and hesitation. Hamlet gazes on
what he could have been and must become. Militarism provides him
with a quasi-spiritual framework of consciousness and a programme
for action that, albeit on a grand and tragic scale, mirrors the relationship between the military subject and the civilian subject found in
contemporary theory. Since Hamlet knows little of Fortinbras beyond
his leadership of this campaign over 'an eggshell', he cannot think of
the possible consequences of such foreign wars of prestige and
honour. As we shall see in a later chapter, had he looked at the way
other dramatists represented this kind of war, he might have felt less
inclined towards Fortinbras as a hero and inspirational leader.

At the end of the play, Fortinbras's treatment of Hamlet's body
can be seen as a compliment repaid. He knows little of Hamlet
ahead of Horatio's story, but seems to recognise in the prince

something of himself, which is not surprising as Hamlet has apparently taken on his mantle. By intuition his first command in Denmark is to give Hamlet a soldier's funeral which, one might assume, would be one he would wish for himself. In a way, Hamlet has become Fortinbras and moved a step further towards his revenge, although 'what is mortal and unsure' and 'fortune, death and danger' prevailed in his personal battlefield, as they did not for Fortinbras in his war against the Poles, even though he fearlessly embraces their threat. In a reciprocal way Fortinbras becomes Hamlet, 'the delicate and tender prince' of Horatio's story, and the guns fire their homage to the dead soldier prince. Horatio still has his story to tell, but in the annals of Danish history this will now be a story of a soldierly prince, mortally wounded in the line of duty, but replaced by a princely soldier from a neighbouring country. Talk of military discipline, the terror and pity of war, and the loss of our better selves can nicely frame the story. For Danish history this will sound more decorous than a narrative of 'carnal, bloody, and unnatural acts', 'accidental judgements' and 'casual slaughters', all of which it might prefer to keep dark.

THE TRAGIC SOLDIER

Another effect of this 'commissioning' of Hamlet can be observed when the play is considered, as it often is, alongside the other three principal tragedies. Hamlet may have been, like Fortinbras, a 'delicate and tender prince' but once he is imagined as a soldier, he fits the set of plays that includes *Othello*, *King Lear* and *Macbeth*. The protagonists of each of these is a soldier of some kind and, given the circumstances of their downfalls, one is reminded of the military theorists' scorn for what they consider to be the malign influence on soldiers of women and domesticity. Othello's reputation as a soldier has secured him employment by the Venetian state. A possible interpretation of this position is that his continuing 'outsider' status is due not only to the general exclusivity of Venetian society and the racism that threads through the play. An additional factor informed Italian militarism: a suspicion of soldiers who did not have a long and ancestral association with the city or region for which they fought, and Shakespeare might have known about that from reading Machiavelli, who also, as we have seen, despised the concept of the mercenary. Italian culture instead lauded the concept of the knight and in reality kept chivalry alive, particularly in the northern city-states, long after its virtual disappearance elsewhere in Europe. Whilst Othello is not a mercenary, and Machiavelli preferred citizen soldiers to the anachronism of knights, Shakespeare's play is edged by concerns about the identity of various kinds of soldier. Othello's self-image is laden with a kind of medievalism, which contrasts with the representations of military matters elsewhere in the play. The best example comes at a crisis point when Othello associates his supposed betrayal by Desdemona with a loss of his occupation:

> I had been happy if the general camp,
> Pioneers and all, had tasted her sweet body,
> So I had nothing known. O, now for ever
> Farewell the tranquil mind, farewell content,
> Farewell the plumèd troops and the big wars
> That makes ambition virtue! O, farewell,
> Farewell the neighing steed and the shrill trump,
> The spirit-stirring drum, th' ear-piercing fife,
> The royal banner, and all quality,
> Pride, pomp, and circumstance of glorious war!
> And O, you mortal engines whose rude throats
> Th' immortal Jove's dread clamours counterfeits,
> Farewell! Othello's occupation's gone.
>
> (III.iii.350–62)

Othello's status is defined in terms of his profession, by comparison with which everything else often seems secondary: the aesthetics of war dim the appeal of Desdemona and the marital bed. Othello is an unusual figure for the English stage of the period for reasons other than the fact that he is one of only a few sympathetically drawn black characters. His fall has an odd parallel with the perceived decline in the status of the English soldier, which obsessed contemporary theorists. He is outwardly still a vision of chivalry, yet this appears to have become a brittle shell, like the knights in late Tudor tournaments who looked good in the tiltyard but would have fared poorly on the field of battle, or so the military writers claimed. Shakespeare's Othello, according to his own description of himself, also seems something of an anachronism. He is outwitted by a species of latterday Vice in the shape of the rather modern and 'political' Iago. Shakespeare seems to use Othello's military identity in a way that increases our sympathy for him: his downfall is associated with a loss of this image of himself, which is defined entirely by his status as a soldier. Fortinbras 'contains' the wayward and dispersed subjectivity of Hamlet in the image of a soldier, whilst Iago prises Othello from his. Tellingly, both plays show that by the early years of the seventeenth century, audiences might well have had their doubts about placing their trust in protagonists whose identity was shaped by their military prowess. This is certainly true of King Lear whom one can imagine had once led armies of knights. His increasing loss of status is measured against the loss of his knights which is understandable, but lacks credibility the more often he mentions it, and particularly by comparison with the loss of faith in his family.

Diverse as the soldiers in *Hamlet*, *Othello* and *King Lear* are they invite audiences to consider the fact that military power is superficial, a matter more of outward display than inner sensibility, and that those who claim it as a badge of masculinity seem to be the most vulnerable men. In Shakespeare's four main tragedies the central figures are protagonists rather than 'heroes', so although we may sympathise with their plight, we are not necessarily invited to respect them. Since Shakespeare makes them all so conspicuously soldiers (by sleight of hand in the case of Hamlet), he may have been contributing the tragedies to the critique he has already offered of military protagonists in the history plays. History meets tragedy in *Macbeth* where military prowess most conspicuously reveals itself as a matter of sheer brutality. One wonders whether the Captain at the beginning of *Macbeth* is the same as the one who tells Hamlet about Fortinbras's exploits against the Poles, travelling from country to country with a special interest in battles involving Norweigans and marvelling at various acts of seeming military excellence. Here in Scotland he reports on the way that brave Macbeth ('well he deserves that name') 'unseamed' the rebel Macdonald 'from the nave to th' chops / And fixed his head upon our battlements' (I.i.22–3). Is this an Englishman's view of Scottish tactics (Macbeth's own head gets this treatment at the end of the play), or simply a rare representation of the reality of hand-to-hand fighting? Whatever the case, it is a stark image that reflects on the way that war legitimises activities that within the walls of castles provoke madness, hallucinations and guilt and does little for the reputation of the soldier as a figure of respect.

Notes

1. I am again using the titles and following the compositional sequence of plays established by Stanley Wells and Gary Taylor (see note 2 in Chapter 5).

2. In *Othello*, for example, Lodovico promises at the end to relate the story to 'the state': the state will learn and reform, acting with knowledge of what has occurred in order to avoid repeating such folly.

3. Nick de Somogyi (1998), *Shakespeare's Theatre of War*, Burlington, VT and Aldershot: Ashgate, p. 235. Another issue is at stake in the differences between the Quarto variants. As de Somogyi explains, Q2 sees a reduction in the significant amount of military imagery in Q1, which he attributes in part to the official moves towards more peaceful international relations in the reign of James Stuart.

4. While writing this I thought of an analogy in the extraordinary occasion of the funeral of the Princess of Wales in 1997. The memorable week between her death and her funeral was made even odder for some when Diana, who not long before had been campaigning for an international ban on landmines, was borne to Westminster Abbey on a gun carriage surrounded by soldiers. Here was a sight that more became the field.

Part IV
Refusal

7

GENTLER CRAFTS

◈

Shakespeare is replete with war and pity. Beyond the histories, where it is unsurprisingly a central theme, and the bloody classical plays, drawn from the heroic martial narratives that were enthusiastically cited by the military theorists, war also penetrated the tragedies and even the comedies to an extent that makes it almost universal in the canon. It is therefore not surprising to find that war similarly absorbed those who wrote before, during and after Shakespeare's productive twenty-year period of writing for the stage. For some, notably Christopher Marlowe, war could be presented as an abstraction. The two parts of *Tamburlaine the Great* present militarism on one level as an extreme medium through which an audience observes how the potential of a protagonist for greatness is tragically squandered, leaving only futility and waste. Generically, war for Tamburlaine is as necromancy is for Faustus, as the allure of sex is for his Edward II, and as the corroding temptation of Machiavellian power is for Barabas in the *The Jew of Malta*. Yet in the context of the Elizabethan theorists' demands for militarism to become less of an abstraction and more of a concrete reification of the emerging state, say, in the form of a standing army whose business was to be conducted by disciplined soldiers, *Tamburlaine* reaches far beyond mere tragedy. The figure of Tamburlaine offers audiences a vision, in a manner that is much more distinct than in Shakespeare, of the way that the militarised male can become detached from any meaningful sense of political process.

Tamburlaine speaks constantly of military discipline and seems to be especially well versed in the contemporary manuals of military theory. In the second part he explains to his sons how he will teach them elements of this theory:

But now, my boys, leave off and list to me
That mean to teach you rudiments of war.
I'll have you learn to sleep upon the ground,

> March in your armour, thorough watery fens,
> Sustain the scorching heat and freezing cold,
> Hunger and thirst, right adjuncts of the war,
> And after this to scale a castle war,
> Besiege a fort, to undermine a town,
> And make whole cities caper in the air.
> (III.ii.53–61)

He proceeds to describe in some detail how to establish and defend a fort, taking most of the technical information about angles, ditches, bulwarks, counterscarps, countermines, and so on from Paul Ive's *The Practise of Fortification*.[1] One is reminded of Thomas Smith's list of the qualities he saw as requisite in the 'expert soldier' described earlier in the military manuals. For Smith, the ideal soldier would be one:

> that has some sight in the mathematicals and in geometrical instruments, for the conveying of mines under the ground, to plant and manage great ordnance, to batter or beat down the walles of any towne or castle; that can measure altitude, lattitudes and longitudes, etc.[2]

Whether in offence or defence, Tamburlaine's expertise is learned, precise and utterly up-to-date in terms of Elizabethan military science. One wonders whether the citizens of Harfleur would have fared better against the marauding Henry V had they read the Elizabethan books Tamburlaine seems to have known. The anachronism gives him an intellectual edge that is lacking in the play's two main sources.[3] *Tamburlaine the Great* sees Marlowe at the height of his powers, and the lyricism of the poetry soars in response to the atrocities that pile one upon another. Throughout the plays Tamburlaine expresses his belief in the general codes of militarism that have fostered and endorsed his military 'professionalism'. Yet the discourse itself is dangerously autonomous: the politics of the siege, as Tamburlaine explains to his sons, lead inevitably to their own brutal conclusion, that the purpose of all this is simply to 'murder the foe' (III.iii.83). Marlowe presents Tamburlaine as grotesque and exaggerated – taunting his caged prisoners, slaughtering the virgins sent to plead for his mercy, slaying one of his own sons for cowardice and finally drowning the inhabitants of Babylon – but Tamburlaine sees himself as a model of militarism.

As an apparatus conceived to show tragic hubris, all this is, to say the least, elaborate. That Tamburlaine simply sickens and dies at the end of Part II (handing over the business of world domination to his remaining sons), instead of suffering a fate to match his own excess, shows Marlowe resisting the accepted formula of tragedy. It is for this reason that there is little correspondence between the figures of Tamburlaine and the Vice-like Richard of Gloucester. At least the latter, like the equally ambitious Macbeth, is visited by ghostly spectres of his conscience. Nowhere in Tamburlaine's progress does he speak of the horrors of his deeds, unless it is to celebrate them, and nowhere does he express any remorse. If there are doubts, they are only over whether or not Amyras is suited to his inheritance:

> Let not thy love exceed thine honour, son,
> Nor bar thy mind that magnanimity
> That nobly must admit necessity.
> Sit up, my boy, and with those silken reins
> Bridle the steeled stomachs of those jades.
> (V.iii.199–203)

There is nothing in the way of redemptive self-knowledge to cloud his final vision, his own spirit guiding his newly crowned son's chariot into further conquests. He dies almost cheerfully:

> The nature of thy chariot will not bear
> A guide of baser temper than myself,
> More than heaven's coach the pride of Phaëton.
> Farwell, my boys! My dearest friends, farewell!
> My body feels, my soul doth weep to see
> Your sweet desires depriv'd my company,
> For Tamburlaine, the scourge of God, must die.
> (V.iii.242–8)

There is certainly no sense of justice for those who suffered as 'collateral damage' as Tamburlaine rampaged throughout the world, and the references to his soul may have seemed to an Elizabethan audience the height of perversity. The popularity of *Tamburlaine the Great* in its day may attest to the morbid desire of its audiences for excessive displays of carnage and brutality: and the scenes of torture and humiliation are as graphic and cruel as anything we see in the modern world. Yet if it is the case that one of the attractions of the play is the lyricism of its language, Tamburlaine's mastery of military rhetoric might have been seen as giving poetic voice to the often rather dull and repetitive polemic of the military theorists whom Marlowe had clearly read. It is as if an early version of 'The Double-Armed Man' himself, later framed and contained in the engravings accompanying William Neade's 1625 text, finds a voice and steps out to bestride the world. Members of an Elizabethan audience, attuned to the atmosphere of conflict that dominated the period when the play first appeared, witnessing musters and militias, and possibly reading the contemporary military theory, may have made the connection between these various textual and non-textual manifestations of war. And perhaps William Neade, with his nostalgia for the longbow and carefully detailed descriptions of drill, may have after all only been trying to 'contain' the excessive military zeal of those earlier military theorists upon whose work Marlowe drew.

Yet even the exaggerated Tamburlaine is susceptible to the 'regressive' power of an alternative discourse of the 'effeminate and faint'. However precise his theory and however determined his action on the battlefield, disciplining his men, murdering the foe and humiliating his prisoners, a nagging doubt remains. As Alan Shepard has noted:

Off the battlefield . . . Tamburlaine is not always the stalwart general, but is sometimes troubled about the power of speech to shape – or better yet, to warp – his martial persona. We see this most acutely in his panegyric to Zenocrate that follows upon the slaughter of the virgins near the end of Part One. His songful praise is far from humble ablution, and seems to hold no hint of self-recrimination, nor threat to his masculinity. Yet he stops himself midway through it:

But how unseemly is it for my sex,
My discipline of arms and chivalry,
My nature, and the terror of my name,
To harbour thoughts effeminate and faint!
                                    (V.i.174–7)[4]

Shepard's *Marlowe's Soldiers: Rhetorics of Masculinity in the Age of Armada* has addressed the representation of warfare in Marlowe's works with a thoroughness that would be hard to emulate. He believes that Marlowe responded to the war fever of Elizabethan London with a range of plays that offered audiences 'a far more complex experience of that war fever than any other contemporary English playwright, Shakespeare included'.[5] His conclusion is worth quoting in full because it presents an inviting link to the plays I shall come to in the remaining part of this study:

Marlowe made it all but impossible to leave a performance of one of his plays fully convinced that soldiers and the warlords who employ them do in fact deserve the absolute epistemic control they were bidding for in the midst of the Armada scares in a London at war. Paradoxically, his plays suggest, state security may in fact actually be endangered by soldiers.

When they buy into the rhetoric of 'epic masculinity,' a code of identity requiring them to eliminate all difference from their local surroundings and from their own characters, soldiers 'protect' the state in ways that may be fatal – to the civilians who cross them and to the state they are aiming to protect.[6]

One way of endorsing Shepard's view of the singularity of Marlowe's treatment of the relationship between early modern military theory, the impact of war on the citizens of London and the potential the theatre had to interrogate this 'war fever' is to investigate alternative responses to war. A range of plays complements the sceptical views on warfare that can be read in interpretations of the work of Shakespeare and Marlowe. Yet these other plays go beyond mere scepticism by celebrating distinctly non-military ways of valuing the world that was emerging during the troubled transition from the medieval to the modern.

A strand of unease about militarism as a code of behaviour for the state or the individual can be found in much earlier English texts. The mid-fourteenth-century *Wynnere and Wastoure* seems radical in its discussion of militarised hierarchies and imposition of taxation upon a merchant class reluctant to finance Edward III's French wars.[7] I am also thinking here of the satirical Middle English *Alliterative Morte Arthure*, a representation of war, myth of nation and chivalry that is much more critical of their tenets than Malory and Caxton's patriotic *Le Morte d'Arthur* of 1485.[8] And Chaucer's *Knight's Tale*, or rather the knight that tells it, has been read controversially as an exposé of a redundant chivalric order. Editors, critics and historians have claimed that such texts stand outside the orthodox traditions of chivalric romance, undermining its values and establishing a critique of the excesses of war.[9]

Before turning to the dramatic texts that may be said both to perpetuate the scepticism of these older ones, but also to include visions of non-military social organisation, I want first to take some account of a contemporaneous work of prose. Thomas Deloney's *The Gentle Craft* was written in about 1596, between Shakespeare's *Richard III* and *Henry V*, and for a number of reasons appears as a significant text in terms of its presentation of war and nation.[10] First, there is such an abrupt discontinuity between the treatment of war in this text and the plays dealt with so far that it can be seen as a portal into the alternative dramatic worlds which actively celebrate a refusal of war. It is in itself the source of a particular play, Thomas Dekker's *The Shoemaker's Holiday* of 1599, but it also very clearly captures the anti-war themes found in many other examples of contemporary drama.[11] It is worth addressing here because it can be seen to be consolidating these themes in a vivid and radical way, almost as a compendium of the concerns Londoners had for the impact of war upon their lives.

Secondly, as we shall see, Deloney's celebration of the long 'history' of shoemakers and their craft refashions the hierarchical chivalric formula underpinning the myths and legends of courtly literature, opening an ideological space for his subsequent privileging of the lives of ordinary people in the London of Henry VI. Here, if anywhere in the prose writing of the Elizabethan and early Stuart period, is to be found an account, however romanticised, of the detail of the way that life was lived for certain groups of Londoners. The plays that I shall address in the next chapter often respond to a similarly democratic impulse, but the clarity of the vision in *The Gentle Craft* is itself worthy of analysis. Shakespeare and Marlowe produced plays that principally featured the nobility, introducing commoners, sometimes as figures of fun, but almost always as in some way subservient to their masters and mistresses, even if modern critics and audiences take an egalitarian approach to this hierarchy. Like the plays, *The Gentle Craft* is a work of fiction, but there is a firm sense of realism that is convincing enough to suggest that this is a fairly authentic encounter with long-dead Londoners, working through their aspirations and setbacks, their petty grievances and their huge desires. Part of this effect is due to the strong evocation of place. Deloney's London was, of course, perhaps the most important centre in Europe for the publication, printing, distribution and consumption of the written word: military treatises, pamphlets and prose works like *The Gentle Craft* itself. It is therefore unsurprising that the city itself is the subject of much of what is being written, and that this writing is aligned to a theatre that both complements and compliments these other forms. In *The Gentle Craft*, London, as in many of the contemporary plays, is captured in a particular period of its evolution that is coming to a close as Deloney is writing. It is not that the text is simply nostalgic about a passing London, and still less is it an evocation of a kind of fading 'Merrie England', as the constant references to warfare and poverty demonstrate. Rather, it seems to be the product of a desire somehow to arrest and record places and people – and the stories that unite them – in the face of the accelerating change and the warlike climate that characterised the last years of Tudor England.

In order to do this, Deloney conjures an optimism and fortitude in the circles of the craftworkers he describes which further underline the appeal of the text and justify its examination in juxtaposition with the plays. It is hard to quantify, but an argument in favour of *The Gentle Craft* can surely be made on aesthetic grounds that relate to its sheer optimism about the potential human beings have to live in communities and eschew warfare. Along with all its socio-political insight, and its openness to students of class and commerce, gender and geography, this is a text that also invites investigation because of its consistent good humour, constant vitality and an elaborate celebration of the human spirit. It is worth repeating that this is not an idealised world, but one where the spirit seems to have to remain optimistic since despair, destitution and danger are never far away – caused not least by preparations for, or the outcome of, war. *The Gentle Craft* is also significant because of the approach it takes to ideas of nation. The plays of Shakespeare and Marlowe foreground matters of national and racial difference, although not necessarily in a racist or nationalist way: Deloney positively emphasises inclusive and multi-ethnic social orders based on craft and community. Given that this positive assertion of community is accompanied by references to international warfare, the text invites a glimpse of toleration and integration which stands in opposition to the xenophobia that characterised the work of the military theorists.

Lastly, *The Gentle Craft* deserves its place in a study that contrasts prose and drama because in a sense it stands between the two. Just as military prose, and even Erasmus's writing, often contained 'dialogues' conducted in specified locations, teasing out argument and counter-argument, Deloney's text is characterised by the generous space given in the text to speech. This in itself may have drawn it to the attention of the playwright Dekker. *The Gentle Craft* may have been seen by some as an early form of novel, but at times it looks more like a script. It is as if Delony wrote with a popular readership in mind, but felt the compelling influence of the playhouse and its possibilities.

THE GENTLE CRAFT

Deloney left the first two parts of what was almost certainly planned as a trilogy. In the first he outlines the mythical origins of the shoemaker's trade, recounting the legend of Hugh and Winifred, patron saints of shoemaking. He then tells the story of the shoemaking princes Crispine and Crispianus and finally, moving from legend to 'history', describes the spectacular rise of Simon Eyre to Lord Mayor of London, including along the way numerous romantic intrigues and subplots set in and around Eyre's expanding household. A significant governing theme is the belief in the essential nobility of the shoemaker. In folklore a shoemaker is likely to be an exiled prince necessarily disguised due to an earlier misfortune. In history he proves an individual of high moral integrity and worth, yet also canny and capable of the occasional sleight of hand in his ambitious social and business dealings.

The second part introduces new figures and plots, all more or less connected to the shoemaking craft. Deloney recounts the story of Richard Casteler and his complex life in pursuit of love for himself and as an object of desire for others. Chapters V–VII of Part II describe the household of the successful cobbler Master Peachey. His qualities are expressed locally by his bravery in confronting two bullying captains who show contempt for his trade. Abroad, he shows his loyalty and commitment by sending a troop of men to defend the Isle of Wight against the encroaching French who have shown disdain for Peachey's king and country. These episodes are evidence of what might be seen as a significant strand in the narratives: the influence of warfare upon the lives of ordinary citizens of Deloney's world. Thus, there is humour, but it is humour in the face of an understated, yet seemingly very present threat to individual and community well-being. There is the external threat to the peaceful islanders from the French, but also the internal threat from unrestrained professional military men. Deloney's text describes his vision of the London of Henry VI, but as with the staged histories of Shakespeare and his contemporaries, there is a clear resonance of the concerns of the present, including the Elizabethan preoccupation with war. *The Gentle Craft* invites its readers to contemplate the idea that in its fictional world conflict is never far away. Although there is a sense of ambivalence towards war, as there is in the theatre of Shakespeare and other contemporary dramatists, the text portrays war's consequences as a dreadful intrusion into the text's system of values, threatening the dominant atmosphere of geniality.

GENRE, CLASS AND COMMUNITY

The various interweaving stories that make up *The Gentle Craft* are evidence of the rich mythology and folklore that underpinned the craft of shoemaking. Other trades – especially weaving – had similar traditions about their origins and values, some of which have survived to the present day as part of the heritage of craftsmen and crafts-women at work in manufacturing. In Deloney's time these elements gave each trade an historical resonance, equivalent, say, to the narratives of aristocratic romance, and yet they also had a topical vitality. It might be said that the health and stability of a particular trade could be measured by the credibility of its folklore and how widely it was understood and transmitted within the community of a particular trade's practitioners.

In terms of genre, critics have seen texts such as *The Gentle Craft* as reflecting a largely metropolitan change in taste, readership and appeal that signalled the end of Elizabethan 'late medieval' romance and pointed ahead to the early novel form of the late seventeenth and early eighteenth centuries. Indeed *The Gentle Craft* is commonly seen as evidence of an expanding readership's weariness with the tradition of courtly romance exemplified by the work of Edmund Spenser, John Lyly and Philip Sidney. Public taste, sometimes described as 'middle-class', was switching to pamphlets about London street life or popular culture in general by writers such as Nashe, Greene and Dekker. Deloney combined features of this kind of writing with the earlier romantic tradition so that 'knights' became artisans and their heroic deeds became more realistic. James Ruoff has described this phenomenon thus:

> Deloney retained much of the polyphonic narration and vagarious events and characterizations still attractive about the courtly romances, but he made ingenious improvisations on the old values by glorifying the craft of shoemaker or weaver as thoroughly as Sidney and Spenser had apotheo-sized true courtesy. Deloney turned the knights and ladies of the courtly romances into fun-loving artisans and lively wenches, and placed them in the familiar environs of Berkshire, Norwich, or London rather than in Fairyland or Mauritania.[12]

Critical debate over this work has for a long time centred on issues of class identity and mobility, as befits a society where these issues were to the fore. Deloney's texts rest on popular unifying ideological motifs, such as anti-Catholicism and nationalism, and seem on the surface to support an organic view of the social formation in which artisans can mix with royalty and 'get by' (despite social inequalities) by dint of quick-wittedness and hard work. However, there are severe tensions in the social world of *The Gentle Craft* just as there are in *The Shoemaker's Holiday*. These texts remain a rich source of evidence for the social diversity of a society that is rapidly becoming urban and class-conscious. Matters of identity are to the fore in terms of gender, class and status, and the issue of warfare in these texts is an example of how they tend to foreground discontinuity and alienation in the social structure, at the same time as they promote social cohesion and consensus.

Three themes emerge in *The Gentle Craft* that are indicative of changing patterns within the social environment from which the text emerged. These are important in terms of the way that Deloney fashions his evocation of the classical/mythical stories of early shoemakers, and even more important with respect to his 'history' of episodes and characters from the more recent past. The first of these is the way that Deloney acknowledges the 'international' social composition of the communities described in the stories and therefore, by implication, of the wider social world of contemporary London. Second is the emphasis given to social standing and mobility, and the recognition that history is altering the status of the retreating chivalric aristocracy and facilitating the emergence of a new class. Third is the presence of war as a backdrop to the mythical and 'historical' perspectives on shoemaking. War, or talk of war, had a part to play in conditioning the social milieu of the Londoners and others for whom Deloney produced his work, making the fictional text intelligible in the light of their own experiences and expectations. It is partly the way that these issues are presented to the reader through a mixture of genres that gives *The Gentle Craft* its curious potential for an unsettling of an idealised or romanticised vision of the chivalric past. Most evident is the way that the text is characterised by the formal mixing of prose and song. The songs perform a variety of functions in the text and are often very funny. Yet on occasion the humour is juxtaposed with what seem more serious debates about the issues to hand.

An example of this is the bawdy song about marriage in Chapter VII of Part I. Crispine sings of marriage, but only in the poignant context of the loss of his brother, pressed into the wars in Gaul. His song is to be followed by 'a deep discourse of the matter' (marriage and sexuality) between Crispine and a journeyman which Deloney does not recount as 'it appertaines not to our matter', leaving it open to the reader's imagination. Indeed, a distinctive formal pattern applies to many of the narratives in *The Gentle Craft* overall that can be said to operate by means of a sudden gathering together or closing off of the strands of a particular story in a short and often abrupt ending. In some respects this pattern has something in common with the style of the joke: a long story is rounded off with a quick punch-line marking the end of the particular episode and building an expectation in the reader of something quite different in the next section. Yet the reader is never certain whether the episode will end joyously – or at least hopefully – or in sudden tragedy; but where it is tragedy, the cause is usually war.

This generic pattern is established early on in Part I with the long story of Hugh and Winifred that ends in Chapter III with their graphic and poignant deaths. The romantic genre expected in an account of such noble protagonists gives way to a sharp realism in the disturbing treatment of their physical remains, leaving only their good names to posterity as the patron saints of shoemaking. There is something quite shocking in this sudden closure and switch of styles. Yet both stylistically and thematically the next chapter goes some way to resolving the tension of this discontinuity by emphasising realism and, as a microcosm of the text overall, privileging the crude but durable culture of the shoemaker. Stealing away Hugh's bones, and characteristically debating their possible function in a series of jokes, the chapter ends with a critical motif of shoemaking culture, the idea of the shoemaker's tools as 'Saint Hugh's bones'. This is carefully set against the theme of war which is to be central to the new narrative of the legend of Crispine and Crispianus, and the one that later threads through the 'history' narratives that conclude the first part and form the substance of the second:

> And it shall be concluded that what Journey-man soever he be hereafter, that cannot handle the Sword and Buckler, his Long Sword, or a Quarter staffe, sound the Trumpet, or play upon the Flute and beare his part in a three mans Song: and readily reckon up his Toole in Rime; except he have born Colours in the field, being a Lieutenant, a Sergeant or Corporall, shall forfeit and pay a pottle of wine, or be counted for a colt: to which they answered all viva voce Content, content, and then after many merry Songs, they departed. And never after did they travell without these tools on their backs: which ever since were called Saint Hughes bones.[13]

The comment on professional soldiering is interesting, especially in view of what is to come in the later story of the shoemakers' antipathy to the invasion of their community by military men. These switches in style and mood may not be surprising if we see *The Gentle Craft* as an example of a form that is emerging against (and informing as a source) the attendant dramatic writing of the period. Deloney, it might be said, had an eye to satirising the romances of an earlier period, but at the same time a committed vision of the serious aspects of nation, class and warfare in his own times. He seems to have sought to engage his readers by distilling a wide range of styles, which would appeal through a sense of contrast and counterpoint.

NATION AND IDENTITY

The uncertainties in the political and social environment from which *The Gentle Craft* emerged were numerous and complex: war and food shortages dominated the contemporary London scene and both find their way into Deloney's account of an earlier London. As we have seen, despite the successful repulsion of the Spanish Armada in 1588, Deloney's England was awash with rumours of renewed incursions, new enemies, foreign spies, Catholic plots and all manner of potentially destabilising phenomena. And all this was set against the realisation that there was little to defend the relatively new Protestant state, in the form of a standing army or a police force, from its internal and external enemies.

Deloney's earlier work casts him as an influential polemicist in this sea of uncertainties, with his broadsides against Catholicism, his invective against the Spanish and his complaints about foreign workers.[14] He seems to have been something of a campaigner for the dispossessed and those falling victim to the food shortages that were a recurrent feature of both urban and rural life in the closing years of Elizabeth's reign. These were mostly the result of failures in the harvest, especially in 1596 when Deloney was probably writing *The Gentle Craft*, but it was claimed in some quarters that their impact was aggravated by an influx of foreigners adding to the number of mouths to feed. Such alarmist thinking was current in the time of Simon Eyre as much as it was in the last decade of the sixteenth century. Deloney, thinking historically or topically, could not have failed to have been sensitive to the presence in London and elsewhere of representatives of foreign societies and cultures. There is a sustained awareness in the text of the 'otherness' of newly arrived settlers from abroad, but it is perhaps surprising to find that although there are exceptional moments, *The Gentle Craft* offers more of a celebration of cultural difference than an invective against immigrants. Foreigners are often central to the plots of the various stories, and whilst their fortunes are mixed and their speech and social skills caricatured, notably in the case of Haunce the Dutchman and John the Frenchman, they are rarely portrayed as being more deserving of such treatment than indigenous figures in the eclectic mix that inhabits the collection of stories overall. The worlds of *The Gentle Craft* reveal a sympathetic awareness of the people of other lands and their customs. The reader can find the 'Dutch Maiden' of Part I, Chapter III, or the 'Egyptian woman' of Part II, Chapter IX, 'that at Black-wall was in travell with child, and had such hard labour, that she was much lamented among all the wives that dwelt thereabout'.[15] In these episodes and others, cultural differences, in the form of national and religious identities, are eventually overridden by the superior values of the community of shoemakers. The contrast with Deloney's early compositions and with the tenor of the military texts is significant. It seems that Deloney had a change of heart with respect to his opinion of foreigners, just as the military texts became more and more affirmative about ideals of nation and state.

RANK AND ECONOMY

Clearly Deloney was aware of the impact of the economic instability of the times about which he wrote and the time in which he lived. *The Gentle Craft* records facets of economic exchange such as conditions of employment, investment and mercantile adventure – all of which speak of the advances made by certain elements in the evolving social formation of the 1590s. Set against this, the wanderings of the various dispossessed and masterless figures in the text, however cheerful, seem all too typical of the grim realities that many endured. Moreover, when there is talk of war there is a hint of the kind of colonial competition that is to characterise succeeding centuries. Indeed, when the 'Sea Captaines' Stuteley and Strangwidge appear in Chapter V of Part II, they are 'bound to sea on a gallant voyage, wherein the King hath no small venture' during which they 'would be seeking out the Coast of Florida'.[16]

Deloney certainly acknowledges the extraordinary social advance that can result from certain kinds of astute commerce. Yet he is at pains, in both his folk history of shoemaking and his realisation of the values attached to the art of shoemaking in the sixteenth century, to celebrate something more than the potential of the individual and an ideology of enterprise. Time and again in *The Gentle Craft* an emphasis is placed on tradition rather than change, and continuity rather than innovation. Above all, the narratives show that shoemakers prosper, and best demonstrate their noble qualities, when they act collectively as part of a specific community. This is not to say that

Deloney wants to return to a lost world of medieval values, rather that he is aware of the tensions between the behaviour of individuals who recognise themselves as part of a community of values and those who step outside that community. David Morrow has noted that:

> Few if any Elizabethan authors have been so commonly identified with a rising entrepreneurial spirit and with the material interests of the bourgeoisie. . . . Concomitantly under-emphasized, overlooked, or treated as merely mystificatory has been Deloney's dependence upon, and celebration of, moral economy, or communal ideology, which, much evidence suggests, made up a key component of the discursive field within which Deloney produced and others consumed his fictions.[17]

Furthermore, Deloney's shoemakers are 'ennobled' (in the sense that they belong to the folk history of shoemaking that denotes the craftsman as 'gentle') by the physicality of the work itself rather than the abstract accumulation of wealth. Indeed, the sense of community is defined to a large degree by a sense of the physical fitness of its members, made strong by their work and judged against competing indices of masculinity derived from elsewhere in the wider social formation.

MAKING WAR VERSUS MAKING SHOES

As we have seen, the military writing of the period helped establish a polarity between military prowess, best realised in overseas campaigns (which had the added benefit of defining nationhood at home) and a non-military quietude exemplified by those men who preferred domesticity. Such 'non-men' were considered weak because of their preference for hearth and home, their preoccupation with their crafts and trades, and their overwhelming desire for the company of women. In this context, *The Gentle Craft* can be seen as a text that radically opposes the argument for military discipline and a formal army that was to gather pace over the course of the seventeenth and eighteenth centuries. In so far as the standing army became a central component of the modern state, this invites modern readers to view Deloney's implied critique of late sixteenth-century militarism as significant indeed. *The Gentle Craft* is full of allusions to war and its consequences. In the story of Crispine, Crispianus and Ursula, Deloney describes the fighting in considerable detail, contrasting its brutality with the tenderness of Ursula's love for Crispine, and comparing the situations and desires of the brother who is pressed into war abroad with the one who pursues love at home. Crispianus makes a fine soldier, of course, but the contrast between the soldier and the lover (and the soldier and the shoemaker) is established as an important theme for *The Gentle Craft* in general.

It is a theme that gains importance as the story gathers pace and becomes more 'historical', leaving behind the early legends about shoemaking. In Chapter III of Part II at the end of the long story of Richard Casteler, Long Meg and 'Gillian of the George', war suddenly enters like a cold draught. The affectionate portrayal of these figures, so firmly rooted in their experiences of London, and with such resonant and persuasive voices, distinguishes this as one of the text's most elaborate and successful narratives. The evocation of place and custom, and the gossip, jokes, trickery and songs, deliver this tale of lost desire and frustrated sexuality at a consistent and measured pace; and yet, as with many of narratives in *The Gentle Craft*, the dénouement is sudden and unexpected. In the value systems of the text overall, Gillian, like the more successful shoemakers, is reconciled to the favoured discourse of domesticity and labour. Meg, on the other hand, is brought down by domesticity's mirror image, and the narrative ends for her with the excesses determined by war:

> Thus Margaret in a melancholy humor went her waies, and in short time after she forsooke Westminster, and attended on the Kings army to Bullen, and while the siege lasted, became a landresse to the Camp, and never after did she set store by her selfe, but became common to the call of every man, till such time as all youthfull delights was banished by old age, and in the end she left her life in Islington, being very penitent for all her former offences.
>
> Gillian in the end was well married, and became a very good housekeeper, living in honest name and fame till her dying day.[18]

War comes into these characters' world as an indiscriminate agent of destruction. So complete and sudden is Meg's fate that its resonance may carry over into the next chapter in which Robin and his fellows sing before the king of the siege of Bullen. In the song Bullen is seen as a 'Lady of most high renowne' and the king as determined to 'obtaine' her 'Maiden-head'.[19] The fusing of sexual violation with military prowess is not uncommon in early modern discourse and this seems like a precursor to Luke Gernon's erotic vision of colonialism referred to at the end of Chapter 4 above. The contrast between the open but innocent desires of Meg, Gillian's former London life and this formalised metaphor of military success as rape is complete. The fact that the account is sung before the king in a public place (and to great acclaim and reward) is an early example of how foreign wars can be turned into domestic capital. The account of the siege recalls, and possibly demystifies, that of Henry V at Harfleur, and the general sense of myth-making here casts new light on the use of the story of Agincourt in Tudor prose histories and in the theatre. Part II of *The Gentle Craft* ends with a more localised form of myth-making as Tom Drum, with his 'old cogging humor', produces a fictional account of his deeds of war in Scotland:

> An hundred merry feates more did he, which in this place is too much to be set downe. For afterward Tom Drum comming from the winning of Mustleborow, came to dwell with them, where he discoursed all his adventures in the wars: and according to his old cogging humor, attributed other mens deeds to himselfe, for (quoth he) it was I that killed the first Scot in the battell, yet I was content to give the honour thereof to Sir Michaell Musgrave, notwithstanding (quoth he) all men knowes that this hand of mine kild Tom Trotter, that terrible traytor, which in despite of us, kept the Castell so long, and at last as he cowardly forsooke it, and secretly sought to flye, with this blade of mine I broacht him like a roasting pigge. Moreover, Parson Ribble had never made himselfe so famous but by my meanes. These were his daily vaunts, till his lies were so manifest that hee could no longer stand in them.[20]

To an Elizabethan readership attuned to the phenomenon of soldiers, both genuine and counterfeit, begging in the streets of London, Deloney's text, with its characteristic mix of humour and social comment, must have seemed highly topical in terms of this aspect of the actual consequences of war.

The military prose of the period lamented the neglect of soldiers (advocating both sufficient training in readiness for war and their post-battle rehabilitation), but *The Gentle Craft* seems to favour codes of masculinity and domesticity that are morally superior to war in the first place. Deloney points to this opposition most clearly in the story of Master Peachey in Chapter V of Part II. Having appeared at the court with his liveried household of shoemakers, Peachey is challenged by the 'gallant Sea Captaines' Stuteley and Strangwidge, who resent what they perceive as a civilian undermining of the authority they claim as military men. The contest between the community of shoemakers and these two adventurers is partly about hierarchy, power and privilege. As sea captains, Stuteley and Strangwidge are symbolic of the Elizabethans' cultivation of a heroic masculinity represented by Drake, Raleigh and the real Thomas Stukeley. David Morrow notes that:

> Stukeley's celebrity endured beyond his death in 1578, in oral and written forms, including Holinshed, [George] Peele's *The Battle of Alcazar* [c. 1589] and the anonymous *The Famous History of Captain Thomas Stukeley*. The picture of Stukeley that emerges from these representations is an ambiguous one. He is courageous and adventurous, but also wholly individualistic, a Catholic double agent whose desire in life – as he reportedly told the Queen herself – was to be a king.[21]

These military figures from Elizabethan England, introduced into a story of the London of Henry VI, must surely have been resonant with the potential for ambiguities, or rather contradictions, that can be detected in the contemporary military writing. The captains are professional – bound for Florida on behalf of the king, we are told – with fine reputations at court and abroad. The real Thomas Stukeley was strong, his body hardened by combat, a good leader of men who respected him, his mind attuned to the disciplines of war.[22] Doubtless he could turn his hand to the science and skills that could be gleaned from contemporary manuals. Yet he also wanted to be a king – subject only to his own autonomous disciplines. In Deloney's tale, written for a London full of soldiers and talk of war, the fact that the military character has to be enacted, and its licence continually demonstrated, reveals its artificiality – nowhere more so than when it is seen in contrast to the values of the alternative corps of the shoemakers.

The gallant Stuteley and Strangwidge parade around London looking to impose their presence and impress the civilian population: in particular they are searching for Peachey and his men. Intruding into the very workplace of the shoemakers, they first suffer a firm rebuff for their arrogance and rudeness, and when the conflict descends into violence, are harried by shoemakers throughout the streets of London:

> Now a plague on them (quoth Stuteley) shall we never be in quiet for these quoystrels? Never were we so ferrited before, swownes we can no sooner look into the streets, but these shoomakers have us by the eares: a pox on it that ever we medled with the rascals: sblood they be as unluckie to be met, as a Hare on a jorney, or a sergeant on a Sunday morning, for ever one mischiefe or other followes it. Captaine Strangwidge (quoth he) there is no other shift but to seek their friendship, otherwise we are in danger every houre to be maimed, therefore to keep our lims sound against we go to Sea, tis best to finde meanes to quiet this grudge.

> Then (said Strangwidge) it were good to do so, if a man knew how: but you may be sure they will not easily be intreated, seeing we have so mightily abused them in speech.
>
> Thus they cast in their mindes divers times by what meanes they might be reconciled: and albeit they sent divers of their friends unto Master Peachie and his men, yet they would not yeeld, nor give consent to be appeased, nor to put up such wrong as they had received without further revenge: so that the Captaines were at length constrained to make sute to the Duke of Suffolk to take up the matter: who most honorably performed their request: and so the grudge ended betwixt them, to the great credit of Master Peachie, and all his men.[23]

The shoemakers, with their love of hearth and home, their dedication to their crafts and trades, and their initial attempts to placate the captains, may have been redolent of the 'non-men' scorned in the military texts as the antitheses of the ideal of masculinity associated with the soldier. Here, though, despite their 'soft' trade, cultivation of community and celebration of work, the shoemakers show that, under threat, they are, well, as tough as old boots. They and their craft are called 'gentle' because of their ethics and inherent 'nobility', not because they are necessarily pacifists. The episode throws into relief the idea that military individualism and its masculine codes are superior to the collective authority of the civilian craftsmen who, though initially restrained, are equal to the ascendant military discourse. As John Simons has noted, 'the violence of Peachey's world is seen in terms of the group rather than through the individual status that the captains afford themselves. It is the class, not the individual that is the hero'.[24]

PROSE TO PLAY

Three elements of *The Shoemaker's Holiday* are derived from *The Gentle Craft*. The first is the general celebration of the craft of shoemaking, including the legend of St Hugh. More directly appropriated are the stories of Crispine and Crispianus. And then there is the central narrative concerning Simon Eyre. The relationship between *The Shoemaker's Holiday* and its source is a subtle and clever one. R. L. Smallwood and Stanley Wells have noted in their edition of the play that:

> Dekker uses the Eyre story only as the central anchor to which he attaches the two stories of the contrasted pairs of lovers, Lacy and Rose, and Ralph and Jane. The interdependence of these parts is made possible by an amalgamation of the roles of Eyre and his wife with those of the shoemaker

and his wife in the Crispine–Crispianus tale, and by the intervention of a rival wooer in both love-plots, whose interference keeps the tension alive, thus postponing, and making more welcome, the happy ending.[25]

The act of transferring material from *The Gentle Craft* to the stage is one of considerable transformation: the theatre opens up the subject matter and introduces new tensions. But there is also the influence of earlier plays in the busy, competitive world of the contemporary stage. *The Shoemaker's Holiday* came not long after Shakespeare's *Henry V*, so raising questions of association in terms of the king at the end of the play: it is Henry VI of Eyre's time, but simultaneously the ideologically and symbolically important Henry V of Agincourt.

How happy the ending of *The Shoemaker's Holiday* is is an open question, precisely because of the suggestiveness of this possible parallel. In the lovers' story all is well, and as in *The Gentle Craft*, we hear of Simon Eyre's plans to build Leadenhall, the centre for the leather trade for which Elizabethans remembered him.[26] It is Shrove Tuesday, a day of celebration established for the apprentices of London as Eyre promised it would be if he ever became Lord Mayor. The king happily accepts Eyre's invitation to share his banquet, prompting critical receptions of the play as an affirmation of a dissolving of class hierarchies. Yet the threat and consequences of warfare were woven into various episodes of *The Gentle Craft*, threatening individuals and, in the story of Peachey and the two captains, invading the shoemakers' overall community. Similarly, as Smallwood and Wells remind us throughout their Introduction, *The Shoemaker's Holiday* is edged by talk of war and especially its intrusions into the lives of the poor. Most notably Ralph Damport, one of Simon Eyre's journeyman shoemakers, finds it impossible to avoid war due to his poverty and returns (genuinely) wounded from France. War wastes the lives of the poor, while the rich can avoid it: meanwhile it continues to define and propagate the reputation of kings.

The concluding scene, celebratory as is, assuring the reputation of the 'gentle craft' of shoemaking and reaffirming for the play's audience Eyre's reputation as a hero of a rising class of Londoners, nonetheless reintroduces the war theme in a deliberate and provocative way. Eyre is keen to speak to Henry of Leadenhall and shroving but the king is equally anxious to speak of furthering the campaign in France:

With all the old troop which there we keep in pay
We will incorporate a new supply.

Before one summer more pass o'er my head,
France shall repent England was injurèd.
(XXI.139–42)

It seems that Henry might have had his eye on the company of shoemakers, who now arrive on the scene, as potentially part of his 'new
supply' for the French wars. Indeed, Eyre describes the group as 'all
gentlemen of the Gentle Craft, true Trojans, courageous cordwainers'
(146–7), ironically using the term 'Trojan' in the sense of 'work like
a Trojan' (as he does in IV.121), rather than in a martial sense. It is
almost as though he is reading the king's mind, and he hastens to
return to the business of business by adding:

[*To the King*] They are all beggars,
my liege, all for themselves; and I for them all on both
my kness do entreat that for the honour of poor Simon
Eyre and the good of his brethren, these mad knaves,
Your Grace would vouchsafe some privilege to my new
Leaden Hall, that it may be lawful for us to buy and sell
Leather there two days a week.
(XXI.153–9)

Henry agrees and the merriment continues, but one is left feeling at
the very end of the play that this is but a temporary suspension of the
real business of the City of London, which for Henry lies abroad in
the battle against the French:

Eyre, I will taste of thy banquet, and will say
I have not met more pleasure on a day.
Friends of the Gentle Craft, thanks to you all.
Thanks, my kind Lady Mayoress, for our cheer.
Come, lords, a while let's revel it at home.
When all our sports and banquetings are done,
Wars must right wrongs which Frenchmen have begun.
(XXI.190–6)

According to Smallwood and Wells, early editions of *The Gentle
Craft* were 'read out of existence by the popular audience to which
they were directed' and this comment hints at the popularity of
this kind of writing.[27] And if *The Gentle Craft* was popular in its
time, so was *The Shoemaker's Holiday*, along with a host of other
plays that offer a marked contrast with those of Shakespeare and
Marlowe in terms of how they deal with war. They present alternative paradigms of peaceful human co-existence, or recommend a
dependence on God's will to bring peace, or simply satirise the

military imperative that took men and women from the streets of London to die or be maimed abroad. Together, they constitute at least a refusal of the military codes and operations of the military theorists and in some ways they sought to establish opposing traditions and sets of values.

It may be that it was due to the popularity of *The Gentle Craft* and the *Shoemaker's Holiday* that Saint Crispin's Day became a holiday for London shoemakers in the seventeenth century, as it had been in effect for their colleagues in parts of Kent.[28] Although it was abrogated at the Reformation, the feast of Crispianus was restored in 1561, probably in part because of the association with Agincourt. For Elizabethan theatre audiences the king's prediction in Shakespeare's *Henry V* had been realised in a material way:

> This story shall the good man teach his son,
> And Crispin Crispian shall ne'er go by
> From this day to the ending of the world
> But we in it shall be rememberèd,
> We few, we happy few, we band of brothers.
> For he today that sheds his blood with me
> Shall be my brother; be he ne'er so vile,
> This day shall gentle his condition.
> And gentlemen in England now abed
> Shall think themselves accursed they were not here,
> And hold their manhoods cheap awhiles any speaks
> That fought with us upon Saint Crispin's day.
>
> (IV.iii.56–67)

What is interesting, and even symbolic in view of the work of Deloney and Dekker, is the duality in the meaning of 25 October. The tension at the end of Dekker's play is reproduced in a contest for the meaning of the feast. On the one hand, it belongs to a chain of significance with links stretching back to Henry's victory in France and all that it implies: God and nation, war and manhood – and speeches and images that, mostly due to Shakespeare, have endued to the present. Alternatively, the date conjures up the largely peaceful community of shoemakers: patriotic but not exclusive, and endlessly desirous of work, wine and each other's company.[29] That the first submerged the second set of associations for Saint Crispin does not mean that the shoemakers' values have entirely disappeared; they remain, as it were, as an undercurrent. It is simply that Henry V, just as when he was up against the French majority at Agincourt, seemed the more inspired leader in the field of ideas.

Notes

1. Paul Ive (1589), *The Practise of Fortification, Wherein is shewed the manner of Fortifying all sorts of situations*, London. See P. H. Kocher (1942), 'Marlowe's Art of War', *Studies in Philology*, Vol. XXXIX, 207–25; and Nina Taunton (2001), *1590's Drama and Militarism*, Burlington, VT and Aldershot: Ashgate, pp. 58–9.
2. Thomas Smith (1600), *The Arte of Gunnerie*, London, sigs. Aii. R–v.
3. The sources are Petrus Perodinus (1553), *Magni Tamerlanis Scytharum Imperatories Vita*, London; and Thomas Fortescue (1571) *The Forest*, a translation of Pedro Mexia's *Silva de Varia, Leccion*, London, neither of which has much to say about military discipline or strategy.
4. Alan Shepard (2002), *Marlowe's Soldiers: Rhetorics of Masculinity in the Age of the Armada*, Burlington, VT and Aldershot: Ashgate, p. 37.
5. Ibid., p. 218.
6. Ibid., p. 219.
7. See Stephanie Trigg (ed.) (1990), *Wynnere and Wastoure*, Oxford: Oxford University Press.
8. Anon., *The Alliterative Morte Arthure* (1983), ed. Valerie Krisna, Lanham, MD: University Press of America; Sir Thomas Malory, *Caxton's Malory* (1983), ed. James W. Spisak, 2 vols, Berkeley and Los Angeles, CA: University of California Press; Sir Thomas Malory (1998) *Le Morte Darthur: The Winchester Manuscript* (1998), ed. Helen Cooper, Oxford: Oxford University Press.
9. See Thomas Bestul (1974), *Satire and Allergory in Wynnere and Wastoure*, Lincoln, NB: University of Nebraska Press; Juliet Vale (1982), *Edward III and Chivalry: Chivalric Society and its Context 1270–1350*, Bury St Edmunds: Boydell Press. It was pleasing to note Nick de Somogyi (1998), *Shakespeare's Theatre of War*, Burlington, VT and Aldershot: Ashgate, p. 7 remarking on the seriousness of a book dismissed by some scholars: Terry Jones (1980), *Chaucer's Knight: the Portrait of a Medieval Mercenary*, 2nd rev. edition, London: Methuen.
10. *The Gentle Craft* was published in 1597 (Part I) and 1598 (Part II), although there is much speculation over the accuracy of these dates. Most modern editions have been based on surviving seventeenth-century versions: a single copy of 1627 (Part I) held by the University of Sheffield and two copies of 1639 (Part II) held in the British Library and the Bodleian Library in Oxford. The provenance of an earlier edition (dated 1599 and held by the Biblioteka Gadańska in Poland) is uncertain, but it is of immense interest because it includes several additional pages and indicates that the author intended to produce a third part. I have included these additions in my own edition of the text: Thomas Deloney [1597/8] (2007), *The Gentle Craft*, ed. Simon Barker, Burlington, Vermont and Aldershot: Ashgate. Quotations are from this edition.

11. Thomas Dekker, *The Shoemaker's Holiday* [1599] (1999), ed. R. L. Smallwood and Stanley Wells, Manchester: Manchester University Press. Quotations are from this edition, which is arranged into scenes but has no act divisions.
12. James E. Ruoff (1975), *Macmillan's Handbook of Elizabethan and Stuart Literature*, London and Basingstoke: Macmillan, p. 107.
13. Deloney, *The Gentle Craft*, pp. 21–2.
14. See Ian W. Archer, Anthony Fletcher, John Guy and John Morrill (1991), *The Pursuit of Stability: Social Relations in Elizabethan London*, Cambridge: Cambridge University Press; David J. Morrow (2006), 'The Entrepreneurial Spirit and "The Life of the Poore": Social Struggle in the Prose Fictions of Thomas Deloney', *Textual Practice*, 20.3, 395–418, in which he notes that Deloney co-authored 'A Complaint of the Yeoman Weavers Against the Immigrant Weavers', a letter sent to the French and Dutch churches in London and printed for wider distribution. Deloney was jailed in 1595 for his part in this polemic. See also Andrew Pettegree (1986), *Foreign Protestant Communities in Sixteenth-century London*, Oxford: Clarendon Press; and Alan Shepard and P. J. Withington (2000), *Communities in Early Modern England: Networks, Place, Rhetoric*, Manchester: Manchester University Press.
15. Deloney, *The Gentle Craft*.
16. Ibid., p. 106.
17. Morrow, 'The Entrepreneurial Spirit and "The Life of the Poore"', p. 396.
18. Deloney, *The Gentle Craft*, p. 100.
19. Ibid.
20. Ibid., p. 144.
21. Ibid., p. 402. Strangwidge was also an historical figure, killed during an attack on the French coast.
22. See Juan E. Tazón (2003), *The Life and Times of Thomas Stukeley (c. 1525–78)*, Burlington, VT and Aldershot: Ashgate. Tazón provides an excellent guide to diverse historical and literary accounts of the life of Stukeley, especially showing that he achieved fame and notoriety across Europe. Stukeley's expedition to Florida is addressed in detail, although Deloney's representation of Stukeley as Stuteley is not mentioned.
23. Deloney, *The Gentle Craft*, p. 109.
24. John Simons (1983), *Realistic Romance: The Prose Fiction of Thomas Deloney*, Contexts and Connections: Winchester Research Papers in the Humanities, Winchester: King Alfred's College.
25. Dekker, *The Shoemaker's Holiday*, p. 203.
26. Strictly speaking Eyre rebuilt Leadenhall, probably long before he became Lord Mayor. Smallwood and Wells note that the name was recorded as early as the thirteenth century and that Sir Richard Whittington gave the hall to the city in 1411. Ibid., p. 200.

27. Dekker, *The Shoemaker's Holiday*, p. 203. It is fascinating to speculate on how an earlier edition of Part I of *The Gentle Craft* than those known to Smallwood and Wells has come to be in the Biblioteka Gadańska in Poland. Someone suggested to me that it might have been carried there by a member of the touring companies of actors known to visit northern Poland in the time of Shakespeare. Or perhaps it crossed the Channel in the bag of soldier who could read of home as he went to war.

28. I am indebted to Linda Hutjens for this suggestion. See Linda A. Hutjens (2004), 'The Renaissance Cobbler: the Significance of Shoemaker and Cobbler Characters in Elizabethan Drama' PhD thesis, Toronto: University of Toronto. In a wide-ranging and persuasive discussion of the numerous plays of the period that feature or refer to shoemakers, Hutjens examines the status of the shoemaker and the symbolism of the trade in terms of early modern economics and social class. That her list of plays which refer to shoemakers does not include *Henry V* seems entirely right, despite some critics' assertions that it should. Of special interest is her insight into the status of St Crispin's Day as a public holiday, and the history of the term 'gentle craft' itself.

29. The aspirations and values of the guilds that grew from the various communities of urban workers seem somewhat different from those represented by Deloney and Dekker, or are at least more sober than those that Henry sees in the 'mad' Simon Eyre.

8

BEYOND HISTORY

∽

Was 1603 the end of histories? There is an approach to the relationship between early modern drama and its representation of warfare that understands that, by the early years of the seventeenth century, the comparative tranquillity of England's foreign policy under James Stuart reduced popular interest in warfare as a conspicuous subject for the stage. The argument is based partly on the fact that, with the exceptions of *The Tragedy of Macbeth* and *All is True (Henry VIII)*, Shakespeare stopped writing history plays at the accession of James to the English throne. *Macbeth* is thus regarded as an exceptional return to the history genre because it celebrates James's lineage, flatters his abiding interest in witchcraft and simultaneously offers a convenient vehicle for tragedy, a form that continued to absorb the playwright for a number of years. *Henry VIII*, opening as it does with a description of the diplomacy of the Field of the Cloth of Gold in 1520 and ending with the christening of Elizabeth in 1533, avoids depicting the wars that characterised Henry's reign. It concentrates instead on domestic political and religious intrigue, and foregrounds Henry's troubled relationship with Rome. Whatever the nature of the international conflict that underpins this late play, all is smoothed over by the vision of peace promised in Cranmer's prophecy concerning the life of the infant princess. The idea that the drama of the period forsakes history is a neat formulation that almost holds true for Shakespeare's commitment to the history play as a form. Yet in terms of militarism it does not quite work for the overall play of history as Shakespeare's later tragedies and classical plays demonstrate; and since warfare and history are so intimate we might want to suggest that wherever the former appears, there is something to be said about the latter. Moreover, just as James's reign did not see the end of international tension or a cessation of demands for military preparedness, Shakespeare's contemporaries and successors continued to display a strong interest in militarism, and sometimes, by means of parody and imitation, at the expense of Shakespeare himself. Later in this chapter I shall examine some examples of the way that Shakespeare's military world came under scrutiny in the dramatic work of some of his contemporaries and followers. But before coming to this extensive but sometimes obscure set of plays I should like to look at a selection of texts from earlier in the period which casts some doubt on both the military orthodoxy of the Tudors and the ideals espoused by their military theorists.

GORBUDUC, OR THE TRAGEDY OF FERREX AND PORREX

This early play by Thomas Sackville and Thomas Norton was first staged in 1561 and printed around ten years later.[1] It was performed for Queen Elizabeth at Whitehall on 18 January 1562. King Gorbuduc decides to divide his kingdom between his two sons, Ferrex and Porrex. Like Lear, he does this against the advice of his courtiers and with severe consequences. Porrex invades Ferrex's lands and kills him, only to be killed in turn by his mother in an act of revenge. The play concludes with a popular rebellion in which both Gorbuduc and his queen die, the arrival of Albany, who has seen the opportunity for material advantage in the midst of this chaos, and the outbreak of a general civil war. Early in the play Gorbuduc was warned by one of his counsellors against dividing up the kingdom in the following terms:

Within one land one single rule is best:
Divided reigns do make divided hearts,
But peace preserves the country and the prince.
Such is in man the greedy mind to reign,
So great is his desire to climb aloft,
In worldly stage the stateliest parts to bear,
That faith and justice and all kindly love,
Do yield unto desire of sovereignty,
Where egal state doth raise an egal hope
To win the thing that either would attain.
Your grace remb'reth how in passed years
The mighty Brute, first prince of all this land,
Possessed the same and ruled it well in one;
He, thinking that the compass did suffice
For his three sons three kingdoms eke to make,
Cut it in three, as you would now in twain.
But how much British blood hath since been spilt
To join again the sundered unity!
What princes slain before their timely hour!

What waste of towns and people in the land!
What treasons heaped on murders and on spoils!
Whose just revenge even yet is scarcely ceased;
Ruthful remembrance is yet raw in mind.
The gods forbid the like to chance again.

(I.ii.259–82)

Eubulus' advice raises a number of issues. Clearly a warning against the evils of civil conflict, the speech invites the audience to consider the virtues of peace and unity in contrast with the images of a war that will spread throughout the land. Yet peace is itself unstable since it exists, even when the state is unified, only in spite of the seemingly natural ambition of warlike men who will always seek to gain sovereignty. Moreover, the present peace of the state was itself forged out of war after Brute's earlier mistake. The sense of a cycle of disorder is profound and can be registered against the play's Senecan overtones, which imply a parallel between acts of revenge and issues of war. The role of heaven, forbidding an action that might cause war, is demoted here to somewhere far below the actions of humans, a hierarchy that may have been unsettling for an audience that included a monarch who claimed divine authority for her own proclamations of peace and war. The play is caught up in its generic provenance in the classics and the Morality Play tradition. Gorbuduc's advisers have emblematic names: 'Eubulus' ('wise counsellor') and 'Philander' ('friend to man'), for example. The episodic structure, dumb shows and use of a Chorus combine to make it entirely reminiscent of earlier religious drama. Yet it also sets the scene for an anthropocentric attitude to the business of war and state authority, one that will steadily permeate the drama that is to come. Instability in the theological framework that governs the acquisition and use of sovereign power is heightened at the point where Ferrex is urged by Hermon to take up arms against his brother. An account of war and kingship is presented that offers the audience the unsettling notion that the gods sanction in kings what they forbid in ordinary citizens. The pursuit of mortal ambition and aspirations to sovereignty may be continued through war as long as that sovereignty, and the licence that goes with it, are finally secured by those who seek them. In effect, the audience is presented with a heaven (albeit a pre-Christian one in the early part of the play) which both forbids and sanctions war at the same time:

The gods do bear and well allow in kings
The things that they abhor in rascal routs.

> When kings on slender quarrels run to wars,
> And then in cruel and unkindly wise
> Command thefts, rapes, murders of innocents,
> The spoil of towns, ruins of mighty realms;
> Think you such princes do suppose themselves
> Subject to laws of kind and fear of gods?
> Murders and violent thefts in private men
> Are heinous crimes and full of foul reproach;
> Yet none offence, but decked with glorious name
> Of noble conquests in the name of kings.
>
> (II.i.144–55)

This advice, although considered wicked in the context of the play, nonetheless sets out a position on the authority of kingship that will sit uneasily beside the claims that are to be made about the issue in the military theory that is beginning to emerge during this period. The vision of a divine sanctioning of warfare is exactly that which will be allowed by those authors who derived their command of the subject from their selective readings of the Bible. War can be justified because kings are especially empowered by divine authority. At the same time kings are not entirely subject to the laws of gods, and in this instance, tend towards the kinds of military activity ('thefts, rapes, murders of innocents') that Shakespeare is later to associate with the marauding Henry V at Harfleur.

Gorbuduc was performed several years before the opening of the public theatres and thus used the staging devices of the Morality Play with its visual balancing of good and evil exempla of human behaviour. Good figures contend with figures of evil, working their influence on central, often equally emblematic figures. This helps increase an effect that suggests that no single discourse is privileged above a range of alternatives and there is certainly very little to offer the audience in the form of a resolution of the conflicting positions about warfare. King Gorbuduc, paradoxically a kind of royal Everyman, defies the empirical evidence of what can happen when a kingdom is divided as it was under the historical Brute. His sons debate with their followers the status of their 'name', implying that whoever may be the more worthy prince, both are superior in status to the gods to whom they pay lip-service at best. And the Chorus represents a vision of a state given over to the dictates of secular ambition expressed through martial supremacy:

> The lust of kingdom knows no sacred faith,
>   No rule of reason, no regard of right,

No kindly love, no fear of heaven's wrath;
  But with contempt of gods and man's despite,
Though bloody slaughter doth prepare the ways
  To fatal sceptre and accursed reign.
                         (III.i.170–5)

Towards the end of the play, with the old king murdered by the people and both his sons dead, Eubulus gives a long description of the chaos imagined by the Chorus. Internal division has made Britain vulnerable, leaving it open to the threat of invasion from abroad:

Lo, Britains realm is left an open prey,
A present spoil by conquest to ensue.
Who seeth not now how many rising minds
Do feed their thoughts with hope to reach a realm?
And who will not by force attempt to win
So great a gain, that hope persuades to have?
                         (V.ii.191–6)

Gorbuduc promotes the ideal of a state unified under a single monarch since the splitting of the realm is bound to lead to the apocalyptic description of civil strife described in Eubulus' final speech. Moreover, the devolution of power to a parliament is also considered a waste of time, or even dangerous, since:

Alas, in parliament what hope can be,
When is of parliament no hope at all.
                    (V.ii.223–4)

That a single earthly authority should take precedence over power-sharing would seem a theme fit for a relatively new queen sitting in an audience all too familiar with the wounds caused by civil war in the past. Yet two issues are set out in *Gorbuduc* that are to prove contentious in both the body of drama that is to come and the military theory that will accompany it. The first is that of the divine agency around which the play ends with a curious kind of 'turn'. The 'gods' who have previously been shown to lack the power to intervene, their authority claimed by both sides in a dispute (or simply defied altogether), are replaced by a single Christian entity to which a rather plaintive appeal is made in the play's closing moments:

While yet the prince did live whose name and power
By lawful summons and authority
Might make a parliament to be of force
And might have set the state in quiet stay.

But now, O happy man whom speedy death
Deprives of life, ne is enforced to see
These hugy mischiefs and these miseries,
These civil wars, these murders, and these wrongs
Of justice. Yet must God in fine restore
This noble crown unto the lawful heir;
For right will always live and rise at length,
But wrongs can never take deep root to last.
                                          (V.ii.268–79)

In view of what has transpired this wished-for outcome seems a little
weak. The whole play has seen the unreliability of the gods with
respect to human ambition, various interpretations of sovereignty
and the cyclical nature of war and revenge. The play may be an affirmation of the agency of the true Christian God summoned to replace
the pagan deities, but this seems to stretch its theology somewhat.
Rather, the audience is left relying on the forlorn word 'must' in
line 276: God will provide, eventually. It is another exit strategy.
Gorbuduc can be viewed as establishing an agenda of issues for the
ideas about militarism, God and the state which will be discussed in
the prose and drama that is to follow. At this point the play raises
some doubts about the certainty of God's presence and the clarity of
Christian doctrine in these matters. Those who remain at the end of
the play hope for and await divine guidance, yet there is little to
suggest that the Christian God is going to be any less protean than his
pagan predecessors.

    The second issue concerns notions of the spectacle of power and its
ability to usurp due political process. Ferrex and Porrex are obsessed
with their reputations and status and both finally demonstrate this by
recourse to violence. It is a play that works through in microcosm
some of the larger debates that were to be conducted later in the pages
of military theory and on the stages of the later Elizabethan and early
Stuart theatres. This is a play about cruelty and ambition set in a
distant and pagan court. Yet its focus upon civil war, for Elizabethan
audiences, may have provided an immediacy that was partly fuelled
by the tendency of the Tudors to use foreign campaigns as unifying
motifs at home: Henry and France; Henry and Scotland; Elizabeth and
Spain; Elizabeth and Ireland. Certainly, the emerging military theorists' recommendations to a king such as Gorbuduc would have been to
instigate a foreign war that would override internal dissent and dis-
unity. This strategy is added to the agenda that is to be worked
through in a sequence of subsequent plays.

CAMBISES, KING OF PERSIA

Like *Gorbuduc*, Thomas Preston's tragedy dates from around 1561, although the earliest extant edition is from 1584.[2] If the military texts are going to recommend foreign war as a means by which to promote internal unity, then this play dramatises the result of such a policy. King Cambises decides to wage war against Egypt in order to enhance his reputation at home in Persia. His advisers agree with the plan, noting that the name, reputation and power of Persia will all be validated by victory. Moreover, the war will bring the monarchy closer to heavenly virtue and reinforce a sense of justice. One counsellor reflects on this:

> Through Maris aid the conquest wun, then deed of hapy prince
> Shall pearce the skies unto the throne of the supernal seat,
> And merit there a just reward of Jupiter the Great.
> But then your Grace must not turne backe from this pretenced
>   will;
> For to proceed in vertuous life imploy indevour stil;
> Extinguish vice, and in that cup to drinke have no delight;
> In judgement you do office beare, which have the skil in lawes;
> We thinke that you accordingly by justice wil deale,
> That for offence none shal have cause, of wrong you to appeale.
>   (28–36)

For the period of his absence at the wars Cambises appoints one of his judges, Sisamnes, as acting governor and the play develops around this figure's gradual corruption under the influence of a Vice figure named Ambidexter. Upon his return, Cambises learns of his deputy's misdemeanours and has him arrested, tried and executed, making a point of gratuitously summoning Sisamnes' son to witness his father's death. The play continues with Cambises summoning the figures Cruelty and Murder to eliminate his brother, and he then executes his own fiancée for objecting to this act. *Cambises*, unlike *Gorbuduc*, has an active and very visible deity in the form of Divine Justice who eventually intervenes, making Cambises stab himself accidentally with his own sword.[3] The play is characterised by its fulsome reflections on war and monarchy. On the one hand, Cambises is the very model of the military theorists' idea of strategy in the sense that he follows their recommendations in pursuing a foreign campaign in order to bolster his domestic reputation and strengthen the state. That this fails so miserably not only undermines the strategy itself, but also opens up a further dimension. It is revealed that although Ambidexter encourages Sisamnes in his venality, the judge had actually been waiting for the king to depart in order explore the possibilities for self-promotion. Furthermore, Cambises is himself corrupted by the experience of war, departing as a just if somewhat conceited sovereign, but returning to wreak havoc on the innocent. In a piece that belongs very clearly to the later stages of the Morality tradition, its principal Vice assumes a persona of warlike subjectivity that parodies the more serious militarist strands of discussion in the play. Ambidexter mimics Cambises' rhetoric of militarised absolutism, tries to rally the ordinary soldiers Huf, Ruf and Snuf (the Baldoph, Pistol and Nim of this play), and declares himself a reluctant but inspired and manly soldier:

> Stand away, stand away, for the passion of God!
> Harnessed I am, prepared to the field;
> I would have been content at home to bod,
> But I am sent forth with my speare and shield.
> I am appointed to fight against a snaile,
> And Wilken Wren the ancient shall beare;
> I dout but against him to prevaile, –
> To be a man my deeds shall declare;
> If I overcome him, then a butter-fly takes his part.
> But you shall see me overthrow him with a fart.
>   (126–35)

These early plays offered their audiences an opportunity to observe the contradictions and discontinuities in the relationship between monarchical government and military endeavour in a mixture of serious critique and parody. The military theorists, whose work began to be published in considerable volumes in the 1580s, may have been responding in part to what was seen on the stage. The correspondence between the issues discussed in their prose and those dramatised in the developing public theatres is certainly close enough to suggest such a dialectical relationship.

A LOOKING GLASS FOR LONDON AND ENGLAND

An example of such correspondence comes in another play from the 1580s (but published in 1594), which examines the general moral decay in England described by the military theorists. In Thomas Lodge and Robert Greene's *A Looking Glass for London and England* the city and the country must take up an active stance against the domestic ills which threaten to leave the state vulnerable to foreign invasion.[4] The figure of Jonas states:

O London, maiden of the mistress isle,
Wrapped in the folds and swathing clouts of shame,
In thee more sins than Ninevah contains:
Contempt of God, despite of reverend age,
Neglect of law, desire to wrong the poor,
Corruption, whoredom, drunkenness, and pride.
                              (V.v.75–80)

Lodge and Greene do not clearly set out the remedy for these ills, but
the play is a good starting place for an examination of the kinds of
solution offered in the military prose for such behaviour, but transferred, and given a very different treatment, in the theatre. The complaints are those that could be found in a range of pamphlets, books
and ballads: irreligious behaviour, a lack of respect for the old and
widespread illegality – and the usual range of sinful submission to
worldly appetites. These kinds of complaint sometimes mirror those
found in military theory with regard to a softening of men's behaviour. Lack of discipline is established as both the cause and effect of
a preoccupation with love and sex, and the decorum that this entails:
the 'merry meetings' that Richard of Gloucester objected to so ful-
somely. As we have seen, true virility, argue the theorists, lay with war
rather than women.

CAMPASPE

John Lyly's *Campaspe* of 1584 is a love story set in the court of
Alexander the Great, where the influence of love and 'womanly
niceness' has begun to undermine the usual martial atmosphere.[5]
Alexander, whose military prowess, past campaigns and military discipline have made him the most powerful soldier in the world, finds
himself competing for the attention of Campaspe with a languid
painter, Appelles, who represents all those values disdained by the
military theorists. In the following quotation, Alexander's power and
authority are affirmed by his courtier, Hephestion, who still regards
Alexander as equal to the task of subduing neighbouring states,
despite the distractions on the home front:

> Occasion cannot want if will doe not. Behold all Persia swelling in the
> pride of their owne power, the Scythians carelesse what courage or fortune
> can do, the Eygptians dreaming in the soothsayings of their aurgues and
> gaping over the smoake of their beasts intralls. All these, Alexander, are
> to be subdued, if that world be not slipped out of your head which you
> have sworne to conquer with that hand.[6]

Alexander's reluctance to go to war is due to his intense love for Campaspe but also, the text implies, to his quiet assimilation of some of the values of the intrusive Apelles. Towards the end of the play, Alexander concedes victory in love to Apelles, and leaves to fight the Persians. Superficially, this seems like a dramatisation of the argument found in the military prose. Alexander had only temporarily lost 'himself', becoming for a while more like Shakespeare's Prince Harry than a military commander from Antiquity, but as with Harry, all is well in the end, as war restores men to an appropriate register of masculinity and virtue.

In the theatre though, unlike in the military prose, the alternatives to war, such as love, passivity and intellectual pursuit (and painting), are contrasted with the stringencies of the field of battle. Two regimes of masculinity collide in the play, leaving the audience to contrast the warlike excesses of Alexander with the songs, love-making, philosophising and tranquillity of Apelles. By comparison with the sanitised descriptions of war in the military texts, where soldiers operate in stylised formations to the beat of the drum and in the spirit of Saint George, *Campaspe* offers visions of war that are far less sanitised. As Hephestion knew he still could be, Alexander is ruthless in his work. He comes across as a slightly absurd figure, while Apelles 'matures' to reach the status of the soldier himself, a development that is rather disturbing to those around him. This curious turn of events gives some legitimacy to the pro-war arguments of the theorists (and Hephestion) but for an audience at least it shows that the mantle of militarism can be assumed at will if necessary, and is far from 'natural'. In the end the play seemed to offer little fixed point of view in making such a contrast between the two versions of masculinity. There is space and a need for both, it seems to invite us to think. Yet the disciplined anti-sentimentality and single viewpoint on the issue of masculinity promoted by the theorists seem to be undermined, left indeed for Richard of Gloucester in the play Shakespeare was shortly to write.

THE THREE LORDS AND THREE LADIES OF LONDON

A number of plays produced around the crisis year of 1588 resist the urgency found in the contemporary military theory in terms of their constant and mutual demands for the establishment of a force to defend England and undertake prestigious foreign campaigns. In Robert Wilson's *The Three Lords and Three Ladies of London* of

1588 London is personified as a 'A Lady very richly attired . . . having two Angels before her, with bight rapiers in their hands'. In the preface, London addresses the audience:

> Lo, gentles, thus the Lord doth London guard,
> Not for my sake but for his own delight;
> For all in vain the sentinels watch and war,
> Now may my foes in vain both spurn and spite,
> My foes, I mean, that London represent,
> Guarded from heaven by angels excellent.
>
> This blessing is not my sole benefit:
> All England is, and so preserv'd hath been,
> Not by man's strength, his policy and wit,
> But by a power and Providence unseen;
> Even for the love wherewith God loves our Queen,
> In whom, for whom, by whom we do possess
> More grace, more good, than London can express.[7]

The image, linking peace to God's willingness to defend Elizabeth, resists 'man's strength, his policy or wit', and makes military preparedness redundant. Celebrating the magnificence of the Crown, the play suggests that a 'natural' position for England is to rely on divine protection rather than armed preparedness. Whilst this seems an absurd position, it corresponds to a degree with the mythology that began to emerge from the moment of the defeat of the Armada that Drake's success could be attributed to God's intervention and protection.

THE BATTLE OF ALCAZAR

This idea of divine protection as opposed to military preparedness is geographically extended in George Peele's *The Battle of Alcazar*, which according to its editor, Walter Greg, was probably written in 1588, although it was not printed until 1594.[8] The play examines the military adventures of Thomas Stukeley, the anachronistically placed Stuteley of *The Gentle Craft* who was so decisively dealt with by the shoemakers prior to his voyage to Florida on behalf of Henry VI. As Juan Tazón has noted, Stukeley had long featured in a number of Elizabethan ballads and was later to appear in *The Famous Historye of the Life and Death of Captaine Thomas Stukeley* (printed in 1605, but performed in 1596), for which 'no author has yet been convincingly identified'.[9] Along with the ballads, Peele's main source,

John Poleman's *The Second Part of the Booke of Battailes*, published nine years after the historical Stukeley's death, had helped secure Stukeley's reputation. This was a publication tellingly written 'for the profit of those that practise armes, and for the pleasure of such as love to be harmlesse hearers of bloudie broiles'.[10] In *The Battle of Alcazar* Stukeley is shown to be a military man capable of operating with an autonomy that prefigures that of Caius Martius in Shakespeare's *Coriolanus*. Here the Captain is on his way to Ireland, on a mission backed by the Pope and aimed at undermining Elizabeth's claim to that country. Having landed at Lisbon he explains to the authorities his own independence and that of his men:

> Lord Governor of Lisbourne understand,
> As we are Englishmen, so are we men,
> And I am Stukley so resolute in all,
> To follow rule, honor and Emperie,
> Not to be bent so strictly to the place
> Wherein at first I blew the fire of life
> But that I may at libertie make choise
> Of all the continents that bounds the world.
>   (451–8)

The Portuguese are intent on a war against the Moslems in Africa, but in persuading Stukeley to join this, instead of continuing the expedition to Ireland, they explain that such an attempted violation of Elizabeth's sovereignty would be entirely fruitless. Britain and Ireland, Stukeley is told firmly, enjoy defences that are capable of thwarting any mere military offence and are defined by a combination of God's hand, natural barriers against invasion and allied agencies from classical mythology:

> To invade the Iland were her highnes raignes,
> Twere all in vaine, for heavens and destinies
> Attend and wait upon her Majestie,
> Sacred, imperiall, and holy is her seate,
> Shining with wisdome, love and mightines.
> Nature that everie thing imperfect made,
> Fortune that never yet was constant found,
> Time that defaceth everie golden shew,
> Dare not decay, remove or be impure,
> Both nature, time and fortune all agree,
> To blesse and serve her roiall majestie,
> The wallowing Ocean hems her round about,
> Whose raging flouds do swallow up her foes,

And on the rockes their ships in peeces split,
And even in Spaine where all the traitors dance,
And plaie themselves upon a sunny daie,
Securely guard the west part of her Isle,
The South the narrow Britaine sea begirts,
Where Veptune sits in triumph, to direct
Their course to hell that aime at her disgrace,
The Germaine seas alongst the East do run,
Where Nenus banquets all her water Nymphs,
That with her beautie glansing on the waves,
Distaines the checke of faire Prosperina,
Advise thee then proud Stukely ere thou passe,
To wrong the wonder of the highest God,
Sith danger, death and hell doth follow thee,
Thee and them all that seeke to danger her.
(732–59)

In terms of a perceived autonomy of the military subject, this play and *The Famous Historye*, are of immense interest. Stukeley becomes detached from any real sense of cause, offering his services where he likes, even to Spain itself. He loses the loyalty of his men and the backing of the Church, but ends up revealing himself 'for the last time as a true soldier, faithful to the end to his role as a rash leader'.[11] Stukeley epitomises the potential detachment of the soldier, especially as a leader, but set against the historically 'God-given' victory over the Spanish Armada, it radically undermines the accelerating demands of the military theorists for the creation of yet more and more such militarised subjects. Clearly the idea that a combination of natural defences and God's special protection of Elizabeth's realms was a fanciful one, but its ideological force as a counterweight to the urgency of the theorists' arguments makes these kinds of plays very suggestive indeed.

THE WOUNDS OF CIVIL WAR

Thomas Lodge's play, another from the year of the Armada, features a Roman soldier, Sylla, who embodies many of the virtues of the classical soldier referred to by the military theorists:[12] he is disciplined, intelligent, effective and successful. His foreign campaigns have increased the reputation and power of Rome abroad; his army is feared, but seen as a model by neighbouring states; and his victories are always decisive and conducted according to the laws of war. In theory, his person, his army and his strategies read like extracts from the military prose. Yet instead of increasing the internal security of Rome, Sylla's foreign campaigns have led to civil war, and opposing factions have competed for power during his absence abroad. Confronting his domestic enemies and erstwhile friends he says:

> Ungrateful men! Whilst I with tedious pain
> In Asia seal'd my duty with my blood,
> Making the Daranians faint for fear,
> Spreading my colours in Galatia,
> Dipping my sword in the Enetians' blood,
> And foraging the fields of Phocida,
> You called my foe from exile with his friends;
> You did proclaim me traitor here in Rome;
> You raz'd my house, you did defame my friends.
> But, brawling wolves, you cannot bite the moon,
> For Sylla lives, so forward to revenge,
> And woe to those that sought to do me wrong.[13]

The play has something of the tone of *Coriolanus* and although it lacks Shakespeare's subtlety and control, it demonstrates once again the autonomy of the militarised leader. Sylla, however, is presented much more carefully as a product of military discipline than Caius Martius as he moves from seeing himself as a representative of the state to an individualised warrior emphasising, as he does here, his personal sacrifice. He dwells on the spilling of his own blood in the conduct of his duty and assures that blood will be spilt at home in revenge for his betrayal. *The Wounds of Civil War* avoids the sense of tragedy that pervades *Coriolanus* and thus objectifies its relationship with contemporary military texts. By comparison with the practicalities of war and the politics of a militarised state observed in this play, the military theory seems at best an abstraction, at worst to recommend a policy that will potentially create forces in the state that will destroy it. The 'tragedy' of the *Wounds of Civil War* is not vested in its protagonist but in the flawed structures of a political system that cannot tolerate what it has created.

THE DOWNFALL OF ROBERT, EARLE OF HUNTINGTON

The setting of Lodge's play may seem remote to those thinking about military affairs at the turn of the century. However, the military writers employed examples from the classical world to illustrate their arguments as frequently as the dramatists used them to make those same arguments seem more complicated and less assured. Anthony Munday's *The Downfall of Robert, Earl of Huntington* would have drawn the matter of the benefits of foreign campaigns into an English context. Munday was considerably attuned to matters of war and reputation, having attempted in an earlier play to rescue the image of Sir John Oldcastle from associations with Shakespeare's Falstaff.[14] In the play about the Earl of Huntington, from around 1601, the body of the state is torn apart by the absence of its king in spite of the fact that Richard I is busy enhancing England's international status with his engagement in the Crusades. John is an evil figure in the play, as he had remained in the folklore that in part informs it, yet it nonetheless dramatises a situation from English history that is very much like that of Sylla's. The play attacks the simple equation offered in the military writing that a powerful military leader ensures the security and discipline of the state by waging foreign wars. As John notes:

> Richard is king,
> In Cyprus, Acon, Actes, and rich Palestime:
> To get those kingdoms England lent him men,
> And many a million of her substance spent,
> The very entrails of her wombe was rent.[15]

The king's crusades produce a new status for England, and in the play the poor willingly make sacrifices in order to finance Richard's adventures, yet the absence of the king allows the internal evil and corruption embodied in the figure of John to come to the fore. The play invites the audience to consider that the idea of a strong military leader with constant foreign disputes is a contradictory one. Clearly the solution would be for a monarch to have a foreign campaign but not to have to go on it in person. Yet the military theorists celebrated those leaders in the past, like Henry V, who had actively participated in battles, thus redeeming monarchs who might otherwise be flawed, such as Richard III. The story the theorists told was that only battle itself could ennoble individual soldiers or monarchs. Even if an exception could be made for Elizabeth herself, the field of battle remained the proving ground.

SOLIMAN AND PERSEDA

Some plays from the period simply illuminate what the military texts keep dark about those fields of battle. As has been noted, the theorists, not unlike some strategists in the contemporary world, rarely discuss the brutalities of combat. If such matters were raised in the sixteenth century it is with an assertion of the moral standing of the soldier that is the proof of his sacrifice, or a quite literal sanitising of the situation by suggesting that the wounded should be treated by surgeons in the field.[16] Often the theorists simply stylise killing. Thomas Kyd is best known for *The Spanish Tragedy* (c. 1585), a play in which the protagonist, Hieronimo, experiences agonies of injustice that proceed from anti-chivalric behaviour on the battlefield.[17] In *Soliman and Perseda* (1591), however, Kyd distils the business of war, showing that the only victor in any battle is Death.[18] The play is an elaboration of the play-within-the-play that features in *The Spanish Tragedy*. Debating the outcome of a complex and bloody conflict between Christian and Moslem, Death, Fortune and Love assess their comparative strengths and weaknesses in terms of their influence on human activity. Death weighs his own part and, rightly in the context of the play, proclaims victory:

> By wasting all I conquer all the world:
> And now, to end our difference at last,
> In this last act note but the deeds of Death.
> Where is Erastus now, but in my triumph?
> Where are the murtherers, but in my triumph?
> Where's judge and witness, but in my triumph?
> Where's false Lucina, but in my triumph?
> Where's Basilisco, but in my triumph?
> Where's faithful Piston, but in my triumph?
> Where's valiant Brusor, but in my triumph?
> Their loves and fortune ended with their lives,
> And they must wait upon the car of death.
> Pack, Love and Fortune! Play in comedies:
> For powerful death best fitteth tragedies.[19]

In an echo of the compromise that Henry VIII tried to extract from John Colet, Kyd goes on to assert that Death will triumph over all those who participate in wars, except those who are friends of Elizabeth. Despite this caveat, the play is a graphic representation of the outcome of war which complements *The Spanish Tragedy* itself and stands in stark opposition to the energies of the theorists of the time, who became increasingly bellicose in the years following the Armada.

THE LIFE AND DEATH OF JACK STRAW

One focus of the theorists' contempt in the last decade of the sixteenth century was their perception that the people most likely to be called on to participate in the military organisations thought necessary to prepare for war were simply unwilling to do so. As we have seen, there was considerable hostility to the systems of militia or trained bands, and such institutionalisation of militarism could actually lead to civil unrest. In addition, in many areas of the social formation there was a reluctance to raise the taxation involved in supporting such institutions. All this put into relief the idealised notions of discipline, professionalism and moral righteousness espoused by the military writers. The theatre cannot have helped the situation for such enthusiasts. The anonymous play *The Life and Death of Jack Straw* was first staged during the closing years of the sixteenth century.[20] It is of particular relevance to issues of commitment and refusal in terms of the state's military ambitions since it dramatises a popular rebellion that had originated in part with the unwillingness of the people to support a monarch's war with France. The real Jack Straw's late fourteenth-century revolt was concerned with a range of issues that have been identified with a growing class consciousness defined as 'communism' by one mid-twentieth-century mainstream historian: but the emphasis in the play is on a poll tax that will underwrite the war.[21] Despite parliamentary approval for the campaign, payment from all quarters is slow in arriving. The Lord Treasurer discusses the situation with the Archbishop:

And yet, Lord Archbishop, your grace doth know
That, since the latest time of parliament,
Wherein this task was granted to the King
By general consent of either house,
To help his wars, which he intends to France,
For wreak and just recovery of his right,
How slow their payment is in every place,
That better a king not to command at all,
Than be beholding to ungrateful minds.
ARCHBISHOP:
Lord Treasurer, it seemeth strange to me,
That, being won with reason and regard
Of true-succeeding prince, the common sort
Should be so slack to give, or grudge the gift
That is to be employed for their behoof.
Hard and unnatural be the thoughts of theirs
That suck the milk, and will not help the well.[22]

The centrality of the war to the state is profound ('mother's milk') and the way that war is represented as fought on behalf of everyone is allied here to notions of the just war and the 'naturalness' of consent. The play further dramatises a conflict between two forms of authority over the issue of conflict itself. On the one hand, the king hopes to sway the rebels to his cause by taking a sympathetic position:

My lord, I hope we shall not need to fear
To meet those men, that thus do threaten us.
We will, my lord to-morrow meet with them,
And hear, my lord, what 'tis that they demand.[23]

The purpose here is, as it were, to put into practice something of the arguments of the Elizabeth military theorists. The people are to become 'knowing' with respect to the war and its justification. On the other hand, the king adopts this approach against the counsel of his advisers who would prefer to see direct and merciless punishment. The problem in the reign of the real Richard II was that he had insufficient troops known to be loyal enough to subdue the 'common sort'. This understandably is not discussed in the play, yet still the focus shifts to an alternative approach, the best resort of an absolute monarch without a reliable army, a dazzling image of Divine Right:

BISHOP:
Your grace herein is very well advised,
With resolution fitting your degree,
Your grace must show yourself to be a king
And rule like God's vicegerent here on earth.
The looks of kings so lend both life and death,
And when a king doth set down his decree,
His sentence should be irrevocable.[24]

Neither approach, hard or soft, is taken to a real conclusion. The king ends up compromising and decides to execute the ringleaders, including the eponymous Jack Straw, but offers the majority of the rebels clemency. What emerges from the play is a very clear contest over the kinds of power available to an absolute monarch; but more importantly it demonstrates the centrality of military concerns (and taxation) to ideas of national identity and popular consent.

THE KNIGHT OF THE BURNING PESTLE

Such matters of high policy were paramount to the military theorists, but they were also concerned with the detail of military organisation as it was regularly played out in the musters and gatherings of trained bands in London and elsewhere. These displays, associated in London with specific locations such as Mile End, drew crowds of onlookers and provided evidence for the theorists of the paucity of any effective military preparedness. Their lament over the poor quality and undisciplined behaviour of those involved was entirely justified. Moreover, had they visited the theatre they might have felt that their concerns were being parodied in a number of contemporary plays. If, like so many across the centuries, they had looked to derive from Shakespeare at least a degree of comfort in the rhetoric of military figures such as Henry V or Julius Caesar, they may well have seen them parodied as well.

First performed in 1608 and published in 1613, Francis Beaumont's *The Knight of the Burning Pestle* depends in part for its humour on its audiences' knowledge of both military exercises and Shakespeare's plays.[25] It belongs to the world of *The Gentle Craft* and *The Shoemaker's Holiday*, with its inversion of the chivalric romance, and mocking celebration of artisan culture. There is also a strong element derived from *Don Quixote*, thought to have circulated in one form or another before the first official English translation of 1612. *The Knight of the Burning Pestle* was apparently rejected by audiences at the Blackfriars but was more successful in the Caroline period, and received well by an appreciative audience at the private Cockpit theatre. Whatever interpretation one places on its depiction of social class, the play nonetheless depends for its appeal on its relationship to militarism and militarism's London apparatus.

A central figure is Rafe, a grocer's apprentice who, inspired by reading of chivalry in *Palmerin of England*, becomes the Knight of the Burning Pestle. He embarks on a series of adventures in which various rather ordinary locations are imagined as fantastic settings for romantic encounters and demonstrations of chivalric prowess. In what might seem a subversive way, the play reaches its conclusion by blending these motifs of chivalry with a parody of the musters of soldiers. This fusion of the old and the new precisely parallels the ideological method of the military texts that were available for purchase not far from some of the locations mentioned in the play. The end of the play includes a complex set of references to a range of recent plays by a number of playwrights, including *The Spanish Tragedy*, but when Rafe addresses his gathering of mustered 'soldiers', the references are clearly to Shakespeare:

'Tis a fault, my friend: put it in again. You want a nose, and you a stone. Sergeant, take a note on't, for I mean to stop it in the pay. Remove, and march! Soft and fair, gentlemen, soft and fair! Double your files! As you were! Faces about! Now, you with the sodden face, keep it there! Look to your match, sirrah; it will be in your fellow's flask anon! So, make a crescent now! Advance your pikes! Stand and give ear! Gentlemen, countrymen, friends, and my fellow soldiers, I have brought you this day from the shops of security and the counters of content to measure out in these furious fields honour by the ell and prowess by the pound. Let it not, O, let it not, I say, be told hereafter the noble issue of this city fainted; but bear yourselves in this fair action like men, valiant men and free men! Fear not the face of the enemy nor the noise of the guns; for believe me, brethren, the rude rumbling of a brewer's car is far more terrible, of which you have daily experience; neither let the stink of powder offend you since a more valiant stink is nightly with you. To a resolved mind, his home is everywhere: I speak not this to take away the hope of your return, for you shall see (I do not doubt it), and that very shortly, your loving wives again and your sweet children, whose care doth bear you company in baskets. Remember then, whose cause you have in hand and, like a sort of true-born scavengers, scour me this famous realm of enemies. I have no more to say but this: stand to your tacklings, lads, and show to the world you can as well brandish a sword as shake an apron. Saint George, and on, my hearts.

(V.ii.44–76)

The speech begins by parodying the military drill of London's trained bands and then proceeds to borrow from Shakespeare's *Julius Caesar*: 'Gentlemen, countrymen, friends'. What follows seems to mimic the high military rhetoric of *Henry V*, turned on its head with the odd obscene reference: 'Let it not, O, let it not, I say, be told hereafter . . .' Towards the end, however, the speech turns on elements of Richard III's speech before Bosworth. Richard raised the issue of his soldiers' wives and denounced Richmond's forces in the kinds of terms that Rafe ironically reserves for his own men. Finally, there is Saint George. Clearly there is fun here at the expense of Shakespeare, but there is also a serious point about the formulaic nature of the heroic and inspiring leader's speech.

The theatre of the later Jacobean and Caroline periods continued to feature soldiers and issues of war. With some exceptions, however, the principal theme was that of the boastful soldier, parodied for the entertainment of the more socially elevated audiences of the private theatres. Philosophical issues to do with the just war and the relationship between the military leader and his troops tended to retreat a little, but the politics of soldiering were to the fore. Soldiers in the work of Philip Massinger in particular are absurd figures who dwell on past campaigns but often infect the civilian societies into which they have retired. The stereotype appears in a number of his plays including *The Duke of Milan* (1623), *The Bondman* (1624) and *The Roman Actor* (1629). *The Bondman* proved controversial as it parodied the king's favourite, George Villiers, for his military adventures abroad. Alternatively, soldiers returning from war are likely to become involved in intrigue and revenge, as Melantius does in Beaumont and Fletcher's *The Maid's Tragedy* (1611) or in various works from the 1630s by James Shirley. Plays and fragments of plays from the years following the closure of the theatres show that the unfolding events inspired more plays about war, such as *Il Pastor Fido* and a kind of interlude by 'Mercurius Pragmaticus' called *The Leveller's Levelled*, both from around 1647.

THE CHRONICLE HISTORY OF PERKIN WARBECK AND THE MARTYR'D SOULDIER

Two further Caroline plays are worth considering for their unusual attitudes to war. John Ford's *Perkin Warbeck* dealt with Henry VII's relations with Scotland, which were unsettled by James IV's support for the pretender to the throne.[26] James is presented in the play as a dogmatic defender of Divine Right and a purveyor of arbitrary justice. A contrast is made with Henry VII, who reluctantly recognises that the disputes with Scotland may result in war. Clearly the play flatters one king and traduces the other, but Henry's utterances on warfare are extremely ambivalent. Once again the old spirit from the military texts is paraded as the king begins to understand the benefit that can be drawn from using a foreign war as a means to bolster popularity at home. Henry notes, rather wistfully, that:

> We must learn
> To practise war again in time of peace
> Or lay our crown before our subjects' feet.
> (III.i.103–6)

Yet the foreign war does offer domestic salvation, an end to Perkin Warbeck's rebellion and, in Elizabethan terms, a legitimising of a rationale for war, which by the 1630s must have seemed ideologically irresistible. However, a second notable text from very late in the Caroline period, despite its imperial and racist overtones, offers some relief from this dominant position and something of an alternative rationale. Henry Shirley's *The Martyr'd Souldier* was staged in Drury Lane in 1638 and published in the same year.[27] The play includes some of the most violent images of war and its consequences of any dealt with in this book and makes for uneasy reading in the context of today's regimes of torture. The plot involves the relationship between Genzerick, King of the Vandalls [sic] and his Christian enemies. At the beginning of the play the king, 'sicke on his bed', is cheered up by his courtiers who, since he cannot by affected by music, read him accounts of their victories against the Christians:

> No, no; no Musick;
> But if you needs will charme my o're-watcht eyes,
> Now growne too monstrous for their lids to close,
> If you so long to fill these Musicke-rooms,
> With ravishing sounds indeed; unclaspe that booke,
> Turne o're that Monument of Martydomes,
> Read there how Genzerick has serv'd the gods
> And made their Altars drunke with Christian blood,
> Whil'st their loath'd bodies flung in funerall piles
> Like Incense burnt in Pyramids of fire.
> (I.i.28–37)

The first scene is taken up with readings from the book, images which are acted out as the war against the Christians is rehearsed:

ANTONIO:
Thirty faire Mothers, big with Christian brats,
Upon a scaffold in the Palace plac'd
Had first their dugges sear'd off, their wombes ript up,
About their miscreant heads their first borne Sonnes
Tost as a sacrifice to Jupiter.
(I.i.51–5)

The point of the play is that, despite this gruesome beginning, the Vandalls one-by-one become converted to Christianity, including most surprisingly, their torturer-in-chief, Bellizarius. Christian prisoners and converted Vandalls then begin to defy Genzerick's oppressive regime and receive the support of divine intervention from the Christian God:

BELLIZARIUS:
Prepare your tortures now you scourge of Christians,
For Bellizarius the Christians torturer;
Centuple all that I have ever done;
Kindle the fire and hacke at once with swords;
Teare me by piece-meals, strangle, and extend
My every limbe and joint; may devise more
Than ever did my bloody Tyrannies.

O let me never lose the sight of men
That I may see an Angell once again.
　　　　　　　　(I.ii.116–24)

The intervention of God stops these cruelties and a range of other acts of war on the fields of battle nearby, and slowly everyone in the play observes the power of Christianity, from the ordinary soldiers to the king himself:

SOULDIER:
Strange, my Lord, beyond a wonder,
For 'tis miraculous. Since you forsooke
The bloody fight and horrour of the Christians
One tortur'd wretch, whose sight was quite extinct,
His eyes no farther seeing than his hands,
Is now by that Eugenius, whom they call
Their holy bishop, cleerly restor'd again
To the astonishment of all your army.
　　　　　　　　(I.i.56–63)

Resisting this power until the end, Genzerick is struck by a bolt of lightning and replaced by Hubert, a military commander who has become a Christian soldier. The play ends with the establishment of a Christian union between the warring factions. War becomes redundant because God always intervenes, saving the wounded and restoring life to the dead, but since everyone is now converting to Christianity, there will be no more cause for war anyway. Furthermore, it is decided that the new state will be based on close consultation between monarch and people, which will extinguish both tyranny and popular dissent. Hubert claims that:

Violent streames
Must not bee stopt by violence; there's an art
To meete and put by most boysterous wave;
'Tis now no policy for you to murmure
Nor will I threaten. A great counsell by you
Shall straight be call'd to set this frame in order
Of this great state.
　　　　　　　　(V.i.501–7)

The Martyr'd Souldier is an extraordinary text and it would be easy to be cynical: hell turns into Switzerland in a few short acts. Obviously, the play is a piece of orthodox Christian polemic, and one which too easily ignores the inter-Christian warfare that dominated Europe in the seventeenth century and could never be far from English minds.

Alternatively, though, the play can be seen as a rebuttal of the compromises of Christianity in relation to real wars, from the Crusades through to the recent one with France, Spain and Scotland. There is Christian hegemony, the pagans drawn into the 'civilised world' through an appeal to their hearts and minds. Yet there is also something of Colet in this version of Christianity, a vision of an alternative dimension where the Charity texts are held to be about the community rather than the individual. Other possible analogies are available. Hubert is perhaps a model for Charles Stuart, calling for a conference with his people in order to 'set' the 'frame' for the state: if he will no longer threaten, they will no longer militate against monarchy. It is a gruesome but suggestive text in terms of its view of Christian justifications for war.

Such a text, although aesthetically unappealing, nonetheless has something to add to the way that war was represented in the theatres of Shakespeare and his contemporaries. In some ways these obscure and sometimes wayward texts do indeed lie 'beyond history' in the sense that the familiar, domesticated and critically 'overwritten' Shakespeare belongs to a very certain history of war and nation that is difficult in itself to interrogate, although we can and should try. Not that long ago Shakespeare practically monopolised examination of the drama of the late sixteenth and early seventeenth centuries and his voice was easily allied to a widespread set of assumptions about his orthodox and conservative 'view' of English history. However, despite thirty years of theory and our reconnection to a host of near-forgotten plays, this view of a warlike Shakespeare has not gone away.

Notes

1. Thomas Sackville and Thomas Norton (*c.* 1571), *Gorbuduc, or Ferrex and Porrex*, ed. Irby B. Cauthen (1970), London: Edward Arnold. References are to this edition.
2. Thomas Preston (1561), *Cambises, King of Persia*, in John Matthews Manly (ed.) (1897), *Specimens of the Pre-Shaksperean Drama*, London: Ginn. References are to this edition.
3. Looking at the plot of *Cambises* it is worth noting its original title: *A lamentable tragedy mixed ful of pleasant mirth, conteyning the life of Cambises king of Percia*.
4. Thomas Lodge and Robert Greene (1594), *A Looking Glass for London and England*, London.
5. John Lyly (1584), *Campaspe*, in Manly (ed.) (1897), *Specimens of the Pre-Shaksperean Drama*. References are to this edition.
6. Ibid., p. 301.

7. Robert Wilson (1588), *The Three Lords and Three Ladies of London*, ed. W. Carew Hazlitt, *Dodsley's Old English Plays*, Vol. V.
8. George Peele [1594] (1907), *The Battle of Alcazar*, ed. Walter W. Greg, Oxford: Oxford University Press. References are to this edition.
9. Juan E. Tazón (2003) *The Life and Times of Thomas Stukeley (c. 1525–78)*, Burlington, VT and Aldershot: Ashgate, p. 7. Anonymous [1605] (1975), *The Famous Historye of the Life and Death of Captaine Thomas Stukeley. With his Marriage to Alderman Curteis Daughter, and Valient Ending of his Life at the Battaile of Alcazar*, ed. Judith C. Levinson, Oxford: Oxford University Press.
10. John Poleman (1587), *The Second Part of the Book of Battailes, Fought in our Age*, London.
11. Tazón, *The Life and Times of Thomas Stukeley*, p. 11.
12. Thomas Lodge [1588] (1874), *The Wounds of Civil War*, ed. W. Carew Hazlitt, *Dodsley's Old English Plays*, Vol. VII.
13. Ibid., pp. 174–5.
14. Anthony Munday (1600), *Sir John Oldcastle*, London.
15. Anthony Munday (1600), *The Downfall of Robert, Earle of Huntington*, OEDr, Sig, G4v.
16. An example would be William Clowes (1588), *A Proved Practice for All Young Chirurgians, concerning burnings with Gunpowder, and Sword, Halbard, Pike, Launce, or such other*, London. This text provides information about the medical treatment of the injured by trained surgeons and appeals for the long-term care of soldiers after the wars are ended.
17. Thomas Kyd [1585] (1989), *The Spanish Tragedy*, ed. J. R. Mulryne, London: A. & C. Black.
18. Thomas Kyd [1591] (1874), *Soliman and Perseda*, W. Carew Hazlitt (ed.), *Dodsley's Old English Plays*, Vol. V.
19. Ibid., pp. 373–4.
20. Anon. (1590–1600), *The Life and Death of Jack Straw*, W. Carew Hazlitt (ed.), *Dodsley's Old English Plays*, Vol. V.
21. See May McKisack (1959), *The Fourteenth Century: 1307–1399*, The Oxford History of England Series, Oxford: Clarendon Press, p. 421.
22. Anon., *The Life and Death of Jack Straw*, p. 384.
23. Ibid., p. 392.
24. Ibid.
25. Francis Beaumont [1613] (1986), *The Knight of the Burning Pestle*, ed. Michael Hattaway, London: A. & C. Black. References are to this edition.
26. John Ford [1633] (1968), *The Chronicle History of Perkin Warbeck*, ed. Peter Ure, London: Methuen. References are to this edition.
27. Henry Shirley (1638), *The Martyr'd Souldier*, London. References are to the 1638 folio.

9

THE ABANDONED SOLDIER

⊘

Harvest time in a village in England. When I was in Temple Grafton in the summer of 1992 I learnt something about Ray Peace and Ronnie Williams which came as a surprise. Despite the odds against their surviving many more of their bombing missions over Europe, both expressed a deep satisfaction that they had avoided conscription into the Army. The point was to do with the proximity of the enemy. As 1942 drew to a close, the period of Churchill's 'Hinge of Fate', there was already speculation over the means by which an allied force might have to regain territory that had been occupied by the Nazis. It was predicted – rightly as it turned out – that this would involve intense close quarters combat, which Ray and Ronnie felt fortunate to have avoided in their own wartime careers. Their work, and even that of their colleagues in the fighter squadrons, set them at a distance from their enemy, and besides this they felt that when their time came they would rather go quickly and in one piece rather than be 'shot up' and sent home in pieces.

The world of 1942 now seems in some ways as remote as that of Shakespeare and his contemporaries, and yet there are continuities that connect them with each other and both those worlds with our own. Much of the military writing of the late sixteenth and early seventeenth centuries was driven not by an enjoyment of killing or an obsession with order, but by uncertainties about the governmental apparatus that was to evolve in order to protect and promote the interests of a recognisably modern state. That in the time of Shakespeare the state hung on to myths about divine monarchy does not detract from the idea that the beginning of the modern era was under way and a *sine qua non* of the idea of the state was, as it is now, a standing army. Despite 'troubles' about its borders and various kinds of modification, devolution and changing alliance, the 'Britain' of Shakespeare's later years survives as a now quite elderly 'nation'.

The other continuity is war. In the history of Britain, as in most recognisably modern states, war and nation are intimately connected and both have provided fruitful subject matter for a variety of cultural forms and the criticism that attends those forms. I have tried to explain how one brief period gave rise to an enormously influential body of theory devoted to an understanding of the direction that the modern state should take in terms of its military apparatus, from the detail of weaponry to the relationship between the soldier and God. My case has been that the theatre, form against form, interrogated some of the assumptions and theoretical predisposition of this military theory, often on behalf of those who would be called on to fight at close quarters or who had a moral objection to institutionalised killing. At the same time it has been necessary to work against a common conception that Shakespeare was unambiguously a supporter of war fought on behalf of the nation-state. My own view is that Shakespeare's is a fairly conservative voice in these matters. He balances the pity of war against its perceived necessity whilst paying attention to what he seems to think of as its aesthetics. On the other hand, he shared with many of his contemporaries an obligation to reflect the interest some of his audience may have had in refusing the imposition of war in the name of God and nation. The opportunities for dissent through theatrical representations were limited, as they were for those who used Shakespeare to critique totalitarian states in the post-war twentieth century, so what we get may always be a compromised view. It may also be that prose texts, such as Deloney's *The Gentle Craft*, enjoyed far more licence as vehicles for anti-war sentiment than the heavily regulated public theatre. There is, however, a chink in most of these dramatic texts through which to glimpse the enormity of war as a means of settling disputes or bolstering the flagging image of a monarch or politician.

The figure that emerges most commonly from the military prose and fictional texts is the masculine heroic warrior. This is an ideal that pre-dated Shakespeare and has been passed down the centuries through the cultural artefacts of successive generations. A common view held by soldiers I have spoken with is that part of their motivation comes from being endlessly compared to this normative ideal.[1] The British Army's central and regimental archives and histories record the history of this figure, and the competitive nature of training regimes ensures it is always at hand to shape and occasionally bully the recruit who falls short of expectations. The ideal manifests itself in what can only be described as a 'hardness' – a certain physical manner that is accompanied by a specialised diction and self-possession. It is the acquisition of this, or rather the training that encourages it, that is sometimes espoused as an ideal remedy for the problem of wayward youth in modern Britain.[2] It can also be seen in the swagger of political leaders as they stand shoulder to shoulder with their allies, often aboard aircraft carriers, sometimes dressed in some curious quasi-military garb, directing far-away wars. This heightened masculinity is a fiction that Shakespeare and his contemporaries knew only too well could be acted out, just as surely as they knew that many of the 'returned soldiers' in the streets of Elizabethan London were in fact counterfeiting their battle wounds through self-mutilation.[3]

Whilst many who serve or have served in the armed forces readily subscribe to this image of masculinity, which has corresponding mores among female recruits, there are also those who regard it as a form of ideological control. In fact, many aspects of military service have come under close scrutiny in Britain and elsewhere in recent years, partly because of the conditions imposed on recruits by an increased level of warfare itself. Soldiers and ex-soldiers (and their families) have started complaining: about the inadequacy of their weapons and clothing, military housing, the bullying some have experienced during training and exercises, pay and pensions, and, above all, about their treatment when wounded or retired. A frequent lament is that the dead are treated with due dignity and ritual, but once no longer able to act 'in theatre' the retired, wounded or mentally damaged are ignored and in many cases tempted by suicide. Much of this disquiet has found expression in soldiers' and ex-soldiers' internet blogs. Some of these express profound disillusion with the causes they are paid to fight for. It is as though what has been traditionally 'kept dark' about some aspects of service life has suddenly been revealed. One aspect of the treatment of war in the plays of Shakespeare and his contemporaries was that the military subjects, and especially those in positions of leadership, were dangerously prone to a degree of autonomy that could manifest itself in acts of cruelty. In other cases disaffected soldiers could change sides to find a more accommodating cause. In the modern world this autonomy has expressed itself in the numerous acts of torture that have been exposed in connection with the 'war against terrorism'. Yet for every latterday Tamburlaine there is a twenty-first-century general willing to speak to the media about the cause, or the treatment of personnel, in a way that would have been unthinkable just a few years ago. Just as in the age of Shakespeare, the militarised subject, honed to perfection according to the disciplines of war, can turn against those who have created the institution that has produced him. Soldiers speaking out, or admitting their fears, or too sympathetic to the enemy, were discouraged in the military theory of the early modern period just as they attract controversy in the modern world. Aggrieved ex-service personnel and their families who lobbied the British Parliament in 2006 brought with them to Trafalgar Square a large sculpted head entitled 'The Abandoned Soldier'. The face of the soldier was cracked and distressed: the contrast with the smooth faces of the warriors on nearby plinths and those found on the many effigies commemorating the two world wars was complete.

Those soldiers whose disillusion extends beyond the issue of conditions to the cause itself are sometimes asked about how warfare can end. The response includes the idea that if people could get closer to war then it would stop altogether. This sentiment echoes that of war correspondents who claim that the images transmitted from theatres of war are too sanitised and that if the reality was shown, people would find alternatives to war. However, as seems to have been the case in Shakespeare's day, the capacity for war to be smoothed over in the name of tragedy is immense. Pity floods the channels of dissent and refusal, and acts of remembrance and evocations of sacrifice restore the dead to their place on the memorials and in the grateful hearts of the nation. The compelling aspect of the drama of the early modern period is that it came at a crossroads for the emerging nations. Were they to heed the sanctions against war of the reforming theologians or simply to adapt their weapons and tactics to suit the times? This moment of uncertainty was captured in the theatre and in other forms of popular fiction. There was a glimmer of hope that war might pass into history as an atavism.[4] What happened, of course, is that the dramatic literature of the time, and especially that of Shakespeare, was distilled for its patriotism, its celebration of warlike heroism and its numerous role models. Henry V's speeches have found their way not only into the boardroom as inspiration for company managers but also into the White House and the backpacks of its soldiers.[5] The period itself has long been seen as an inspiration to empire-builders in business and the world as one of individual enterprise and exploration.[6] Meanwhile, some of those businesses are active in producing weapons that will further sanitise war, ensuring the relative safety of those who operate them and avoiding the problem of 'proximity'.

On the way to work each morning I walk along one of Cheltenham's pleasant central thoroughfares. 'The Promenade' has on one side what must be some of the most expensive shops in the country, and on the opposite side there is a series of monuments set among gardens and trees. Cheltenham's reputation as a popular spa resort was established in the Georgian period, so it is not altogether surprising to find an ornate fountain within which sits Neptune, saluting passers-by with his trident. Cheltenham is also a town characterised in part by its longstanding associations with militarism and defence. Historically, it was favoured as a place of retirement for British officers. One reason for this, I have heard said, is because its mild but slightly damp climate reminded these colonels and majors of places they had served in the Empire. In our own troubled times Cheltenham has a significant role to play in the 'war against terrorism' since it is the location of the Government Communications Headquarters (GCHQ) of which, of course, I may say nothing more.

Along from Neptune and spaced at regular intervals are three less flamboyant and rather more serious monuments, all evoking a sense of loss and remembrance. Furthest from Neptune is a statue commemorating local people who died in the Boer Wars in South Africa of 1899–1902. A uniformed figure stands atop a plinth, his rifle reversed and his pith helmeted head forever bowed. Shrouded in silence, he seems a perfect representation of the pity summoned for those who were killed in that now almost forgotten colonial campaign. As with many similar monuments his sombre and timeless vigil is deeply symbolic of our attitudes to war and nation, and to militarism and its consequences. Closest to Neptune is a statue commemorating one of Cheltenham's famous sons. It reads:

EDWARD ADRIAN WILSON
BA MB CANTAB FZS
BORN IN CHELTENHAM 1872
CHIEF OF THE SCIENTIFIC STAFF
ARTIST AND ZOOLOGIST OF THE
BRITISH ANTARTIC EXPEDITION
1910–1913
HE REACHED THE SOUTH POLE
JANUARY 17 1912
AND DIED WITH CAPTAIN SCOTT
ON THE GREAT ICE BARRIER
MARCH 1912

Scott's expedition to the South Atlantic has been derided by some as a late empire adventure in patriotism, little more than a race to reach the South Pole before the Norwegians did. Flawed as the enterprise certainly was, Wilson stands as an example of a masculinity that devoted itself to science, the arts and the challenge of a journey that he undertook despite chronic poor health. The figure provides a stark contrast with those of young men and latterly young women recruited to take part in military activities in the name of glory and sacrifice. Each November a ceremony takes place in front of the third monument, the war memorial to the dead of the two world wars which stands between Wilson and the soldier from the South African campaign. Local clergy conduct the Remembrance Sunday service each November and personnel from the local Royal Air Force base guard the memorial for the duration. They stand like statues themselves at each corner in uniforms that would have been recognisable to Raymond Peace and Ronald Williams.[7] You have to stand on tiptoe to read the inscription, but you find it is partly in the words of William Shakespeare, prompting you to act like a soldier, in the eternal name of war and nation:

> Remember the men of Cheltenham who gave their lives for you in the Great War. If they were strangers to one another here in their common home they served and wrought and died in many lands near and far as a band of brothers. Learn from themselves to live and die that when you have followed them and are no more seen you may like them be remembered and regretted.

Notes

1. One of these soldiers directed me to Ben Elton (2005), *The First Casualty*, London: Black Swan, a novel about the First World War, where he had found what he considered an apt description of another source of motivation for soldiers. In the book, Douglas Kingsley, a policeman who is also a conscientious objector, is sent to the trenches to investigate a murder. Witnessing the carnage, Kingsley notes that he had heard soldiers speaking 'not of the fear of death but the fear of being found wanting, of having *let the side down*. Robert, Kingsley's brother, had spoken of it often in his letters. "I am afraid of fear," he had written, "I only want to do my best." They all wanted to do their best. Indeed, after a yearning for home, Kingsley had read, the fear of letting the side down was the principal emotion expressed by the doomed generation that sat in ditches in France. Comrades living cheek by jowl in fear and squalor, dependent only on each other for comfort and support, and in each man's heart the deep-seated desire not to let his mates down and the secret fear that when the ultimate test came, he might' (p. 352).
2. One notes that in Scotland there are plans to offer youngsters aged 16 and 17 the option of residential courses in military training run by the Territorial Army. Plans in the UK to raise the school leaving age to 18 raise the spectre of a similar kind of training across the UK.

3. Thomas Dekker in *O PER SE O* of 1612 describes in detail the science of self-mutilation which involved plates of copper, bandages and arrested gangrene which wrote onto the bodies of pretend soldiers a seemingly authentic message of self-sacrifice in the name of national identity. Thus the streets of London were full of individuals who could claim to have fought on behalf of the military idealism of the soldier subject, but whose integrity could not be proved.

4. I suppose an equivalent moment in modern history was the decision of the new revolutionary government in Russia to withdraw troops from the First World War. Say what you like about the Bolsheviks, but this a considerable, if short-lived, rejection of warfare. See Michael Melancon (1990), *The Socialist Revolutionaries and the Russian Anti-War Movement 1914–17*, Columbus, OH: Ohio State University Press.

5. See Norman Augustine and Kenneth Adelman (1999), *Shakespeare in Charge: The Bard's Guide to Leading and Succeeding on the Business Stage*, New York: Hyperion Books; Paul Corrigan (2000), *Shakespeare on Management: Leadership Lessons for Today's Managers*, London: Kogan Page; Richard Olivier (2002), *Inspirational Leadership: Henry V and the Muse of Fire*, Rolinson, NH: Spiro Press. There was also the now famous quasi-Shakespearean speech delivered by Lieutenant Tim Collins as the Royal Irish Regiment prepared to enter Iraq. He urged his soldiers to be 'ferocious in battle but magnanimous in victory', spoke of Iraq's history and the humanity of its people, and reminded them of the significance of the 'mark of Cain'. See transcript in the *Sun*, Wednesday, 21 May 2003, p. 5.

6. One telling example from recent British history was the gift given to General Pinochet as he was departing London in 2000, as a token of regard and acknowledgement of his help during the war in the South Atlantic. Andy Beckett explains: 'A cargo hoist had to be used to lift Pinochet into the plane. There was a small delay. A present had arrived for the general from a well-wisher. As television crews began to gather beyond the perimeter fence, it had to be carried out to the aircraft. The gift was a signed silver plate: a reproduction of those cast in 1588 to commemorate Sir Francis Drake's victory over the Spanish Armada. No one could accuse Margaret Thatcher of lacking a sense of history.' See Andy Beckett (2002), *Pinochet in Piccadilly: Britain and Chile's Hidden History*, London: Faber and Faber, p. 256.

7. It is not my intention to belittle these acts of remembrance or the comfort they afford. I attend the Cheltenham ceremony each year with my father who fought at sea during the Second World War. And I remember being deeply moved by the attempts of the custodian at the Scottish National War Memorial in Edinburgh Castle to get visiting tourists to remove their hats and caps as they entered the Hall of Honour. Many simply did not understand this mark of respect and were astonished by his polite urgings.

BIBLIOGRAPHY AND FURTHER READING

Achesome, James (1629), *The Military Garden, Or Instructions For All Young Soldiers*, London.

Adams, Robert P. (1962), *The Better Part of Valour: More, Erasmus, Colet and Vives, on Humanism, War and Peace 1496–1535*, Seattle, WA: University of Washington Press.

Addison, Paul and Crang, Jeremy (eds) (2006), *Firestorm: the Bombing of Dresden: 1945*, London: Pimlico.

Alexander, Catherine M. S. and Wells, Stanley (eds) (2001), *Shakespeare and Sexuality*, Cambridge: Cambridge University Press.

Alfar, Cristina Leon (2005), 'Fantasies of Female Evil: The Dynamics of Gender and Power in Shakespearean Tragedy', *Shakespeare Quarterly*, 56: 1, 110–12.

Allen, P. S., Allen, H. M. and Garrod, H. W. (eds) (1905–47), *Opus Epistolarum Des. Erasmi Roterodami*, Oxford: Oxford University Press, Vol. IV.

Anderson, Perry (1974), *Lineages of the Absolutist State*, London: Verso.

Anonymous (fourteenth century) *Wynnnere and Wastoure*, ed. Stephanie Trigg, Oxford: Oxford University Press.

Anonymous (fourteenth century) *The Alliterative Morte Arthure* (1983), ed. Valerie Krisna, Lanham, MD: University Press of America.

Anonymous (1530?), *Ordre or Trayne of Warre, that a Prynce, or a Heed Captayne, ought to take, that will Conquere, or assege a place, or keepe or defende a place, where he dowteth to be assay led in his owne countree, or to marche or travers the countree of his enemys or to make gwerne gwerneable*, London.

Anonymous (1590), *A Journall, wherein is truly sette downe from day to day, what was doone, and wirthy of noting in both the Armies, from the last comming of the Duke of Parma into France, vntill the eighteenth of May 1592*, London.

Anonymous [1590–1600] (1874), *The Life and Death of Jack Straw*, in W. Carew Hazlitt (ed.), *Dodsley's Old English Plays*, Vol. V.

Anonymous (1591), *Ordinances Set Forth by the King, for the rule and government of his Majesties men of warrs. Read and publist at Caen the 30. March 1591*, London,

Anonymous [1605] (1975), *The Famous Historye of the Life and Death of Captaine Thomas Stukeley. With his Marriage to Alderman Curteis*

Daughter, and Valient Ending of his Life at the Battaile of Alcazar, ed. Judith C. Levinson, Oxford: Oxford University Press.

Anonymous (1622), *A Spiritual Chaine and Armour of Choice for Sion Souldiers*, London.

Anonymous (1638), *Directions for Musters*, Cambridge.

Anonymous (1639), *Mars, His Triump: an Exercise performed the XVIII. of October, 1638. in the Merchant-Taylors Hall By Certain Gentlemen of the Artillery Garden London*, London.

Anonymous (1641), *The Exercise of the English, in the Militia of the Kingdome of England*, London.

Anonymous (1642), *Militia Old and New. One thousand six hundred forty two. Read All or None: And then Censure*, London.

Anonymous (1642), *Englands Savety in Navie and Fortifications; The Common Interest both of King and People*, London.

Anonymous (1642), *A true Abstract of i List, In which is set down the severall entertainments allowed by His Majesty to the Officers and other Souldiers of his Army. With the copy of an Oath given to all the Officers and Souldiers at their entertainment into the King's Service. Also some few speciall Orders ordained in His Majesties Army*, London.

Anonymous (1642), *A True Description of The Discipline of War Both for Horse and Foot, used in His Majesties Army, under their Excellencies William Earle of New-Castle, and Prince Robert. With the order and Manner of their marching and exercising in the field*, London.

Anonymous (1643), *A True Relation of Prince Rupert's Barbarous Cruelty against the Town of Birmingham*, London.

Anonymous (1643), *Prince Rupert's Burning Love to England Discovered in Birmingham's Flames*, London.

Anonymous (1647), *Il Pastor Fido*, London.

Aquinas, Thomas (1895), *Summa Theologica, Opera Omnia*, Vol. VIII, Rome.

Archer, Ian W., Fletcher, Anthony, Guy, John and Morrill, John (1991), *The Pursuit of Stability: Social Relations in Elizabethan* London, Cambridge: Cambridge University Press.

Aristotle, *The Politics* (1962), trans. T. A. Sinclair, London: Penguin.

Ascham, Roger (1545), *Toxophilus, the schole of shooting conteyned in two bookes. To all Gentlmen and yomen of Englande, Pleasainte for theyr pastyme to rede, and profitable for theyr use to follow, both in war and in peace*, London.

Ashplant, T. G., Dawson, Graham and Roper, Michael (2000), *Routledge Studies in Memory and Narrative*, London: Routledge.

Augustine, Norman and Adelman, Kenneth (1999), *Shakespeare in Charge: The Bard's Guide to Leading and Succeeding on the Business Stage*, New York: Hyperion Books.

Bainton, Roland H. (1961), *Christian Attitudes to War and Peace*, New York: Abingdon Press.

Barish, Jonas (1981), *The Anti-Theatrical Prejudice*, Berkeley and Los Angeles, CA: University of California Press.

Barker, Simon (1983), 'Images of the Sixteenth and Seventeenth Centuries as a History of the Present', in *Literature, Politics & Theory*, ed. Francis Barker, Peter Hulme, Margaret Iverssen and Diana Loxley, London and New York: Methuen.

Barker, Simon (1986), 'Coriolanus: Texts and Histories', in *Assays: Critical Approaches to Medieval and Renaissance Texts*, ed. Peggy Knapp, Pittsburgh: University of Pittsburgh Press, Vol. IV.

Barker, Simon (1990), 'The Armada Year: Literature, Popular Histories and the Question of Heritage', in *Comunicazione Sociale e Testo Letterario*, ed. Daniela Corona, Palermo: Università di Palermo.

Barker, Simon (1992), ' "The Double-Armed Man" – Images of the Medieval in Early Modern Military Idealism', in *From Medieval to Medievalism*, ed. John Simons, Basingstoke: Macmillan.

Barker, Simon (2001), 'Dressing up for War: Militarism in Early Modern Culture', *Dressing up for War: Transformations of Gender and Genre in the Discourse and Literature of War*, ed. Aránzazu Usandizaga and Andrew Monnickendam, Amsterdam and New York: Rodopi.

Barker, Simon (2003), ' "Allarme to England!"; Gender and Militarism in Early Modern England', in *Gender, Power, and Privilege in Early Modern Europe*, ed. Penny Richards and Jessica Munns, Harlow: Longman.

Barker, Simon (2005), ' "It's an actor, boss. Unarmed": the Rhetoric of *Julius Caesar*', in *Julius Caesar: New Critical Essays*, ed. Horst Zander, London and New York: Routledge.

Barnes, Thomas (1626), *Vox Belli, or an Alarum to Warre*, London.

Barnett, Correlli (1970), *Britain and Her Army, 1509–1970: A Military, Political and Social Survey*, New York: William Morrow.

Barret, Henry (1562), *A briefe booke unto private captaynes leading ffootmen*, London.

Barret, Robert (1598), *The Theorike and Pracktike of Moderne Discourses in Dialogue wise*, London.

Barriffe, William (1639), *Military Discipline: Or The Yong Artillery Man, wherein is discoursed and showne the Postures both of Mushet and Pike: THE EXACTEST WAY, &C. Together with the Motions which are to be used, in the exercsing of a Foot-Company. With divers and severall formes and figures of Bottelli; with their reducements; very necessary for all such as are studious in the Art Military*, London.

Barry, Gerrat (1634), *A Discourse of Military Discipline Divided Into Three Bookes, Declaring The Partes and sufficience ordained in a private Souldier, and in each Officer; Servinge in the Infantry, till the election and office of the Captaine General; And the Laste Booke Treatinge Of Fire-Workes of rare executions bt sea and lande, as also of firtisasions*, Brussels.

Barton, Anne (1994), *Essays, Mainly Shakespearean*, Cambridge: Cambridge University Press.

Barwick, Humfrey (1594), *A Briefe Discourse, Concerning the force and effect of all manuell weapons of fire and the disability of the Long Bowe of Archery, in respect of other of greater force now in use*, London.

Bassille, Theodore (1542), *The new pollecye of warre, wherein is declared not only how ye mooste cruell Tyrant the great Turke maye be overcome, but also all other enemies of the Christian publicke*, London.

Battenhouse, Roy (1941), *Marlowe's Tamburlaine: A Study in Renaissance Moral Philosophy*, Nashville, TN: Vanderbilt University Press.

Beaumont, Francis [1613] (1986), *The Knight of the Burning Pestle*, ed. Michael Hattaway, London: A. & C. Black.

de Beccarie de Pavie, Raimonde, Sieur de Fourquevaux (1589), *Instructions for the Warres, Amply learnedly and politiquely discoursing the method of Military Discipline*, London.

Beckett, Andy (2002), *Pinochet in Piccadilly: Britain and Chile's Hidden History*, London: Faber and Faber.

Belsey, Catherine (1980), *Critical Practice*, London and New York: Methuen.

Belsey, Catherine (1985), *The Subject of Tragedy: Identity and Difference in Renaissance Drama*, London: Methuen.

Bender, H. (1959), 'The Pacifism of the Sixteenth-Century Anabaptists', *Mennonite Quarterly Review*, XXX, pp. 7–9.

Benjamin, Walter (1967), *Versuche über Brecht: Herausgegeben und mit einem Nachwort versehen von Rolf Tiedemann*, Berlin.

Bennett, Andrew and Royle, Nicholas (2004), *An Introduction to Literature, Criticism and Theory*, 3rd revised edition, Harlow: Pearson.

Benveniste, Emile [1966] (1971), *Problems in General Linguistics*, Miami, FL: University of Miami Press.

Berek, Peter (1982), 'Tamburlaine's Weak Sons: Imitation as Interpretation Before 1593', *Renaissance Drama* 13: 55–82.

Berger, Harry (1991), 'On the Continuity of the Henriad: A Critique of some Literary and Theatrical Approaches', in *Shakespeare Left and Right*, ed. Ivo Kamps, London: Routledge.

Bernard, Richard (1629), *The Bible-Battels or the Sacred Art Military. For the rightly wageing of warre according to Holy Writ. Compiled for the use of all such valient Worthies, and vertuously Valerous Soutldiers, as upon all just occasions be ready to affront the Enemeies of God, our King, and Country*, London.

Bestul, Thomas (1974), *Satire and Allergory in Wynnere and Wastoure*, Lincoln, NB: University of Nebraska Press.

Bevington, David (1986), *Tudor Drama and Politics*, Cambridge, MA: Harvard University Press.

Bingham, John (1616), *The Exercise of the English in the service of the high and mighty Lords of the united Provinces in the Low Countries*, London.

Black, Jeremy M. (ed.) (1987), *The Origins of War in Early Modern Europe*, Edinburgh: Donald.

Black, Jeremy M. (1996), *The Cambridge Illustrated Atlas of Warfare: Renaissance to Revolution 1492–1792*, Cambridge: Cambridge University Press.

Blackwell, Basil (1954), *Shakespearean Production*, London: Faber and Faber.

Blackwell, Basil (1956), *A Royal Propaganda 1956. A Narrative Account of Work Devoted to the Cause of Great Britain During and after the Second World War*, MS, BL 11786.f.13.

Blandy, William (1581), *The Castle, or pictures of pollicy shewing forth . . . the duety, quality, profession of a perfect and absolute souldier, the martiall feates, encounters, and skirmishes lately done by our English nation.*

Blandy, William (1591), *The Castle, or picture of pollicy shewing forth most lively the face, body and partes of a commonwealthe, the duety, quality, Profession of a perfect and absolute Souldier*, London.

Blese, John R. E. (1989), 'Rhetoric and Morale: A Study of Battle Orations from the Central Middle Ages', *Journal of Medieval History* 15: 201–26.

Bogdanov, Michael and Pennington, Michael (1990), *The English Shakespeare Company*, London: Nick Hern Books.

Bourke, Joanna (1996), *Dismembering the Male*, London: Reaktion Books.

Bourke, Joanna (1999), *An Intimate History of Killing*, London: Granta.

Bourke, Joanna (2001), *The Second World War: A People's History*, Oxford: Oxford University Press.

Bowen, Barbara (1959), *Gender in the Theatre of War, Shakespeare's Troilus and Cressida*, London: Garland.

Boynton, Lindsay (1967), *The Elizabethan Militia*, London: Routledge & Kegan Paul.

Braen, Gordon (1985), *Renaissance Tragedy and the Senecan Tradition: Anger's Privilege*, New Haven, CT: Yale University Press.

Brecht, Bertolt (1965), *Der aufhaltsame Aufstieg des Arturo Ui*, Berlin: Suhrkamp Verlag.

Brecht, Bertolt (1981), *The Resistible Rise of Arturo Ui*, ed. John Willet and Ralph Manheim, London: Methuen.

Breight, Curtis, C. (1996), *Surveillance, Militarism and the Drama in the Elizabethan Era*, Basingstoke: Macmillan.

Breitenberg, Mark (1996), *Anxious Masculinity in Early Modern England*, Cambridge: Cambridge University Press.

Brewer, Ebenezer Cobham (1898), *Dictionary of Phrase and Fable*, London: Cassell.

Brewer's Dictionary of 20th-Century Phrase and Fable (1991), London: Cassell.

Bristol, Michael (1985), *Carnival and Theatre: Plebeian Culture and the Structure of Authority in Renaissance England*, London: Methuen.

Bruster, Douglas (1992), *Drama and the Market in the Age of Shakespeare*, Cambridge: Cambridge University Press.

Butler, Judith (1990), *Gender Trouble: Feminism and the Subversion of Identity*, New York: Routledge.

Calbi, Maurizio (2005), *Approximate Bodies: Gender and Power in Early Modern Drama and Anatomy*, New York and London: Routledge.

Callaghan, Dympna (ed.) (2006), *The Impact of Feminism on Renaissance Studies*, Basingstoke: Palgrave Macmillan.

Carlton, Charles (1992), *Going to the Wars: The Experience of the English Civil Wars 1638–1651*, London and New York: Routledge.

Cheney, Patrick (1998), *Marlowe's Counterfeit Profession: Ovid, Spenser, Counter-Nationhood*, Toronto: University of Toronto Press.

Cheshire, Geoffrey Leonard (1961), *The Face of Victory*, London: Hutchinson.

Cheyney, Edward P. (1926), *A History of England*, 2 vols, London: Longman.

Churchill, Winston S. (1948–54), *The Second World War*, 6 vols, London: Cassell.

Churchyard, Thomas (1579), *A generall rehearsall of warres*, London.

Clark, Suzanne (2000), *Cold Warriors, Manliness in Trial in the Rhetoric of the West*, Carbondalo, IL: Southern Illinois University Press.

Clayton, Giles (1591), *Approved Order of Martiall Discipline*, London.

Clode, C. M. (1869), *The Military Forces of the Crown*, London: John Murray.

Clowes, William (1588), *A Proved Practice for All Young Chirurgians, concerning burnings with Gunpowder, and Sword, Halbard, Pike, Launce, or such other*, London.

Cockle, M. J. D. (1900), *A Bibliography of English Military Books up to 1642 and of Contemporary Foreign Works*, London: Simpkin, Marshall, Hamilton, Kent & Co.

Colon Semenza, Gregory M. (2001), 'Sport, War and Contest in Shakespeare's *Henry VI*', *Renaissance Quarterly*, 54, 1251–72.

Corbett, J. S. (1900), *The Successors of Drake*, London: Longman.

Cormack, Elizabeth (1998), 'Britannia Rules the Waves? Images of Empire in Elizabethan England', *Early Modern Literary Studies*, 4.2 special edition, 1–20.

Corrigan, Paul (2000), *Shakespeare on Management: Leadership Lessons for Today's Managers*, London: Kogan Page.

Cotter, Jarrod (2005), *Living Lancasters: Keeping the Legend Alive*, Stroud: Sutton.

Courtney, Richard (1994) *Shakespeare's World of War: The Early Histories*, Toronto: Simon & Pierre.

Coward, Barry (1980), *The Stuart Age*, 3rd edition, Harlow: Longman.

Crosby, Alfred W. (2002), *Throwing Fire: Projectile Technology Through History*, Cambridge: Cambridge University Press.

Cruickshank, C. G. (1966), *Elizabeth's Army*, London: Oxford University Press.

Cruso, John (1632), *Military Instructions for the Cavallerie*, London.

Curt, Henry (ed.) (1905), *Niccolò Machiavelli – 'The Arte of Warre' and 'The Prince'*, . . . *Englished by P. Whitehorne*, London.

'D. I.' (1631), *Lawes and Ordinances touching military discipline*, The Hague.

Dawson, Graham (1994), *Soldier Heroes: British Adventures, Empire and the Imagining of Masculinities*, London: Routledge.

De La Noue, François (1587), *The Politicke and Militarie Discourses, Of the Lord De La Noue, Wheretoare Adjoyned certaine observations of the same Author, or things happened during the three late civil warres of France with a true declaration of Manie particulars touching the same*, translated by E.A., London.

De La Noue, François (1589), *The Declaration of the Lord de la Noue, upon his Taking Armes*.

De Maisse, (1590s?), *A Journal of All That Was Accomplished by Monsieur de Maisse, Ambassidor in England*, ed. G. B. Harrison and R. A. Jones, London.

De Mendoza, Bernardino (1597), *Theorique and Practise of Warre, Written to Don Philip Prince of Castil, by Mendoza. Translated out of the Castilian Tonge into Englishe, by Sr. Edwarde Hoby Knight*, London.

De Pisan, Christina (1498), *The Boke of the fayt of armes and of Chyalreye*, London.

De Saussure, Ferdinand [1916] (1974), *A Course in General Linguistics*, trans. Wade Baskin, London: Fontana.

De Somogyi, Nick (1998), *Shakespeare's Theatre of War*, Burlington, VT and Aldershot: Ashgate.

Deakin, Quentin (2000), *Expansion, War and Rebellion, Europe*, Cambridge: Cambridge University Press.

Dekker, Thomas [1599] (1999), *The Shoemaker's Holiday*, ed. R. L. Smallwood and Stanley Wells, Manchester: Manchester University Press.

Dekker, Thomas (1612), *O PER SE O*, London.

Deloney, Thomas (1966), 'The Queenes Visiting of the Campe at Tilsburie, with her entertainment there', in J. W. Ebsworth (ed.), *The Roxburghe Ballads*, Hertford: Stephen Austin and Sons; repr. New York: AMS.

Deloney, Thomas [1597/8] (2007), *The Gentle Craft*, ed. Simon Barker, Burlington, VT and Aldershot: Ashgate.

Digges, Thomas (1587), *A Briefe Report on the Militarie Services done in the Low Countries, by the Erle of Leicester*, London STC 7285.

Digges, Thomas (1590), *An Arithmeticall warlike Treatise named Stratioticos . . . As well concerning the Science or Art of great Artillerie, as the Offices of the Sergeant Major Generall, the Coronall General, and*

Lord Marshall, with a conference of the English, French and Spanish Disciplines, beside sundry other Militarie Discourses of no small importance, London.

Digges, Thomas (1590), *A Discourse of the Great Overthrow Given by the French King*, London.

Digges, Thomas (1604), *Four Paradoxes, or Politique Discourses concerning Militarie Discipline*, London.

Dollimore, Jonathan (1984), *Radical Tragedy*, Chicago: Chicago University Press.

Dollimore, Jonathan and Alan Sinfield (eds) (1985), *Political Shakespeare: New Essays in Cultural Materialism*, Manchester: Manchester University Press.

Dorril, Stephen (2006), *Blackshirt: Sir Oswald Mosely and British Fascism*, London: Penguin.

Drakakis, John (1984), *Alternative Shakespeares*, London: Methuen.

Duffy, Christopher (1997), *Siege Warfare: The Fortress in the Early Modern Period 1494–1660*, London: Routledge.

Duffy, M. (ed.) (1980), *Military Revolution and the State 1500–1800*, Exeter: University of Exeter Press.

Eagleton, Terry (1969), *An Introduction to Literary Theory*, 2nd edition, Oxford: Blackwell.

Edelman, Charles (2000), *Shakespeare's Military Language: A Dictionary*, London: Athlone.

Edmondes, Sir Clement (1581), *Observations upon the five first bookes of Caesars Commentaries, setting forth the practise of the art military, in the time of the Roman Empire. Wherein are handled all the chiefest points of their discipline, with the true reasons of every part, together with such instructions as may be drawne from their proceedings, for the btt direction of our moderne wars*, London.

Elizabeth I (4 October 1588), *Proceedings concerning soldiers pressed for the low countries*, London, STC 8175.

Elizabeth I (13 November 1589), *Proceedings. A Proclamayion against vagarent Souldiers and others*, London, STC 8188.

Elton, Ben (2005), *The First Casualty*, London: Black Swan.

Emmison, F. G. (1970), *Elizabethan Life: Disorder*, Chelmsford: Essex County Council.

Erasmus, Desiderius [1503 and 1509] (1978), *Enchiridion Militas Christiani – Praise of Folly* (1509), trans. Betty Radice, Harmondsworth: Penguin.

Erasmus, Desiderius (1511), *The Praise of Folly*, trans. Leonard F. Dean (1946), Chicago: Chicago University Press.

Erasmus, Desiderius [1516] (1953), *Enchiridion Militis Christiani – The Handbook of the Christian Soldier*, trans. Ford Lewis Battles in the series *Advocaes of Reform from Wyclif to Erasmus*, ed. Matthew Spinka, London: SCM Press.

Erasmus, Desiderius [1516] (1936), *The Education of a Christian Prince*, trans. Lester K. Born, New York: Columbia University Press.

Erasmus, Desiderius [1517] (1936), *The Complaint of Peace*, intro. William J. Hirten, New York: Columbia University Press.

Erasmus, Desiderius [1522] (1965), *The Colloquies of Erasmus*, trans. Craig R. Thompson, Chicago: Chicago University Press.

Everade, John (1618), *The Arriereban. A Sermon preached to the company of the Military Yarde, at St. Andrewes Church in Holborne on St. James his day last*, London.

Field, Maury (1977), *The Structure of Violence: Armed Forces as Social Systems*, Beverly Hills, CA: Sage.

Field, Theophilus (1628), *A Watch-Word, or the Allarme, or a good Take Heed. A Sermon preached at White-Hall in the open preaching place the last Lent before King Charles*, London.

Fitter, Chris (1991), 'A Tale of Two Branaghs: Henry V, Ideology and the Mekong Agincourt', in *Shakespeare Left and Right*, ed. Ivo Kamps, London: Routledge.

Foakes, R. A. (2002), *Shakespeare and Violence*, Cambridge: Cambridge University Press.

Ford, John [1633] (1968), *The Chronicle History of Perkin Warbeck*, ed. Peter Ure, London: Methuen.

Forhan, Kate Langdon (2002), *The Political Theory of Christine de Pizan*, Burlington, VT and Aldershot: Ashgate.

Fortescue, Thomas (1571), *The Forest*, a translation of Pedro Mexia's *Silva de Varia Leccion*, London.

Fortesque, J. W. (1910), *A History of the British Army*, 2nd edition, London: Macmillan.

Foucault, Michel (1979), *Discipline and Punish: The Birth of the Prison*, trans. Alan Sheridan. New York: Vintage.

Fourquevaux, Raymond de Beccarie, Sieur de Pavie (1589), *Instructions for Warres*, trans. Paul Ive.

Freud, Sigmund (1915), *Thoughts for the Times on War and Death*. Penguin Freud Library, Vol. 12, *Civilisation, Society and Religion*, London: Penguina Books, pp. 61–72.

Frontius, Sextus Julius (1519), *The Stratagems. Sleyghtes, and policies of warre, gathered togyther, by Julius Frontius, and translated into Englishe, by Rycharde Rorysine*, London.

Furssell, P. (2000), *The Great War & Modern Memory*, Oxford: Oxford University Press.

Garrard, William (1591), *The Arte of Warre. Being the onely rare booke of Myllitarie profession: drawne out of all our late and forreine services, by William Garrard Gentleman, who served the King of Spayne in his warres foutenn yeeres, and died Anno Domino 1587. Which may be called, the true steppes of warre, the perfect path of knowledge, and the playne plot of warlike exercises; as the reeder hereof shall plainly see expressed*, London.

Gates, Geoffrey (1579), *The Defence of Militarie Profession, Wherein is eloquently shewed the due commendation of Martial prowesse, and plainly proved hoe necessary the exercise of Armes is for this our age*, London.

Gernon, Luke (1620), *A Discourse of Ireland*, London.

Gibbon, Charles (1596), *A Watch-word for Warre*, London.

Gibson, Guy [1948] (1986), *Enemy Coast Ahead*, Manchester: Crécy Publishing.

Giddens, Eugene (2001), 'Honourable Men: Militancy and Masculinity in *Julius Caesar*', *Renaissance Forum*, Vol. 5, No. 2.

Goldberg, Jonathan (1983), *James I and the Politics of Literature: Jonson, Shakespeare, Donne and their Contemporaries*, Baltimore, MD: Johns Hopkins Press.

Göller, K. H. (ed.) (1981), *The Alliterative Morte Arthure: A Reassessment of the Poem*, Bury St Edmunds: D. S. Brewer.

Gosson, Stephen (1598), *The Trumpet of Warre, A Sermon preached at Paules Crosse the seventh of Maie 1598*, London.

Grantley, Darrell and Taunton, Nina (eds) (2000), *The Body in Late Medieval and Early Modern Culture*, Burlington, VT and Aldershot: Ashgate.

di Grassi, Giacomo (1594), *His true Arte of Defence, Plainlie teaching by infallible Demonstrations, apt Figures and perfect rules the manner and forme how a man without other Teacher or Master may safelie handle all sorts of Weapons as well offensive as deffensive; And with a waie or means by private Industrie to obtain Strength, Judgement and Activitie*, London.

Grayling, A. C. (2006), *Among the Dead Cities: Was the Allied Bombing of Civilians in World War II a Necessity or a Crime?* London: Bloomsbury.

Greenblatt, Stephen (1980), *Renaissance Self-Fashioning from More to Shakespeare*, Chicago: Chicago University Press.

Greenblatt, Stephen (1988), *Shakespearean Negotiations*, Oxford: Clarendon Press.

Grisone, Federico (1560), *A newe booke containg the Arte of ryding, and breaking greate Horses, together withthe shapes and Figures of many and divers Kyndesof Byttes, mete to serve divers Mouthes. Very necessary for all Gentlemen, Servingmen*, London.

Grose, Francis (1801), *Military Antiquities*, London.

Gutiarrez de las Vega, Luis (1582), *A compedious Treatisem entitled De re military, containing principle orders to be observed in Martiall affaires*, London.

Hacket, Roger (1590), *A Sermon needful for these times, Preached at Paules Crosse the 14. of Feb. 1590*, London.

Hale, John (1961), *The Art of War and Renaissance England*, Washington: Folger Library.

Hale, John (1983), *Renaissance War Studies*, London: The Hambledon Press.

Hall, Edward (1548), *The Union of the Two Noble and Illustrate Famelies of Lancastre and York*, London.

Halley, Janet E. (1999), *Don't: A Reader's Guide to the Military Anti-Gay Policy*, Durham, NC: Public Planet Books, Duke University Press.

Hammer, Paul (2003), *Elizabeth's Wars; Society and Politics During the Reign of Elizabeth I*, Basingstoke: Palgrave Macmillan.

Hampton, William (1527), *A Proclamation of Warre from the Lord of Hosts, or Endland's warning by Israel's ruin. Delivered in a Sermon at Paul's Cross July the 23. 1626.*

Hancock, Brecken Rose (2004), 'Roman or Revenger? The Definition and Distortion of Masculine Identity in *Titus Andronicus*', *Early Modern Literary Studies*, Vol. 10.1, 1–25.

Happé, Peter (1966), 'The Vice 1350–1605', PhD thesis, London University.

Harrington, Alexander (2003), 'War and William Shakespeare', *Dissent*, Vol. 50.4, 89–91.

Harris, Edmond (1588), *A Sermon preached at Brocket Hall before the Right Worshipfull Sir John Brocket and other gentlemen there assembled fot the Tryning of Souldiers*, London.

Harward, Simon (1592), *The Solace for the Souldier and Saylour*, London.

Hazlitt, Carew W. (ed.) (1874), *Dodsley's Old English Plays*, London: Dodsley.

Hawking, Stephen (1988), *A Brief History of Time*, London: Bantam.

Hedlam Wells, R. (2000), *Shakespeare on Masculinity*, Cambridge: Cambridge University Press.

Hexham, Henry (1637), *The Principles of the Art Militarie: Practised in the Warres of the United Netherlands. Presented by Figure, the Word of Command, and Demonstration*, London.

Higham, Robin (1972), *A Guide to the Sources of British Military History*, London: Routledge & Kegan Paul.

Hillman, David and Mazzio, Carla (eds) (1997), *The Body in Parts: Fantasies of Corporeality in Early Modern Europe*, London: Routledge.

Hogg, O. F. G. (1920), *The Royal Arsenal: its Background, Origin and Subsequent History*, London: Oxford University Press.

Holderness, Graham (2002), *Visual Shakespeare*, Hatfield: Hertfordshire University Press.

Holinshed, Raphael [1587] (1976), *Chronicles of England, Scotland and Ireland*, ed. Vernon F. Snow, 6 vols, New York: AMS Press.

Hookham, Hilda (1962), *Tamburlaine, the Conqueror*, London: Hodder & Stoughton.

Hopkins, Lisa (1996), ' "And shall I die and this unconquered?": Marlowe's Inverted Colonialism', *Early Modern Literary Studies*, Vol. 2.2, 1.1–23.

Hortman, Wilheim (2002), 'Shakespeare on the Political Stage in the Twentieth Century', in Stanley Wells and Sarah Stanton (eds), *The*

Cambridge Companion to Shakespeare on Stage, Cambridge: Cambridge University Press, pp. 212–29.

Howard, Jean E. and Rackin, Phyllis (1997), *Engendering a Nation: A Feminist Account of Shakespeare's English Histories*, London: Routledge.

Huizinga, Johan (1984), *Erasmus and the Age of Reformation*, Princeton, NJ: Princeton University Press.

d'Hurault, Jaques, Sieur de Vieu (1595), *Politicke, Moral, and Martiall Discourses*, trans. Artur Golding, London.

Hutjens, Linda A. (2004), 'The Renaissance Cobbler: the Significance of Shoemaker and Cobbler Characters in Elizabethan Drama', PhD thesis, University of Toronto.

Ive, Paul (1589), *The Practise of Fortification, Wherein is shewed the manner of Fortifying all sorts of situations*, London.

Jackson, Sir Barry (1953), 'On Producing *Henry VI*', *Shakespeare Survey*, Vol. 6, 40–52.

Javitch, Daniel (2002), *Baldassare Castiglione: The Book of the Courtier*, New York: Norton.

Jones, Martin (2000), *Clash of Empires: Europe 1498–1560*, Cambridge: Cambridge University Press.

Jones, Terry (1980), *Chaucer's Knight: the Portrait of a Medieval Mercenary*, 2nd revised edition, London: Methuen.

Jongue, Elbert of (1591), *A Journal, or Brief Report of the Late Service in Britaigne*, London.

Jongue, Elbert of (1592), *A Journall, Wherein is Sette Downe What Was Doone in Both Armies*, trans E. A., London.

Jongue, Elbert of (1600), *The True and Perfect Declaration of the Mighty Army by Sea*, London.

Jorgensen, Paul A. (1950), 'Moral Guidance and Religious Encouragement for the Elizabethan Soldier', *Huntingdon Library Quarterly*, Vol. XIII, 241–59.

Jorgensen, Paul A. (1956), *Shakespeare's Military World*, Berkeley, CA: University of California Press.

Judges, A. V. (1930), *The Elizabethan Underworld*, London: Routledge & Sons.

Kaeuper, Richard W. (1988), *War, Justice and Public Order*, Oxford: Clarendon Press.

Kahn, Coppélia (1981), *Man's Estate: Masculine Identity in Shakespeare*, Berkeley and Los Angeles, CA: University of California Press.

Kamps, Ivo (ed.) (1991), *Shakespeare Left and Right*, London; Routledge.

Keegan, John (1993), *A History of Warfare*, London: Hutchinson.

Kenny, Anthony (1983), *Thomas More*, Oxford: Oxford University Press.

Kershaw, Alex (2006), *The Few: The American Knights of the Air Who Risked Everything to Fight in the Battle of Britain*, Cambridge, MA: Da Capo Press.

Klein, Bernard (2002), ' "Tale of iron wars": Shakespeare and the Uncommon Soldier' in Barbara Korte and Ralf Schneider (eds), *War and the Cultural Construction of Identities in Britain*, Amsterdam: Rodopi, pp. 93–107.

Knowles, Ronald (2002), *Shakespeare's Arguments with History*, Basingstoke: Palgrave Macmillan.

Knox, Macgregor and Williamson, Murray (eds) (2001), *The Dynamics of Military Revolution 1300–2050*, Cambridge: Cambridge University Press.

Kocher, P. H. (1942), 'Marlowe's Art of War', *Studies in Philology*, Vol. XXXIX, 207–25.

Kohl, Ernst W. (1978), 'The Principal Theological Thoughts in the *Enchiridion Milits Christiani*', in R. De Molen (ed.), *Essays on the Works of Erasmus*, New Haven, CT: Yale University Press.

Kott, Jan (1965), *Shakespeare our Contemporary*, London: Methuen.

Kurtz, Martha A. (2003), 'Tears and Masculinity in the History Plays: Shakespeare's *Henry VI*', in Jennifer C. Vaught and Lynne Dickson Bruckner (eds), *Grief and Gender: 700–1700*, Basingstoke: Palgrave Macmillan, pp. 163–76.

Kyd, Thomas [1585] (1989), *The Spanish Tragedy*, ed. J. R. Mulryne, London: A. & C. Black.

Kyd, Thomas [1591] (1874), *Soliman and Perseda*, in W. Carew Hazlitt (ed.), *Dodsley's Old English Plays*, Vol. V.

Langsam, Geoffrey (1951), *Martial Books and Tudor Verse*, New York: King's Crown Press.

Leech, John (1619), *The Trayne Souldier. A Sermon preached before the worthy Society of the Captaynes and Gentlemen that exercise Armes in the Artillery Garden, at Saint Andrew-Undershaft in London, April 20 1619*, London.

Leighton, Alxander (1624), *Specuum belli sacri: or the looking Glasse of the holy war, wherein is discovered the evil of war, the good of war, the guide of war. In the last of these I give a Scantling of the Christian tackticks, from the levying of the Souldier to the sounding of the Retrait*, London.

Lingham, John (1584), *A true Relation of all English Captains as have been slaine in the Low Countries, together with those now living: as also of such as are fled to the enemy*, London.

Lodge, Thomas [1588] (1874), *The Wounds of Civil War*, in W. Carew Hazlitt (ed.), *Dodsley's Old English Plays*, Vol. VII.

Longhurst, Derek (1982), ' "Not for all time, but for an age": An Approach to Shakespeare Studies', in Peter Widdowson (ed.), *Re-Reading English*, London: Methuen.

Low, Jennifer (2000), 'Combat in "Those Proud Titles Thou Hast Won": Sovereignty, Power and Combat in Shakespeare's Second Tetralogy', *Comparative Drama*, Vol. 34.3, 269–90.

Low, Jennifer A. (2003), *Manhood and the Duel: Masculinity in Early Modern Drams and Culture*, Basingstoke: Palgrave Macmillan.

Lupton, H. (1909), *Life of John Colet*, London: George Bell.

Luther, Martin (1526), *Ob Kriegsleute Auch in Seligem Stande Sein Können*.

Lyly, John [1584] (1897), *Campaspe*, in John Matthews Manley (ed.), *Specimens of the Pre- Shakeperean Drama*, London: Ginn.

MacCaffrey, Wallace T. (1992), *Elizabeth I: War and Politics, 1588–1603*, Princeton, NJ: Princeton University Press.

Machiavelli, Niccolò [1521] (1560, 1573, 1588), *The Arte of Warre, written first in Italia by Nicholas Machiavelli and set forth in Englishe by Peter Whitehorne, student of Graies Inne: with an addition of other like Marcialle feates and experiments*, London.

Machiavelli, Niccolò (1584), *I Discorsi* and *Il Principe*, printed by John Wolfe with the fictitious imprint 'Palermo', London.

Machiaveli, Niccolò (1587), *Il Libro dell' Arte della Guella*, printed by John Wolfe with the fictitious imprint 'Palermo', London.

Machiavelli, Nicolò (1587), *Istorie Fiorentine*, printed by John Wolfe with the fictitious imprint 'Piacenza', London.

Malcolmson, Christina (ed.) (2002), *Debating Gender in Early Modern England 1500–1700*, Basingstoke: Palgrave Macmillan.

Malory, Sir Thomas, *Caxton's Malory* (1983), ed. James W. Spisak, 2 vols, Berkeley and Los Angeles, CA: University of California Press.

Malory, Sir Thomas (1998), *Le Morte Darthur: The Winchester Manuscript*, ed. Helen Cooper, Oxford: Oxford University Press.

Mangan, Michael (2002), *Staging Masculinities: History, Gender, Performance*, Basingstoke: Palgrave Macmillan.

Manning, B. (1957), 'Neutrals and Neutralism in the English Civil War', PhD thesis, Oxford University.

Marlowe, Christopher [1590] (1967), *Tamburlaine the Great*, ed. John D. Jump, London: Edward Arnold.

Marshall, Cynthia (2004), 'The Shattering of the Self: Violence, Subjectivity and Early Modern Texts', *Comparative Drama*, Vol. 38, 321–4.

Marshall, Tristan (2000), *Theatre and Empire: Great Britain on the London Stages under James VI and I*, Manchester: Manchester University Press.

Marx, Stephen (1992), 'Shakespeare's Pacifism', *Renaissance Quarterly*, Vol. 45, 49–95.

Massinger, Philip [1623] (1871), *The Duke of Milan*, ed. William Gifford, *The Dramatic Works of Massinger and Ford*, London: Moxon.

Massinger, Philip [1624] (1871), *The Bondman*, ed. William Gifford, *The Dramatic Works of Massinger and Ford*, London.

Massinger, Philip [1629] (1871), *The Roman Actor* (1629), ed. William Gifford, *The Dramatic Works of Massinger and Ford*, London.

Massinger, Philip [1639] (1871), *The Unnatural Combat*, ed. William Gifford, *The Dramatic Works of Massinger and Ford*, London.

Mattingly, Garret (1959), *The Armada*, Boston, MA: Houghton Mifflin.

McKellen, Ian (1996), *William Shakespeare's Richard III*, Woodstock, NY: Overlook Press.

McKisack, May (1959), *The Fourteenth Century: 1307–1399*, The Oxford History of England series, Oxford: Clarendon Press.

Mendoza, Bernadino de (1597), *Theorique and Practise of Warre*, trans. Sir Edwarde Hoby, London.

Melancon, Michael (1990), *The Socialist Revolutionaries and the Russian Anti-War Movement 1914–17*, Columbus, OH: Ohio State University Press.

Meron, Theodor (1993), *Henry's Wars and Shakespeare's Laws: Perspectives on the Law of War in the Later Middle Ages*, Oxford: Clarendon Press.

Meron, Theodor (1998), *Bloody Constraint: War and Chivalry in Shakespeare*, Oxford and New York: Oxford University Press.

More, Thomas (1516), *Utopia*, ed. Edward Surtz SJ, New Haven, CT: Yale University Press.

More, Thomas [1595] (1965), *A Myrrour for English Souldiers; or an Anatomy of an Accomplished Man at Armes, Utopia*, Harmondsworth: Penguin.

Morrow, David J. (2006), 'The Entrepreneurial Spirit and "The Life of the Poore": Social Struggle in the Prose Fictions of Thomas Deloney', *Textual Practice*, 20.3, 395–418.

Morton, H. V. [1927] (2006), *In Search of England*, London: Methuen.

Mulhern, Francis (1978), 'Marxism in Literary Criticism', *New Left Review*, Vol. 108, London.

Mulhern, Francis (1979), *The Moment of Scrutiny*, London: New Left Books.

Munday, Anthony (1600), *Sir John Oldcastle*, London.

Munday, Anthony (1600), *The Downfall of Robert, Earle of Huntington*, London.

Murrin, Micheal (1994), *History and Warfare in Renaissance Epic*, Chicago: University of Chicago Press.

Naunton, Robert (1824), *Fragmenta Regalia: Menoirs of Elizabeth, Her Court and Favourites*, London.

Neade, William (1625), *The Double-Armed Man: By the New Invention: Briefly Shewing some Famous Exploits atchieved by our Brittish Bowmen*, London, reproduced in facsimile with an introduction by Stephen V. Grancsay (1971), York, PA: George Shumway.

Nicol, A. and J. (eds) (1927), *Holinshed's Chronicle as used in Shakespeare's Plays*, London: Dent.

Nicoll, Allardyce (1923), *A History of English Drama*, Cambridge: Cambridge University Press.

Nolan, John S. (1997), *Sir John Norreys and the Elizabethan Military World*, Exeter: University of Exeter Press.

Northumberland, Earle of (1640), *Lawes and Ordinances of Warrs, Established for the better conduct of the Service in the Northern parts*, London.

Odell, G. C. D. (1920), *Shakespeare from Betterton to Irving*, London: Constable.

Olin, John C. (ed.) (1965), *Christian Humanism and the Reformation: Selected Writings of Desiderius Erasmus*, New York: Harper & Row.

Olivier, Richard (2002), *Inspirational Leadership: Henry V and the Muse of Fire*, Rolinson, NH: Spiro Press.

Oman, Sir Charles (1937, repr. 1991), *A History of the Art of War in the Sixteenth Century*, London: Greenhill Books.

Oulter, Walley Chamberlain (1818), *A History of the Theatres of London*, London: C. Chapple.

Parker, Geoffrey (1988), *The Military Revolution; Military Innovation and the Rise of the West, 1500–1800*, Cambridge: Cambridge University Press.

Parker, Geoffrey (ed.) (1995), *Warfare*, Cambridge: Cambridge University Press.

Parker, Geoffrey (ed.) (2006), *The Cambridge History of War*, Cambridge: Cambridge University Press.

Patterson, Annabel (1989), *Shakespeare and the Popular Voice*, Oxford and Cambridge, MA: Basil Blackwell.

Peele, George [1589] (1961), *The Battle of Alcazar*, in Frank S. Hook (ed.), *The Dramatic Works of George Peele*, New Haven, CT: Yale University Press.

Pennington D. and Thomas K. (eds) (1978), *Puritans and Revolutionaries: Essays in Seventeenth-Century Historiography Presented to Christopher Hill*, Oxford: Clarendon.

Peraldus, Gulielmus (*c.* 1236), *Summa de Vitiis*.

Perodinus, Petrus (1553), *Magni Tamerlanis Scytharum Imperatories Vita*, London.

Pettegree, Andrew (1986), *Foreign Protestant Communities in Sixteenth-century London*, Oxford: Clarendon Press.

Philips, J. E. (1970), *Twentieth-Century Interpretations of Coriolanus*, Englewood Cliffs, NJ: Prentice-Hall.

Philips, M. M. (1965), *The Adages of Erasmus*, Cambridge: Cambridge University Press.

Pittman, L. Monique (2006), 'A Son Less than Kind: Iconography, Interpolation and Masculinity in Branagh's *Hamlet*', *Early Modern Literary Studies*, 11.3, 4.1–27.

Pocock, J. G. A. (1975), *The Machiavellian Moment*, Princeton, NJ: Princeton University Press.

Poleman, John (1587), *The Second Part of the Book of Battailes, Fought in our Age*, London.

Pollard, A. W. and Redgrave, G. R. (1926), *A Short-Title Catalogue of Books Printed in England, Scotland and Ireland 1475–1640*, London: The Bibliographical Society.

'Pragmatious, Mercurios' (1647), *The Levellers Levelled or The Independants Conspiracy to Root Out Monarchie*, London.

Preston, Thomas [1561] (1897), *Cambises, King of Persia* , ed. John Matthews Manly, *Specimens of the Pre-Shaksperean Drama*, London: Ginn.

Proctor, Thomas (1578), *Of the Knowledge and Conducte of Warres, Two Bookes, latelye written and sett Foorth, profitable for suche as delight in Hystorys, or Martyall Affayres and necessary for this present time*, London.

Pugliatti, Paola (1993), 'The Strange Tongues of *Henry V*', *Yearbook of English Studies*, Vol. 23.

Pugliatti, Paola (2003), *Beggary and Theatre in Early Modern England*, Burlington, VT and Aldershot: Ashgate.

R. S. (1696), *A Briefe Treatise, To Proove the necessitie and excellance of the use of archerie*, London.

R. W. [Richard Ward?] (1642), *The Anatomy of Warre*, London.

Raab, Felix (1964), *The English Face of Machiavelli: A Changing Interpretation 1500–1700*, London: Routledge & Kegan Paul.

Raleigh, Walter (1458), *A Discourse of Sea-Ports; Principally of the Port and Haven of Dover*, London.

Raleigh, Walter (1650), *A Discourse of the Original and Fundamental Cause of Natural, Customary, Arbitary, Voluntary, and Necessary War*, London.

Rees, Laurence (2005), *Auschwitz: the Nazis and the 'Final Solution'*, London: BBC Books.

Reynolds, E. E. (1965), *Thomas More and Erasmus*, London: Longman.

Rich, Barnabe (1574), *A Right Excelent and Pleasant Dialogue, betweene Mercury and an English Souldier*, London.

Rich, Barnabe (1578), *Allarme to England, foreshewing what perilles are procured when people live without regarde to Martiall Lawe*, London.

Rich, Barnabe [1581] (1959), *His Farewell to Militarie Profession*, ed. Thomas Cranfil, Austin, TX.

Rose, Jaqueline (1993), *Why War?*, Oxford: Blackwell.

Roy, Ian (1994), 'Towards the Standing Army', in David Chandler (ed.), *The Oxford Illustrated History of the British Army*, Oxford: Oxford University Press.

Ruff, Julius R. (2001), *Violence in Early Modern Europe 1500–1800*, Cambridge: Cambridge University Press.

Rule, Margaret (1983), *The Mary Rose: The Excavation and Raising of Henry VIII's Flagship*, London.

Ruoff, James E. (1975), *Macmillan's Handbook of Elizabethan and Stuart Literature*, London and Basingstoke: Macmillan.

Sackville, Thomas and Thomas Norton [*c.* 1571] (1970), *Gorboduc, or Ferrex and Porrex*, ed. Irby B. Cauthen, London: Edward Arnold.

Sanger, Ernest (1992), *Englishmen at War: A Social History in Letters 1450–1900*, Dover, NH: Sutton.

Saunders, Corinne, Le Saux, Françoise and Thomas, Neil (eds) (2004), *Writing War: Medieval Literary Responses to Warfare*, Woodbridge: Boydell and Brewer.

Scott, Jonathan (2000), *England's Troubles: Seventeenth-Century English Political Instability in European Context*, Cambridge: Cambridge University Press.

Scott, Sir Sibbald (1868), *The British Army: Origin, Programme and Equipment*, London: Cassell.

Scott, Thomas (1623), *A Tongue-Combat Lately Happening Betweene Two Englishe Souldiers in the Tilt-Boat of Gravesend, the one going to Serve the King of Spaine, the other to Serve the States generall of the United Provinces. Wherein the Cause, Course and Contiuance of those Warres, is Debated and Declared*, London.

Seebohm, F. (1887), *The Oxford Reformers*, London: Longman.

Segar, William [1602] (1975), *Honor Military and Civill, contained in foure Bookes*, ed. Diane Bornstein, New York: Scholars Press.

Shakespeare, William, *The Oxford Shakespeare* (1987), ed. Stanley Wells and Gary Taylor with John Jowett and William Montgomery, Oxford: Oxford University Press.

Shakespeare, William [1608] (1976), *Coriolanus*, ed. Philip Brockbank, London: Methuen.

Shakespeare, William, *King Richard III* [1592/3] (1981), ed. Antony Hammond, London: Methuen.

Sharp, Buchanan (1980), *In Contempt of All Authority*, Berkeley, CA: California University Press.

Sharpe, J. A. (1997), *Early Modern England: A Social History 1550–1760*, 2nd edition, New York: Arnold.

Sheldon, E. K. (1963), 'Sheridan's *Coriolanus*', *Shakespeare Quarterly*, Vol. XIV.

Shepard, Alan (2002), *Marlowe's Soldiers: Rhetorics of Masculinity in the Age of the Armada*, Burlington, VT and Aldershot: Ashgate.

Shepard, Alan and P. J. Withington (2000), *Communities in Early Modern England: Networks, Place, Rhetoric*, Manchester: Manchester University Press.

Shepperd, Eric (1926), *A Short History of the British Army to 1914*, London: Constable.

Shirley, Henry (1638), *The Martyr'd Souldier*, London.

Shirley, James [1642] (1833), *The Country Captain*, in William Gifford and Alexander Dyce (eds.), *The Dramatic Works and Poems of James Shirley*, London.

Sidney, Sir Philip [1591] (1962), 'Astrophel and Stella', in *The Poems of Sir Philip Sidney*, ed. W. A. Ringler, Jr, Oxford: Oxford University Press.

Silver, George (1599), *Paradoxes of Defence*, London.

Simons, John (1983), *Realistic Romance: The Prose Fiction of Thomas Deloney*, Contexts and Connections: Winchester Research Papers in the Humanities, Winchester: King Alfred's College.
Sinfield, Alan (1992), *Faultlines*, London: Oxford University Press.
Sinfield, Alan (2006), *Shakespeare, Authority, Sexuality: Unfinished Business in Cultural Materialism*, New York and Abingdon: Routledge.
Smail, R. C. (1958), 'The Art of War', in Austin Lane Poole (ed.), *Medieval England*, Oxford: Clarendon Press.
Smith, B. R. (2000), *Shakespeare and Masculinity*, Oxford: Oxford University Press.
Smith, Bruce R. (2001), 'Shakespeare and Masculinity', *Renaissance Forum*, Vol. 5.2.
Smith, Thomas (1616?), *The Arte of Gunnerie*, London.
Smith, Thomas (1660), *The Arts of Gunnerie*, London.
Smythe, John [1590] (1964), *Certain Discourses*, ed. John Hale, New York: Cornell University Press.
Smythe, John (1595), *Instructions, Observations and Orders Mylitarie Requisite for all Chieftaines, Captains, and higher and lower men of charge and Officers to understand, knowe, and observe*, London.
Snyder, R. Claire (1999), *Citizen-Soldiers and Manly Warriors: Military Service and Gender in the Civic Republican Tradition*, Lanham, MD: Rowman & Littlefield.
Spenser, Edmund (*c.* 1596, published 1633), *A View of the Present State of Ireland*, London; reprinted (1970), Oxford: Oxford University Press.
Stockwood, John (1584), *A very Fruitfull and necessarye sermon of the Destuction of Jerusalem*, London.
Stone, Lawrence (1967), *The Crisis of the Aristocracy*, London: Oxford University Press.
Strype, John (ed.) (1924), *Annals of the Reformation and Establishment of Religion in the Church of England during Queen Elizabeth's Happy Reign*, Oxford.
Styward, Thomas (1581), *The Pathwaie to Martiall Discipline, devided into two Bookes, verie necessarie for yong Souldiers, or for all such as loveth the profession of Armes*, London.
Sun Tzu (2005), *The Art of War*, Harmondsworth: Penguin.
Sutcliffe, Matthew (1593), *The Practice, Proceedings, And Lawes of Armee*, London.
Tallett, Frank (1977), *War and Society in Early-Modern Europe, 1495–1715*, London: Routledge.
Taunton, Nina (1998), *Watching the Watch: Surveillance of the Camp in Sixteenth-Century Discourses of War*, Thomas Harriot Seminar Occasional Paper No. 26, Durham: University of Durham.

Taunton, Nina (2001), *1590's Drama and Militarism: Portrayals of War in Marlowe, Chapman and Shakespeare's 'Henry V'*, Burlington, VT and Aldershot: Ashgate.

Taunton, Nina (2001), 'Night Watch: The Nocturnal Camp Scenes in Shakespeare's Henry V and 1590s Militarism', in *Acts du colloque La Nuit chez Shakespeare et ses Contemporains: l'invisible présence*, 23–24 Octobre 1998, Recherches Valenciennoises, Presses Universitaire de Valenciennes.

Taunton, Nina (2001), 'Camp Scenes and Generals; Shakespeare's *Henry V*, and the State of the Art of War', *Shakespeare in Southern Africa*, Vol. 13, 41–52.

Tazón, Juan E. (2003), *The Life and Times of Thomas Stukeley, (c. 1525–78)*, Burlington, VT and Aldershot: Ashgate.

Tillyard, E. M. W. (1944), *Shakespeare's History Plays*, London: Chatto & Windus.

Trenchard, Thomas (1689), *A Short History of Standing Armies in England*, London.

Trigg, Stephanie (ed.) (1990), *Wynnere and Wastoure*, Oxford: Oxford University Press.

Trussell, Thomas (1619), *The Souldier Pleading His Own Cause*, London.

Tute, Warren (1983), *The True Glory*, London: Centurion.

Tyderman, Christopher (2006), *God's War: A New History of the Crusades*, London: Allen Lane.

Udall, John (1588), *The True Remedie against Famine and Warres – Five Sermons*, London.

Vale, Juliet (1982), *Edward III and Chivalry: Chivalric Society and its Context 1270–1350*, Bury St Edmunds: Boydell Press.

Vegetius, Flavius (1572), *The Foure bookes of Flavius Vegetius Ranotus, brieflye contayninge a plaine forme, and perfect knowledge of Martiall Policye, feates of Chivalrie, and whatever pertayneth to warre. Translated out of Latine, into Englishe, by John Sadler*, London.

Von Clausewitz, Carl [1832] (1908), *On War*, London: Routledge & Kegan Paul.

Walton, Clifford (1894), *History of the British Standing Army*, London: Harrison & Sons.

Waltz, Kenneth, N. (2001), *Man, the State and War*, 2nd revised edition, New York: Columbia University Press.

Watts, William or Thomas Roe (1632), *The Swedish Discipline, Religious, Civil and Military*, London.

Webb, Henry, J. (1955), 'Classical Histories and Elizabethan Soldiers', *Notes and Queries*, Vol. 200, 468–9.

Weimann, Robert (1996), *Authority and Representation in Early Modern Discourse*, ed. David Hillman, Baltimore, MD: Johns Hopkins University Press.

Wells, Robin Headlam (2002), *Shakespeare on Masculinity*, Cambridge: Cambridge University Press.

Wernham, Robert B. (1986), *After the Armada: Elizabethan England and the Struggle for Western Europe, 1588–1595*, Oxford: Clarendon.

Whetstone, George (1585), *The honorable reputation of a Souldier: With a Morall Report, of the Vertues, Offices, and (by abuse) the Disgrace of his profession*, London.

Whetstone, George [1586] (1973), *The English Myrror*, New York: Da Capo.

White, Paul Whitfield (ed.) (2001–2), *Marlowe, History and Sexuality: New Critical Essays on Christopher Marlowe, Comparative Drama*, Vol. 35. 3–4, 472–5.

White, Stephen (1979), *Sir Edward Coke and 'The Greivances of the Commonwealth' 1621–1628*, Chapel Hill, NC: University of North Carolina Press.

Wickham, Glynne (1974), *The Medieval Theatre*, Cambridge: Cambridge University Press.

Willet, John (1964), *Brecht on Theatre*, London: Methuen.

Williams, Andrew P. (2001), 'The Image of Manhood in Early Modern Literature: Viewing the Male', *Renaissance Forum*, Vol. 5.2.

Williams, Roger (1618), *The Actions of the Low Countries*, London.

Williams, Sir Roger (1972), *The Works of Sir Roger Williams*, ed. John X. Evans, Oxford: Clarendon Press.

Wilson, Charles (1970), *Queen Elizabeth and the Revolt of the Netherlands*, London: Macmillan.

Wilson Knight G. R. (1940), *This Sceptered Isle*, Oxford: Clarendon Press.

Wilson, Robert [1588] (1874), *The Three Lords and Three Ladies of London*, in W. Carew Hazlitt (ed.), *Dodsley's Old English Plays*, Vol. V.

Wilson Knight, G. R. (1956), *A Royal Propaganda, 1956 A Narrative Account of Work Devoted to the Cause of Great Britain During and After the Second World War*, MS, BL, 11768.f.13. Wilson Knight, G. R. (1964) *Shakespeare Production*, London: Faber and Faber.

Wise, Terence (1971), *A Guide to Military Museums*, Bracknell: Bellona.

Woolf, G. and Wilson, Moorcroft J. (1982), *Authors Take Sides on the Falklands*, London: Woolf.

Wrightson, Keith (1982), *English Society, 1580–1680*, London: Hutchinson.

Yongar, William (1600), *A Sermon Preached at Great Yarmouth upon the 13. of September 1599*, London.

INDEX

DATE DUE

HIGHSMITH #45230

Printed
In USA